P9-DCD-295

A Spy in Canaan

To: Joyce & Joe:
With my very best wishes
Sincerely,
Harvey

A Spy in Canaan

My Secret Life As a
Jewish-American Businessman
Spying for Israel
In Arab Lands

BY
Howard H. Schack
WITH H. Paul Jeffers

A Birch Lane Press Book
Published by Carol Publishing Group

A Birch Lane Press Book
Published by Carol Publishing Group
Birch Lane Press is a registered trademark of Carol Communications, Inc.
Editorial Offices: 600 Madison Avenue, New York, N.Y. 10022
Sales and Distribution Offices: 120 Enterprise Avenue, Secaucus, N.J. 07094
In Canada: Canadian Manda Group, P.O. Box 920, Station U, Toronto, Ontario M8Z 5P9
Queries regarding rights and permissions should be addressed to Carol Publishing Group, 600 Madison Avenue, New York, N.Y. 10022

Carol Publishing Group books are available at special discounts for bulk purchases, for sales promotion, fund-raising, or educational purposes. Special editions can be created to specifications. For details, contact: Special Sales Department, Carol Publishing Group, 120 Enterprise Avenue, Secaucus, N.J. 07094

Manufactured in the United States of America
10 9 8 7 6 5 4 3 2 1

Library of Congress Cataloging-in-Publication Data

Schack, Howard H.
    A Spy in Canaan : my secret life as a jewish-american businessman who spied for Isreal in Arab lands / by Howard H. SChack with H. Paul Jeffers.
        p.   cm.
    "A Birch Lane Press book."
    ISBN 1-55972-178-2
    1. Schack, Howard H. 2. Espionage, Israeli-Arab countries.
3. Spies–Israel–Biography. I. Jeffers, H. Paul (Harry Paul),
1934-   . II. Title
UB271.182S337   1993
327.125694'0174927'092--dc20
[B]   92-21113
                                                         CIP

For Ruth

Entreat me not to leave thee, or to return
from following after thee; for whither thou
goest, I will go; and where thou lodgest,
I will lodge; thy people shall be my people,
and thy God my God.

—Ruth 1:16

And Moses sent them to spy out the land of Canaan, and said to them, Get you up this way southward, and go up into the mountain:

And see the land, what it is, and the people that dwelleth therein, whether they be strong or weak, few or many.

—Numbers 13:17–18

Contents

Preface

This book reveals for the first time how and why I, a quiet, middle-aged, successful Jewish-American businessman, plunged into the world of espionage by volunteering to become an agent for Israel's Institute for Intelligence and Special Operations, which the world knows as the Mossad.

But before recounting what I did on behalf of Israel I feel that I must state what I did not do. I took no money from the government of Israel, not even as reimbursement for expenses. I did not seek profits for my business, though it could have gained richly from the secret information that I unearthed. I never acted against the interests of my own country. I bore no personal animosity against the Arab people.

My only compensation came through knowing that I contributed to the continued existence of Israel.

Although these adventures in espionage may read as if they are fiction, they happened in a dangerous world where human life is held cheap and memories are long. Consequently, I have changed the names of some individuals on both sides of the tragedy of the confrontation between Israel and the Arab world who might find themselves at risk if their identities were revealed.

While I cannot name former and present members of the Institute without whom the events in this story could not have taken place, I can acknowledge those without whose counsel and guidance I could not have written this book: my agent at the William Morris Agency, Mel Berger; my editor, Hillel Black; Rockland County District Attorney Kenneth Gribetz; and Sherri Ralph, who provided invaluable advice.

For his painstaking and resourceful research, insights into the history of the Middle East in the 1970s and 1980s that he gained as a broadcast journalist, and skills as an author of many books that he brought to producing the manuscript, I thank my coauthor, H. Paul Jeffers.

I also must gratefully recognize my wife, Ruth, my four sons, and others in the Schack family in the United States and Israel who unquestioningly and patiently put up with my mysterious and frequent, unexplained absences through two decades. Now they know what I could not explain then.

A Spy in Canaan

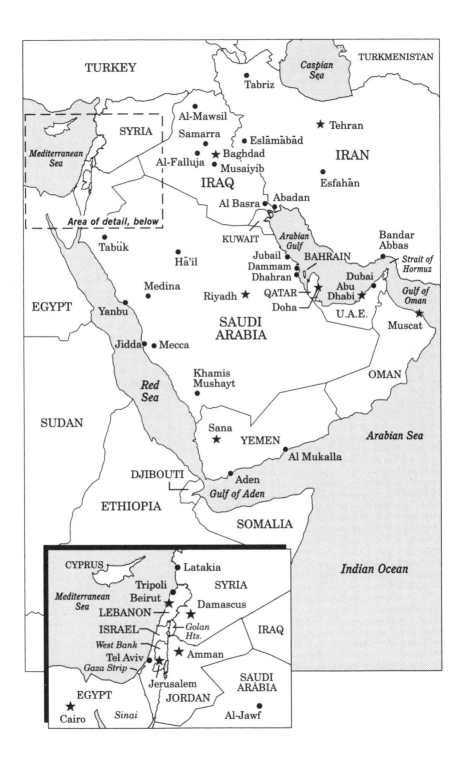

I

Returned Call

 "Initial reports are quite sketchy and unconfirmed," said the newscaster, "but it appears that the attack on Israel began about two hours ago with Egyptian bombing raids on Israeli air forces and missile bases in the Sinai."

With a worried glance at my wife, Ruth, and our four sons, I turned up the car radio.

"There is also word from Cairo that at the same time, an artillery barrage opened up along the entire front," continued the correspondent, reporting from Tel Aviv. "I am also informed that just as the attack was being launched, Prime Minister Golda Meir was convening an unusual Yom Kippur meeting of her cabinet to discuss intelligence reports of some military activity by the Egyptians along the Suez Canal. Informed sources in government say that Israeli intelligence sources had issued a warning of possible hostilities, but apparently no one expected an immediate outbreak of a full-scale war. At this moment, air raid sirens are blaring across Jerusalem."

The next days were filled with agonized frustration for the Jewish community. Like millions of others who felt outraged but helpless, I sat in my comfortable den and watched David Brinkley on television reporting that Egyptians had thrown ten combat bridges across the Suez Canal, allowing 80,000 troops to sweep into the Sinai. That vast, uninhabited desert had been occupied by Israel since the 1967 war. Using high-pressure water cannon (purchased secretly from West Germany), the Egyptians blasted through Israeli defensive ramparts while 222 Soviet-supplied MIG fighters ranged overhead to hit 90 percent of their targets at a loss of only five planes. Reeling under the onslaught, Israel's Sinai

Command ordered troops along the Bar-Lev Line to destroy all weapons and retreat.

Watching news coverage of the swift advance of the Egyptians and hearing reports of attacks on Israel's northern borders by the Syrians, I feared that the Arab forces would push all the way to Jerusalem.

Like Jews around the world, on each Passover holiday I had voiced an ancient toast: "Next year in Jerusalem." But it's a long way from Rockland County, New York, to the city astride the Kidron Valley. By airplane it is a little over six thousand miles. To make the trip you need a whole day: two hours to get to Kennedy Airport, ten and a half by jet from JFK to Ben-Gurion Airport at Tel Aviv, and the rest for the drive to the City of David itself, plus the six hours you set your watch ahead because of the different time zones. Arab warplanes journeyed from their bases in Egypt and Syria in minutes.

Despite the annual Passover pledge, not many Rockland Jews in October 1973 had visited Israel. I had done so only twice. Like me, most American Jews had been steeped in the great melting pot that is the United States and did not consider themselves as citizens of the distant Jewish state. In that we were hardly unique. How many Irish-Americans had been back to Ireland? Italian-Americans to Italy? German-Americans to their homeland? And other hyphen-ated Americans to their roots? For the majority of Americans, their immigrant ancestors' passages to a New World were and remained one-way tickets.

My grandparents came to America from Russia. In the process, the family names of Schachnovitsky and Greenberg were clipped to Schack and Green. None of my grandparents ever went back. They were Americans and had no desire to be otherwise. Nor did my father want to be anything but 100 percent American. A good man, steady, hard-working, devoted to his family, and stubborn to the point of being pigheaded, he was both a warrior and survivor. Believing wholly in the American way, he felt there could be no better way to show his love of the system than by running for mayor of our town, not once but several times. Although unsuc-cessful, he never lost faith in the promise of the United States, even while running a small business through the Great Depression. A product of public schools, he treasured the English language. With all its stories and songs glorifying the heritage and culture of the

Old World, Yiddish was not heard in his house, as, indeed, it had been absent in the homes of those other Jews who preferred to assimilate.

This does not mean that Israel had not been important to the Jews of America. Quite the contrary. Since the founding of a Jewish state in 1948 they consistently expected the United States government to be supportive of Israel, as every politician with even a small Jewish constituency understands. And there have always been ways for individual American Jews to bolster Israel. All sorts of fund-raising appeals, charities, and groups dedicated to the cause of a Jewish homeland flourished in the United States long before Israel became a reality.

Like many other Jewish people, I had voted for pro-Israeli candidates and I had given money. That is why, until the radio came on in my car on that dismal, rainy morning of Saturday, October 6, 1973, I felt no guilt, no need to contemplate my attitude toward Israel during the annual review and assessment of transgressions, which my religion calls the Day of Atonement.

One of the two most holy days of the Hebrew calendar (the other is Rosh Hashanah, ten days earlier), Yom Kippur is a day for making peace with God through fasting, confessing one's sins, repentance, rededicating one's life by asking forgiveness from others, and setting New Year's resolutions.

How strictly a Jew keeps the holy days is between him and God. Many are deeply devout. Many are not. Some Jews keep kosher, some do not. Countless numbers observe rituals to the letter, a great many do not. Consequently, Yom Kippur is to some Jews what Easter is to many Christians, the only day of the year that they show up for services. Mostly, I fit the latter category.

Therefore, as I got behind the wheel of my car to go to morning observances of Yom Kippur, I appreciated that I was going to see faces I had not seen since last year, just as they had not seen mine. What none of us expected was that this year would present quite a different test of one's Jewishness, devout or not. Stunned and sickened by the news of this assault on Israel that coincided with one of the most sacred days in Judaism, I was reminded of Japan's Sunday-morning sneak attack on Pearl Harbor in 1941.

As a teenager during the Second World War I looked upon that conflict as an American. The fight was between Japanese and us, Nazis and us. Then, in 1942, I listened to a talk by Rabbi Jacob

Solovaitchik and heard for the first time that Nazis killed Jews in Germany, Poland, Russia, and anywhere Hitler's armies invaded just because they were Jews. It was the first time I had been told that there were places in the world in which being Jewish could be a capital offense. Drafted into the army in the waning months of the war, I did not learn how far the Nazis had gone in exterminating Jews until newsreels showed the American and Allied forces entering the death camps to liberate the survivors.

After the war I followed news accounts of efforts to create a homeland for Jews in Palestine and how that dream culminated in the declaration of the existence of Israel in May 1948, followed instantly by an attack by Israel's Arab neighbors. The warfare that followed ranged from solitary terroristic attacks on Israeli settlements to the all-out war of 1967 and, suddenly, in the autumn of 1973, the most serious onslaught yet.

By midnight on October 6, an Egyptian military force larger than the combined might of NATO was on the move: 800,000 troops, 2,200 tanks, 2,300 artillery pieces, 150 antiaircraft missile batteries, and 550 first-line aircraft. "Israel has been boasting of their Six-Day War of 1967," gloated Egyptian President Anwar Sadat in a TV news bulletin. "Now we can boast of *our* Six-Hour War."

Seething with anger as I watched the report, I looked at my family gathered in our snug, safe house with its cozy fireplace and thanked God that we were Americans. "Don't worry, boys," I said proudly and confidently to my children. "Israel is strong and the United States isn't going to let her down."

Prime Minister Golda Meir appeared on the screen. "We are in no doubt that we shall prevail," she said defiantly.

Gazing at a map on which I had drawn the battle lines as best I could, based on the news reports, I could not escape the danger that Israel faced. Was it possible, I asked myself, that Israel would be overwhelmed? Despite my assurances to my children, how could I be certain that the United States would come to the rescue of a tiny land no bigger than Rhode Island and surrounded by enemies? President Richard Nixon had always been a reliable friend of Israel, the only democracy in the Middle East, and a stalwart ally in checking the hopes of the Soviet Union to win control of the region. But Nixon was embroiled in a fight to save his own skin, as a result of the scandal known as Watergate.

Might American help come too little and too late? Would it come at all? Inevitably, my thoughts reeled back to World War II. Were Jews headed for a new Holocaust? Were we about to witness what the Arab world had long promised, the destruction of Israel? Was this treacherous attack about to make hollow the Jewish vow of "Never again"? Next year on Passover would an Arab Jerusalem be closed to Jews? To me and my wife? To our sons?

Though I was six thousand miles away from Israel and while I was first and foremost an American, recent history had taught me that I must never forget that I had a stake in the survival of Israel. The Jewish soldiers I watched on television were fighting and dying not just for the defense of their own country but for Jews everywhere, even those in the idyllic and peaceful towns and villages of Rockland County, New York.

I wanted to help. But what could I do? Write my congressman and senators? Send a telegram to the president? Join another of the seemingly endless and fruitless demonstrations at the United Nations? Write out another check?

Surely there must be *something* better, I thought.

What did I, a middle-aged Jewish-American businessman, have to offer?

The next day as I sat at my desk in my construction company I realized that before me lay something that might prove useful to Israel. Heaped on my desk were plans and specifications for an offshore naval expansion program in the Red Sea and Persian Gulf that had been put out for bids by Saudi Arabia. These plans had come to me quite routinely. My firm had exactly the experience needed to carry out portions of the project. Reviewing the plans, I wondered if the government of Israel was aware of them.

I had heard stories about Israel's famous intelligence service, Mossad. Surely its agents must be aware of this project, I thought. But what if they were not?

As I pondered the question, I realized that I might be able to provide similar information. I had had dealings with foreign governments that took me all over the globe, bringing me in contact with hundreds of executives who did business worldwide, especially in the Middle East. From my bending elbows with them in scores of hotel bars and cocktail lounges, I saw how readily they had talked about their affairs, openly discussing a military project in an Arab country or a new naval base going up in the Persian

Gulf. Through the years, my ear had been bent by scores of tired businessmen who were a long way from home, like me, and wanting nothing more than to gossip, usually about their work.

Might Israel find it worthwhile to have access to such information? The logical way to find out, I reasoned, was to contact people in the Israeli government who routinely dealt with American businessmen, the Israeli government's commercial consulate in Washington, D.C.

Telling my family nothing of what I had in mind and with the plans in my briefcase, I boarded the Eastern Airlines shuttle to the capital on Monday. The office I sought was in a commercial building a few blocks northwest of the White House. Expecting to be able to walk right in, sit down with an official, and present my proposal, I discovered as I entered a very small reception room that I was not the only one eager to transact business in the office that day. The place was filled with people inquiring about their loved ones who lived in Israel or about family members who were there as students. I waited nearly an hour.

My purpose in coming, I explained to a young man seated at a big desk in one of half a dozen similar rooms, was to volunteer my services on behalf of Israel.

"Doing what?" he asked dubiously.

"I conduct business in the Middle East," I said, "I have access to projects such as public buildings and massive capital development projects from Kuwait to Libya. My credentials permit me to work intimately with Western firms that have construction contracts in those countries."

I then handed him the plans for the Saudi project and explained their importance.

"We appreciate your good intentions, Mr. Schack. But I really don't see how the commercial consulate can be of any help to you in what you propose."

"Then tell me who can."

"Even if I could tell you, which I can't, it would be quite improper for me to do so," he replied. "For me to do so would possibly be a violation of my position in the consulate."

Astounded, I said, "Do you mean to say that I came all the way down here for nothing? Maybe I should talk about this with your supervisor."

"He is not available at this time."

"I'm sorry," I said, getting up and walking in frustration to the door.

The young man rose behind his desk. "Would you leave me your business card? I'll be writing a report on our meeting and will need your particulars. For our records."

Feeling foolish, I put the card on the desk, turned my back, and left. Hailing a taxi to take me to the airport for my return to New York City, I had no trouble envisioning the young man crumpling my card and tossing it into a wastebasket.

Glad that I had not mentioned to anyone else what now seemed like a harebrained idea, I put the matter out of my head and noted with satisfaction and relief that an American who was far better equipped than I at helping Israel was doing so. In an almost last-minute airlift of equipment and supplies that contributed significantly to preventing a total Arab victory, President Nixon, undaunted by the Watergate troubles that I had feared might paralyze him, rushed military assistance.

The aid certainly helped. But all the fresh equipment in the U.S. arsenal would have been useless without the superiority on the ground and in the air that the Israeli Defense Force demonstrated so effectively, stopping the two-front attacks and turning initial defeat into decisive victory.

"The American airlift was obviously of vital importance militarily to Israel at a critical juncture, but it was perhaps even more significant politically," wrote Chaim Herzog in his history, *The Arab–Israeli Wars*. "Its unequivocal nature was undoubtedly a major factor in bringing about a cease-fire, and in turning the United States into the central figure on the stage of the Middle East in the subsequent months."

With the crisis over I went about my business, certain that my moment of bravado had landed in a trash bin, and, I began to think, rightly so. But one day early in 1974 the private phone on my desk rang and a male voice said, "Good morning, Mr. Schack. How are you today?"

Who was this guy calling me on the direct, private phone line to my office?

"I'm fine, thank you," I said warily.

"You recently visited one of our Washington offices," he said. "This call is to assure you that we appreciated your offer and are interested in talking to you. Could you drop in at our New York

City branch? Tomorrow?" He gave me the address. "Ask for Mike. Shalom!"

What a word! It could mean good-bye, as my caller used it. Or hello. Or a word that had had little currency in the history of the embattled nation of Israel: Peace.

As I hung up the phone, I had a nervous feeling. Out of the blue, after months when I had heard not a peep, came this cryptic call from a guy calling himself Mike and asking me to come see him.

Getting up earlier than usual the next morning, I explained to my puzzled wife that I had a breakfast meeting with a business associate. Arriving at the midtown Manhattan address Mike had given me, I had no idea what to expect.

"I'm sorry we kept you waiting so long before getting in touch with you," said the ramrod-straight, athletic figure in a gray flannel suit who greeted me with a firm handshake. "We had to check you out."

"Naturally," I said, having not a clue as to what he meant. What was there to check out?

He led me into a spartan, windowless office. "How is your cousin Menachem these days?" he asked, sitting behind a bare desk while I took a comfortable leather armchair. "He likes his work at Kfar Hahoresh? And his wife and kids? They are well?"

With a look of astonishment, I blurted, "Maybe *you* should tell *me* how they are!"

He smiled. "They're all in good spirits, I assure you. As are all your relatives in Israel. Menachem deported himself superbly in the war, in the great tradition of your cousin, David Soffee, in the Six-Day War."

The young man he named had been killed in action during the battle to take East Jerusalem in 1967.

"I expect Menachem will be getting a promotion soon," he went on. "Of course, you understand that you will have to wait to hear the news of his medal from Menachem before you send him your congratulations. What goes on between us today is a secret."

"You needn't worry on that account," I said.

"I don't doubt it. I've learned that you are an exceptional man. Most of the people I deal with fall into what I call the 'mice' category. They come to me out of one of four motivations. M, for money. Some are I people, ideologically driven. A few find themselves C for compromised and are forced into working for us. And then there are most dangerous of all, the E people—egotists. You don't fit any of the categories."

"I'm pleased to know that."

"The items you left at our office proved most interesting, by the way," he said. "How much do you feel we owe you for them?"

"Beg pardon?"

"How much did you expect to be paid?"

"I didn't expect pay. I thought the information would be helpful. I was not looking for money."

"Really?"

"I guess that's difficult for you to believe, given your line of work. But it's the truth. I'm not in this for money. I make all the money I need. I'm just a businessman who feels that maybe I can make a difference. Either you are interested or you aren't."

"Obviously, we're interested. You're here. We're always on the lookout for persons who present us with a unique opportunity for collecting intelligence."

"Excuse me," I said, shifting anxiously in my chair, "but I am happy to pass on information that I might happen to pick up. I didn't say anything about *collecting*. When you say 'collecting intelligence' what comes to my mind is espionage."

Mike smiled slyly. "What a loaded word!"

"Loaded or not," I said, sinking back in the chair, "are you interviewing me with an eye toward turning me into some kind of cloak-and-dagger guy?"

"Would that trouble you?"

I pictured secret agents like the dashing James Bond. Dispatched on his dangerous missions by the mysterious M, boss of the British secret service, he packed his trusty Walther PPK automatic pistol and high-tech briefcase stuffed with lethal devices dreamed up by a scientific wizard known as Q. Although I was familiar with firearms and owned a gun for personal protection, I was no 007. Another view of international espionage had been provided by John Le Carré in the fictional form of the portly, middle-aged George Smiley, Great Britain's brilliant Cold War nemesis of Karla, the mastermind of Moscow Centre. Much more plausible. But despite a resemblance in age and physique, neither did I see myself as a George Smiley. Yet here I was in a room with a man who knew all about relatives of mine in Israel—even about a cousin who had been killed in the 1967 war.

How much did this man from Israel know about me? Did his dossier include a page about my uncle Murray, the socialist? Or a note about Uncle Sid and Aunt Rose, who claimed to be communists? Did it go so far back that the dossier included the wedding of my mother's parents through a *shidduch,* an arranged marriage?

Had someone discovered and made note of the fact that another relative, Sam Kearns, had been the organist at the Roxy Theater in New York and a conscientious objector? Sam volunteered to be a medic in World War I and nearly lost his life during an artillery attack. And what about my wife's cousin, Saul Beichman, killed in the Battle of the Bulge? Did Saul rate a notation?

Did the cool-mannered man across the desk from me know about the black sheep of my family? Had someone managed to unearth the bootlegger that no one talked about during family reunions?

What could the government of Israel have discerned in all his accumulated data, I wondered, that prompted somebody to turn my offer to provide Israel with information that I might casually discover into full-time espionage?

"Does spying trouble me?" I asked. "If I watch a spy movie on TV I can't sleep at night. Spying scares the hell out of me."

Mike laughed. "That's excellent. The man who is not scared when he ought to be is a dangerous person, to himself and to everyone else."

"I told the people in your Washington office that I would do all that I can for Israel," I said. "But spying? The idea never entered my head. I'm not looking to be a hero. Besides, I would not know what to do. You're right. I'm not one of the mice. I don't want money. I'm not doing this out of ideology. Nobody's forcing me. And I'm not here because I need to puff up my self-image. So if you think I can be of help to Israel, okay. But let's get one thing quite clear. I will never do anything against my own country."

"We wouldn't expect you to," Mike said. "And I can now tell you that my name is Avrum Langatzky. I am Colonel Langatzky of the Institute for Intelligence and Special Operations, better known as the Mossad. Call me Avrum. From now on, if you agree to join the cause, you will be known by your Yiddish name, Hershel. That is, if you do not object."

"Why should I? I've been called Hershel all my life."

"I know."

"Ah ha," I blurted. "You *do* have a file on me!"

"We opened one on the day you visited our Washington office. It's grown rapidly since then, of course."

"Does that mean that your people have been following me and checking up on me?"

"There was no need for that. Almost everything we need to know about anyone in America is available in public records. It's an easy matter to accumulate data on individuals in the United States. Computers have made it even easier. The job is rather more difficult in the countries of Islam. As you know from your own experience, they are among the most closed societies in the world, stricter in some ways than Russia. The Soviet Union, after all, is a political system and therefore corruptible. But the Arab world is built on religion."

"Religious people can't be corrupted?"

"They can," he said, smiling slightly. "It just makes it more difficult."

He offered me a cigarette.

"Thank you, but I don't smoke," I said.

Lighting a Camel, he said, "Besides being a wise thing in terms of your health, that will stand you well in the Arab world."

Exhaling a plume of smoke, he held out the cigarette as if he were studying it. "For me, giving up tobacco was the worst part of working in Muslim countries," he continued. "Except for sucking horrible Turkish tobacco smoke from a water pipe in a coffee shop, a man smoking in public stands out like a sore thumb. Of course, being conspicuous is the last thing an intelligence agent wants to do. Drinking was a similar problem. I like a cocktail before dinner, but if you're hoping to pass as an Arab, best be a teetotaler. Do you imbibe?"

"How interesting. The file you've got on Howard Schack *isn't* so thorough after all."

"There are a few blanks," he said with a shrug.

"I take a drink now and then. But you can put in the file that I can get along quite well without."

"Getting access to solid human intelligence can prove pretty difficult in countries where if you are not a Muslim you are an infidel," he said. "Now, it is true that we can obtain quite a lot of data through technical means. An orbiting spy satellite's cameras can show you the layout of an air base, but it can't peer through the roof of a building and show you what missiles are stored inside. Nor can photo reconnaissance discover that the building in the heart of Baghdad with a red crescent on the roof is a hospital built on top of an air defense command and control center. You need a man on the ground to find that out. In the trade we call that 'HUMINT.' Human intelligence."

"You want me to steal the original blueprints?"

"They don't have to be the *originals*," he said, crushing the cigarette in an ashtray. "How are you with a camera?"

"All right, I guess. Photography is a hobby."

"Hershel, I grow fonder of you every minute!"

"Is there anything else I can tell you?"

"Your file shows that you're a devoted family man. What did they think about your volunteering?"

"I didn't tell them about it."

"Will you tell them about *this* meeting?"

"They would worry. I don't want them worrying. They would try to talk me out of it."

"At your convenience, if you come on board," he said, "we will arrange a series of briefings and a training schedule for you. There will be a lot to learn. We'll provide you with some special equipment—a microfilm camera, a clever device that lets you check telephones for bugging devices, that sort of thing. It will require a little time. Three or four days."

"Just tell me where and when."

The words sounded braver than I felt.

"That answer is exactly what I expected from you," he said, standing and holding out his hand. "You'll be hearing from us presently. Shalom!"

2

Bodyguard of Lies

 Throughout history a few names have become synonymous for all that they stood for. The Minutemen of Lexington and Concord. The Marines of Tripoli, Guadalcanal, Korea, and Khe Sanh. Scotland Yard. The FBI. The Mafia. Hitler's Gestapo and SS. Russia's NKVD and its successor, the KGB. America's World War II spy agency, Office of Strategic Services, and its Cold War offspring, the CIA. And perhaps the most fascinating of all, Mossad.

Before Israel's independence in 1948 intelligence services working for the creation of a Jewish state had been a collection of freebooting outfits accountable to one political faction or another. In the Jewish struggle to win a homeland there had been a plethora of such organizations with names that sounded pretty romantic to me. Then only a teenager, I listened to grown-ups discussing smooth-talking, dapper young men of the Irgun who came to the United States to appeal to "rich" American Jews for funds. With glamour on their side and guilt as a weapon they raised large sums of money to help finance the war for independence. Later, I read in the newspapers of how the Irgun had blown up half of the King David Hotel in Jerusalem, killing more than two hundred people, civilians as well as British soldiers. Another group, the Haganah, had an intelligence-gathering arm known as the Shai. Aliyah Beth, set up during the years of the British Mandate, smuggled illegal immigrants from Europe into Palestine and after independence brought Jews out of hostile Arab countries. Responsibility for internal security in the new state fell to the Shin Beth, an agency akin to the Federal Bureau of Investigation.

With statehood achieved in May 1948, Israel's first prime minister, David Ben-Gurion, took steps to forge these earlier units into a cohesive organization. He was rather unsuccessful. So in September 1951 he revamped everything, bringing everyone under one roof, so to speak, and answerable to him. For the agency's title he reached back into history and took the name of an organization that had smuggled Jews into Palestine in the 1930s and 1940s: Mossad Letafkidim Meyouchadim. Recognizing that this new entity would be called upon to perform a wide variety of tasks other than "intelligence," Ben-Gurion added the phrase "special assignments" to its title and its mandate. Under a provision of Israeli law (Article 29 of the Basic Law), the Mossad was authorized "to carry out on behalf of the State" any act whose implementation was not entrusted to any other authority. Because there was no other Israeli law governing intelligence and related special assignments, Mossad had a virtual free hand to act.

One of the most spectacular of these actions took place in 1960 when Mossad agents plucked the transport manager of the Nazi Holocaust, Adolf Eichmann, off a street in Buenos Aires to bring the banal technocrat of the "Final Solution" to justice and a hangman's noose in Israel.

Of course, I had no way of knowing it at the time, but the amiable Colonel Avrum Langatzky had volunteered for that enterprise. One of a team of Mossad agents who maintained a discreet surveillance of a man living with his wife and son under the name Ricardo Klement, Langatzky had assisted in the actual kidnapping. He then stood guard until Eichmann could be spirited out of Argentina disguised as one of the crew of an El Al plane that had carried Israeli officials to Buenos Aires for a celebration of Argentina's 150th year of independence.

Four years earlier, Langatzky had joined a Mossad team that provided security for a secret meeting involving Prime Minister Ben-Gurion, Israeli Army Chief of Staff Moshe Dayan, and officials of Great Britain and France in planning the attack on Egypt in 1956 that wrested control of the Suez Canal from the hands of pro-Soviet President Gamal Nasser. Earlier, as a fledgling agent, he had served in Ethiopia and in Djibouti as a support and communications officer. Rising steadily through the ranks, Langatzky had become, by the time I met him, a "gathering officer" responsible for finding, investigating, and clearing potential agents.

In 1966 Mossad operatives had persuaded a sympathetic Christian pilot in the Iraqi air force to defect by flying his Soviet

MIG-15 fighter plane to Israel. In 1969 from the French seaport of Cherbourg Mossad agents had hijacked missile boats intended for the Egyptian navy and sailed them to Israel, announcing to the world, "They now belong to us." It was the Mossad that had set out to avenge the murders of Israeli athletes and others at the Munich Olympic Games of 1972. In 1973 it had carried out an assassination raid into Beirut, Lebanon, against leaders of the Palestine Liberation Organization.

The first Mossad agent to die after independence had been Jacob Bokai. A Syrian-born Jew, he infiltrated the ranks of Palestinian refugees streaming out of Israel in 1949. Quickly recognized, he was arrested and hanged in Jordan. Three years later, Salah Shalom and Joseph Basri were caught in Iraq and hanged side by side in the central square of Baghdad. Between 1957 and 1965, Eli Cohen, using the name Kamil Amin Taabes, successfully spied for Israel in Syria, sending back data by radio until his signals were traced by sophisticated Soviet-supplied homing devices. He went to the gallows in a Damascus square.

How many others paid with their lives in the name of gathering intelligence for Israel was known only to the keepers of the Mossad files.

That this vaunted intelligence service discerned something of promise in Howard Schack had sent me from Colonel Langatzky's spartan office feeling scared, excited, and a little proud. And why not? I had just been invited to join the most romantic and successful brotherhood in the world.

Being a member of organizations had never appealed to me, although for business and political reasons I had joined several. As soon as I reached the required age, I had plunged into the Order of Masons and membership in the Consistory (Scottish Rite) of the Valley of New York, rising to Thirty-second Degree. Then I joined the Shriners, advancing to Orator of the Mecca Temple in New York City.

Presently, I belonged to Kiwanis and numerous other bodies in which secrecy was not required: the Chamber of Commerce, the American Ordnance Association, the U.S. Naval Institution, the World Radio Organization and the American Radio Relay League (I had been a ham operator for years), and the Republican party.

But suddenly, as I left the elevator and crossed the small lobby of the pedestrian midtown office building that served as a disguise for the real work being done within its walls, not far from the United Nations, I realized that the organization to which I had committed myself would require a lot more from me than paying dues and attending meetings. I had committed myself to an undertaking that could lead to me hanging by the neck from an Arab rope. By the time I retrieved my car from a parking garage I was wondering if I had made a terrible mistake.

I prided myself on having built a marriage in which Ruth and I kept no secrets. For twenty-five years she had been a partner in all my undertakings, sharing her insights on personal, family, and business matters during spirited dinner table discussions or in moments of quiet pillow talk. Suddenly I faced the prospect of lying to her.

During dinner that evening I dreaded a moment that I knew had to come, when she would ask how my day had been, whom I had seen or done business with. After all the years we had been together, I was certain that if I were to lie she would sense it. Nor could I try to dismiss the question with a generalization. I had always been specific at such times, even on the most routine and boring of days. At my wit's end and hoping to conceal my anxiety, I hoped that for once she would choose not to inquire.

Of course, she did, asking, "How was your day in the city?"

"Oh, you know how it is," I said. Scrambling for a way to answer, I decided to be flippant. "It was a typical day in New York. I was nearly run down by a lunatic messenger on a bicycle, I got mugged twice. And I had to slug a traffic agent to keep the car from being towed away."

Uncertain whether to believe me, our four sons stared at me in amazement.

"And then there was the meeting I had this morning," I went on. "A *secret agent* who wants me to become a spy for Israel."

The boys groaned.

"Be serious," Ruth said, chuckling.

"But I *am* being serious," I replied with a smile.

"Yeah, sure, Dad," scoffed my eldest. "Now would you please pass the potatoes?"

Having told the truth and feeling blameless for not being believed, I did so happily, and the conversation proceeded to less threatening matters.

Although I had several appointments outside of my office the next day, I canceled or postponed them, remaining at my desk to take the call from Langatzky that I was certain would come. It did not. Nor the next day. Nor all that week. Nor the next. By the end of the third week I could not escape the obvious conclusion that despite his glowing expressions concerning me, Colonel Langatzky apparently had decided that the flesh-and-blood reality of Howard somehow had not measured up to the promise of Hershel. On one hand I found this to be a great relief. On the other, I felt disappointed.

The one thing I felt grateful for during those disappointing days was that I had confided in no one concerning my meeting with Langatzky, other than to disguise it as a joke, and therefore had no reason to feel embarrassed because nothing had come of it.

With springtime in the offing and summer approaching, the period when the construction field was busiest, my thoughts of Colonel Langatzky faded away. I plunged into the work of my company that I had been neglecting while waiting for a call from Langatzky to a higher duty that apparently was not going to come.

Nevertheless, in the five months between the outburst of rage on the Day of Atonement 1973 that had sent me scurrying to Washington to offer my services to Israel and the approach of Passover in the spring of 1974, I could not escape occasional thoughts of how I might have proven useful to Israel.

A case in point landed upon my desk. Awaiting my signature in March was paperwork required to put in a bid for a subcontract for architectural ornamentation, one of my firm's specialties, for a vast petrochemical plant that was being constructed in Saudi Arabia. Signing the bid, I felt confident that my company would win it and that I might soon be on my way to that country. This appeared to be exactly the kind of situation that was bound to provide me with information that Langatzky had talked about and that I had supposed might be of use to Israel should there ever be a new conflict involving Saudi Arabia. The chief bankroller of Israel's hostile Arab neighbors, that oil-rich Arab nation was still smarting over the failure to crush Israel in the Yom Kippur War.

Going about daily routines of both family and business, I reconciled myself to the fact that I was not going to be the answer to Israel's prayers that I had thought I might be. Every week I made frequent trips to New York City for meetings, driving down the tree-lined Palisades Parkway on the New Jersey side of the Hudson

River. I set the radio on an all-news station and listened to reports on the diplomatic aftermath of the war in which the United States emerged as the dominant power broker between Israel and her two most powerful adversaries, Syria and Egypt. Secretary of State Henry Kissinger was shuttling back and forth between the three nations in hopes not only of preventing another war but of pushing out the influence of the Soviet Union and keeping up the flow of Arab oil to the West.

The Arab nations had launched an oil embargo, creating in the United States the greatest gasoline and fuel oil shortage since the Second World War. Within days, all Arab oil-producing nations tightened the tap. The spot oil market jumped from a few dollars a barrel to seventeen. The "energy crisis" was born. Lights in Times Square went dim. Lines formed at gas stations and the American passion for big cars waned. Detroit-made "gas guzzlers" began to look like dinosaurs. Millions worried about a winter without heat. Prices soared.

With the world's economy feeling the pinch, I could not fail to notice that a result of the Yom Kippur War and the oil squeeze had been a shift in American Middle East policy. The United States had become increasingly sensitive to the power of Arab nations to choke off petroleum. It seemed to me that in future confrontations Israel might not be able to rely on automatic support from the United States and other Western industrialized nations who were ever more dependent on Arabian oil. I felt it was evident that Israel ought to welcome all the help it could get from any quarter, including me.

The depth of resentment of those who blamed Israel for the Arab oil embargo presented itself on a chilly Tuesday in March. As I drove into New York City on the Palisades Parkway, a car passed me, revealing a bumper sticker with the motto: PUT A JEW IN YOUR TANK.

Because it was mid-morning the traffic going toward New York was light. Conscious of the need to save gasoline, I proceeded well below the speed limit. Glancing into the rearview mirror, I noticed another car gaining on me. As it drew nearer, headlights flashed. As it overtook me and drew up alongside, I saw the driver gesturing for me to pull over.

"That's great," I thought. "He's trying to signal me that there's something wrong with my car."

With a second look I was astonished to see that the driver of the plain green sedan was Colonel Langatzky.

As I stopped, he pulled in behind me, got out, came to my car and into the front seat. "Long time, no see, Hershel," he said. "I hope I didn't scare you."

"Not at all. I'm used to this sort of thing. It happens all the time."

"That's good," he said with a laugh. "I like a man who has a sense of humor."

"Wouldn't a simple phone call have been sufficient?"

"That's an important lesson, Hershel. Never do the obvious and never expect it. I'll be brief. Your presence is requested at lunch today. That is, if you're still interested in doing some work for our firm."

I had planned to lunch with a business associate, but after waiting so long for a contact and then having it take place in such a melodramatic manner I was not going to let anything keep me from accepting Langatzky's invitation.

"Where and when?" I asked.

"Noon. At the Second Avenue Delicatessen. Where else would three Jewish businessmen go for lunch?"

"*Three?*"

"I'll be introducing you to a friend from the Institute who has expressed an interest in you. He's a fascinating fellow. I'm sure you'll like him. Shalom, Hershel."

With that, he drove away.

At Second Avenue and Twelfth Street, the restaurant stood in the heart of a section known as the East Village but storied in the lore of the New York of a previous generation as the Jewish Rialto. The area had been the heart of the Yiddish theater. There, playhouses between Houston and Fourteenth streets specialized in melodramas and musicals and starred such entertainers as Molly Picon, the Adlers (Jacob and his children Luther and Stella), Boris Thomashefsky, Eddie Cantor, Al Jolson, Milton Berle, and a host of others. They performed in productions based on the American Dream in which the immigrant makes good. By 1973 the immigrants had turned that theme into reality and had long since moved away. Many of them left their Jewishness behind as they went uptown or out of town to assimilating suburban locales in Long Island, Westchester County, and Rockland County.

Through all of this sociological change the Second Avenue Kosher Restaurant and Delicatessen remained steadfast, serving borscht, shashlik, knishes, pastrami, and brisket to a multiethnic clientele in a vaguely Eastern European atmosphere scented by sour pickles. Anxious and impatient and thinking that the Second Avenue Deli was the last place I would have expected spies to meet, I arrived at noon. I felt very cloak-and-dagggerish as I discovered Colonel Langatzky waiting on the sidewalk. In a three-piece, blue pin-striped suit he looked more the American business-man than I.

"Change of plans, Hershel," he said, taking my arm. "We'll be meeting David over at Washington Square Park. We'll walk, if you don't mind. It's not far."

"I know where it is," I said. "You could have called me and told me there was a change."

"Don't be upset, Hershel. This is the way things work. It's the way we go about our business with new people."

"You've had plenty of time to check me out. Either you trust me or you don't. I've been waiting to hear from you for months. I think it's time you shit or get off the pot."

"I apologize for making you wait so long. I was out of the country, and David, who will be your handler from now on, was busy also. Please understand that we are a small firm." He smiled. "Okay? May we go? David will be waiting. I make a point of never keeping David waiting. Believe me, the fuse to his temper is even shorter than yours."

Expecting to meet a duplicate of Colonel Avrum Langatzky, an athletic, thirtyish businessman in a suit and tie, I found myself being introduced to a rather short and tweedy professional man. David, my handler, might have stepped into Washington Square Park for a breather between teaching classes in ancient history or mathematics in one of the New York University buildings sur-rounding the park. He was eating a hot dog purchased from a pushcart vendor.

"It's not the Second Avenue Deli," he said, holding up the mustard-and-sauerkraut-drenched frankfurter, "but I hope you'll join me. It's still the best lunch in town for the money. My treat. Then we'll talk. Just the two of us."

I turned to Langatzky. "You're not staying?"

"I've done my part," he said. "You belong to David now. Good luck, Hershel."

"An outstanding man," David said, nodding at Langatzky as he sauntered toward Fifth Avenue. "He's quite high on you, by the way, Hershel. If he weren't, you and I would not be here today. In your work with us you'll meet different people who will debrief you and pass along information. But Langatzky will always be in charge. I'm his deputy. Anyone you deal with will always be acting on our behalf."

He paused and surveyed the park. "Let's walk," he whispered. "That's a lesson in spycraft, by the way. When you can, walk while you talk. And it's nice to have trees around, in case someone's got a long-distance listening device."

Munching my hot dog as we strolled toward the south side of the square, my imagination shifted into overdrive. Could it be possible that in the heart of Greenwich Village someone had his eyes and ears trained on us? Suddenly I felt as if everyone whom we passed might be a spy.

"As you might well imagine," David said, "we have to be very wary of what we in the intelligence community call walk-ins. You just don't throw your arms around some guy who comes in off the street and says he wants to join up. You check him out. When it comes to vetting a walk-in, such as yourself, there is no one better in the Institute than Lanny. By the way, that's who you're working for: the *Institute*. Never, never, never speak of Mossad. Leave the 'M word' to the amateurs who write spy novels. That is not to say that the authors of thrillers get it wrong. Some of them are quite good. But in their need to maintain tension and excitement they miss the truth about intelligence work. It is not, believe me, all cloaks and daggers. It's details, painstakingly gathered, bit by bit, like picking up tiny pieces of glass to fit into a mosaic. Sometimes good intelligence work is nothing more than buying a bunch of postcards or clipping an article from a scientific journal. I guess you could say we're like a bunch of pack rats, gathering this and that. That's what you'll be doing. You'll be a gatherer. We have a word for such helpful people. *Sayanim.* It means, literally, 'helpers.' I'm your *katsa.* Your handler. From this moment on, I'm your one and only contact."

"How do I contact you? Do you have an office here in the city?"

"I've got lots of offices," he said with a smile. "But at present I'm working out of Montreal. Because of the special and happy relationship between Israel and the United States, we feel that it's a more congenial arrangement not to conduct business with friends like you on American soil. The U.S. government would not be too keen about it if Israel ran intelligence operations involving U.S. citizens *in* the States; not that we ever would. Montreal is close and convenient. From now on, when I call for a meeting between us I'll use the term 'home base.' I will be referring to Montreal. Once you are up and running, we'll meet for debriefings in safe houses closer to your immediate area of concern—Rome, Athens, London, and so forth. These cities are the natural stopovers for a man doing business in the Middle East. But your home base will always be Montreal. Okay with you?"

"Montreal is fine. I conduct a lot of business in Canada."

"I know. Can you clear some time to come up next week?"

An image of my desk calendar flashed in my head, a full slate of meetings related to the Saudi Arabian bid. Although switching dates would be difficult, I felt that I must not exhibit hesitancy. "That will be no problem," I said, "Just tell me where I must be and when."

"Monday through Wednesday. Don't drive up. Take the train. We'll meet at ten o'clock Monday morning at the Hyatt Hotel. Do you know it?"

"Of course. I'll make a reservation right away."

"No need," he said. "It's been done. You are booked for Sunday night only. Then you'll move into a house we keep up there."

"You were pretty sure of yourself, weren't you? Booking me in a hotel before I even agreed to come."

"Not at all, Hershel," he said, lightly tapping my shoulder with a fist. "I'm sure of *you*." He gripped my hand and shook it briskly. "You'll have no trouble arranging this trip? Your wife won't insist on coming along?"

"She's accustomed to me going on business trips without her."

"You'll find the hardest part of your job, Hershel, is not being able to share with loved ones. It's perfectly natural for you to be troubled by all the duplicity and deceit that will be expected of you. I can only suggest that when you struggle with all those questions that you ponder the words of Winston Churchill in the Second World War: 'Sometimes Liberty requires a bodyguard of lies.' "

3

The House on Rue Sanguinet

 As I anticipated, Ruth found nothing out of the ordinary in my sudden announcement that I would be traveling to Canada for a few days, leaving Sunday night and returning on Thursday, though she did wonder why I chose to go by train rather than by car.

"There's a good deal of paperwork to look over," I said, noting how easily I could make up a lie. "Rather than spend the weekend on it, I can take care of it on the way."

She drove me into the city. Dropped off at Grand Central Terminal with an hour to spare, I browsed in a bookstore and, despite my aversion to thrillers about spies, picked up a copy of Ian Fleming's *From Russia With Love* and, on an impulse, Philip K. Kitti's *History of the Arabs*.

Like everyone in my generation who grew up in the era before air travel became commonplace, I retained a special fondness for trains and railroad stations, I experienced a wave of nostalgia whenever I found myself in Grand Central, a magnificent monument to a bygone age when it seemed that all long-distance trains bore romantic names, such as the 20th Century, Broadway Limited, and the train for which I held a ticket, the Montrealer.

Seated in the waiting room, I flipped through the spy novel and found myself reading a page in which James Bond gazed vaguely at one of the most romantic signs in the world, "Orient Express," and noted that the great trains were also going out all over Europe. I had seen the movie based on the Ian Fleming book and vividly remembered the scene in which Sean Connery as James Bond struggled in a compartment of the famous train with a murderous villain. Just the memory of it gave me a chill.

Closing the book and slipping it into a pocket of my coat, I looked up at a pair of well-dressed young men on the bench opposite me. As our eyes met, theirs shifted in the way that eyes do when caught staring. Immediately the pair rose and walked away. When they did not leave the waiting room, my imagination instantly concocted them into a duet of spies with orders to prevent me from reaching my destination. With the announcement that the Montrealer was ready for boarding, they followed me to the gate and onto the platform, then into the same car, cementing my idea that they were watching me.

A few minutes after I chose a seat a portly, elderly woman asked me to help her place a shopping bag from Bloomingdale's in the overhead luggage rack. Standing to put the bag away, I saw that the two men had sat together on the opposite side of the car, two rows behind. Again, they averted their eyes.

Between chatting with the woman and trying to read about Saudi Arabia in my travel book, I remained acutely aware of the presence of the two men all the way to Montreal. Upon arrival they got in the line of passengers waiting for taxis ahead of me and departed the depot in separate cabs, much to my relief.

I had visited Montreal often and found it to be a charming mixture of the New World and the Old. But as I checked into the Hyatt, I could not shake off the memory of the men on the train and the feeling that they had been watching me. Though my reason argued that this was a ridiculous idea, I had great difficulty sleeping, awakening at every sound, however distant or routine. Shortly after dawn I was out of bed and in the hotel coffee shop for breakfast. At seven I sat in the lobby to wait. For what, I did not know.

Exactly at ten David pushed through the revolving door and strode toward me across the lobby. "Good morning, Hershel," he said cheerily as I stood to greet him. "You had a good trip?"

"Please don't think I'm paranoid," I whispered, "but I think I was followed on the way up here."

He glanced around anxiously. "I want to hear about it," he said, "but not here. Come with me."

He led me to the elevators. Entering one, he pressed the button for the top floor. "Useful things, elevators," he said as we ascended. "An empty one going up is ideal for conversations that you don't want overheard."

"What do you do if it stops and someone gets on?"

"I get off."

By the time we arrived, uninterrupted, at the twenty-fifth floor with its revolving restaurant I had described the two men in detail.

"You did very well, Hershel," David said, holding down the DOOR OPEN button. "I'm impressed."

"Beg pardon?"

"You were right about those men, my friend. You *were* being watched. I assigned the two men to watch you."

"*That's* why you insisted I come up here by train," I exclaimed. "You were setting up a test."

"Not a test. Just a practical introduction to spycraft. Congratulations on spotting them."

"They were pretty obvious."

"Yes, they carried out their orders well. You see, I wanted them to be obvious. They were supposed to decoy you away from the person who was really watching you. I had *three* people on your tail."

I gasped. "Who was the other one?"

"The elderly woman carrying the bag from Bloomingdale's who sat beside you on the train."

"Oh my God!"

"There's a cardinal rule of intelligence work for you, my friend. Always anticipate the unexpected and provide against it. While you were being a charming conversationalist the woman took note of your reading material. With your James Bond paperback and a tome on Arabs you quite inadvertently offered clues as to your real purpose on being on that train."

"Come on. That's stretching things quite a bit."

He let go of the button. The door closed.

"Intelligence consists of accumulating numerous facts that appear to be inconsequential," he continued as the car remained motionless. "Added up, little things can tell a much different story. Anyone might pick up a spy novel to read on a train. But why does a man on his way to Canada buy a book about the Arabs? As Sherlock Holmes once put it, 'The little things are infinitely the most important.' "

When the car jerked a little and began a descent I pressed the button for my floor.

"Why did you do that?" he demanded.

"Aren't we going to my room?"

"Avoid meetings in hotel rooms, Hershel. We're going to an address on rue Sanguinet."

When we arrived I noted that a television camera observed us from the wall of a townhouse near City Hall in the heart of Old Montreal. As David pressed the button of an intercom, I read the name on a brass plaque on the door:

DIVERSIFIED INTERNATIONAL CONSULTATIONS, LTD.

A woman spoke through the intercom. "Do you have an appointment?"

"Mr. Mike sent me," David answered.

Opening the door, a muscular young man said, "Good morning, sir. May I see your pass, please?"

"Good morning, Ari," David said, flashing a small photo ID.

Ari stepped aside to let us enter.

"If he recognized you," I said, "why did he ask for your pass?"

"Rules, Hershel. Rules. If you make rules, you follow them!"

As we stood in a vestibule, Ari punched buttons on a panel adjacent to a second door.

As a buzzer sounded and Ari opened the inner door, David said, "The first order of business this morning is to get your picture taken."

"For your files?"

"For a passport, actually," he said as we crossed a small foyer.

"I already have a passport," I said.

"Have you ever used it to visit Israel?"

"Of course."

"Did an immigration official stamp it?"

"I believe so."

"No good," he said, shaking his head. "No one who has been to Israel can enter an Arab country. We will provide you a fresh one."

"Are you telling me that you are going to give me a phony U.S. passport?"

"Oh, it won't be a phony. It will be the genuine article. It will be an exact duplicate of your own, but without the Israeli immigration stamps. We will also produce several others, each in a different name. They will be available as needed, depending on your assignments. For your first undertaking you will receive a Canadian passport, in case you find that being yourself would be unwise or unhealthy."

As he opened a door to a room crammed with photographic, video, and audio equipment, I thought that if I looked around the room I would find "Q" demonstrating his newest wizardry to a sanguine James Bond who, before long, would be putting it to use.

Wordlessly, the young man who had greeted us at the door fiddled with a Polaroid camera and snapped several pictures of me with all the facility of a clerk in a driver's license bureau.

"Your bedroom is on the second floor," David said, escorting me out of the equipment room. "Your luggage will be brought from the hotel. We will also settle your bill. Since time is of the essence, we don't want you wasting it on routine matters."

"Thank you," I said, wondering if the person who would fetch my one suitcase had orders to inspect its contents. "That's very thoughtful and efficient of you."

Opening a door, David showed me a bedroom that was smaller than the one at my hotel but much more homey looking.

"We'll be working in the room next door," he said.

We entered a plain but pleasant room.

"Your task for us," David said, "will be to observe anything of actual or potential military significance. We call such people 'warning agents.' Your construction business is ideal cover. We are interested in everything. As an example, power transmission lines. What could be more mundane? But to a trained intelligence analyst they speak volumes. They are arrows pointing to a source of the power. You can also tell whether that source is an ordinary fossil fuel plant or a nuclear one. Highways also provide clues. Americans assume, for instance, that your country's magnificent network of interstate highways that President Eisenhower started building in the 1950s was constructed for the mere convenience of civilian travelers and to speed interstate commerce. But that was not the intent. Those splendid highways were required by the Cold War, just as Hitler's building of Germany's autobahns was meant for tanks, not for the convenience of Herr and Frau Hun and their kinder on a weekend outing. Show me a paved road cutting through an Arabian desert, Hershel, and I will show you that it has a military purpose."

Going far beyond my initial idea of simply reporting on what I happened to see or overhear, David spent the afternoon teaching aggressive, deliberate, and calculated *spying*.

Explaining procedures for filing written reports, he threw at me an alphabet of code words. *Bravo* stood for new technical information. *Echo* signified construction sites of military significance. *Foxtrot* meant military movements or sites. If I put *Sierra* at the top of a report it meant that my information had something to do with special operations or techniques that might be especially sensitive. *Tango* was economic intelligence. *Zulu* conveyed geographical intelligence.

Another glossary included code names designating sections of the Institute to which my reports might be directed for action. Nevlot was a department that carried out break-ins. Schicklut stood for listening department specialists; Yarid, the security department. Tsiomet recruited people like me. Yahalomim were the handlers and controllers of communications. "Home office" was the term for Mossad headquarters. "Home base" could be any control point in a given area, such as Montreal. The Mossad intelligence analysis unit bore the name Melucha. Kidon, or bayonet, was the "wet squad," that is, assassins.

"How's your Hebrew, by the way?" David asked.

"Not very good. I know a few words," I answered.

"Forget them. And don't learn any others. If you're ever caught and interrogated under drugs, they'll come out. And if you have anything that could connect you even in the remotest way to Israel or being Jewish, a Magen David on a ring, for instance, get rid of them. They could be the death of you, believe me."

His eyes turned to my Masonic ring.

"That's very nice," he said, "and I'm sure you're proud of it. But it gives you away, Hershel. Leave it at home."

At lunch I met Ibrhaim, a young man with a Middle Eastern accent shaded by overtones of Oxford University English that gave him the air of a Lawrence of Arabia. He accompanied each course of the simple meal with an informal lecture on the recent history of the Middle East that was half lecture, half gossip.

He began with the architect of the Yom Kippur War, President Anwar Sadat of Egypt.

"He is by far the cleverest of all the Arab leaders," he said. "The manner in which he planned the war was impressive. That he kept it secret until the date of the attack was even more so. He fooled our best intelligence analysts. But all of this pales in comparison to the way in which he appears to have turned a military defeat into an advantage. He has jolted the government of the United States into publicly acknowledging Arab grievances. He has also had a bit of luck. Secretary of State Henry Kissinger likes him."

At first I thought this remarkable young man's presence to be a coincidence, having no relationship to me, but as he spoke I saw that his lecture was part of my crash course in espionage. He had come to the table prepared to brief me on the status of all of the Arab powers arrayed against Israel in 1974.

"From Morocco on the shores of the Atlantic to Oman on the Arabian Sea," he said, "the Arabs are showing signs of overcoming the three historic hindrances to power: disunity, distrust, and defeat. You might say that they have, at last, discovered oil. Although the boycott that they have imposed has not been wholly successful, it has changed the equation. The West, especially the United States, is being forced to recognize that they best not put all their eggs into one basket. That is why, now more than ever, Israel must have eyes and ears everywhere."

In the afternoon I received a crash course from a young man whom David identified only as "a visiting lecturer." His subject was the equipment of my strange and exciting new world.

He began with the tapping of phones—how to do it and how to detect it.

"But phones aren't the only things that can be bugged," he said. "Look at this room. Ordinary-looking, isn't it? Yet there are a dozen places to install a bug. The lamps. Bookcases. Vases. Behind the chairs."

Going around the room, he revealed a tiny microphone with a built-in transmitter in each of the items he had named.

"Don't worry," he said, grinning. "They're not hooked up. But if they were they could be transmitting our words to listeners as close as the house across the street or one a mile away. Or they could be uplinked to a satellite so that our conversation could be listened to half the world from here."

Crossing the room, he stood by a window. "With the right equipment," he said, tapping a knuckle against the glass, "the vibration of the pane as we speak can be detected, just as if this window were a microphone."

From a desk drawer he brought out a tiny camera. "It's got a built-in four-legged stand," he said, extending the legs and placing the camera on the desk. "They are designed for photographing documents."

Picking up the camera, he placed it in the palm of my hand.

"It looks like a toy," I said.

"But this baby is capable of shooting up to five hundred pictures without changing film," he said. "It's yours. Fully loaded and ready for business."

After dinner, the youth who had opened the door for us when we arrived at the house and then took my picture instructed me on self-defense. A roll of coins for use in public phones, I was shown, could be effective as a weapon when rolled into a fist. A pocketknife would do nicely if I had to slit a throat.

"Do you carry one?" he asked.

"Yes. I have a Swiss army knife that my sons gave me for my birthday a few years ago."

"It may turn out to be the best gift you ever got. May I see it, please?"

I fished out the red pocketknife and handed it to him.

Running his thumb along the edge of the longest of its blades, he shook his head. "Too dull. This couldn't slice a wedge of cheese, much less a man's throat. Get it sharpened. And never be without it from this day on."

He handed me the folded knife. "Nobody is going to issue you a license to kill like James Bond," he said. "But if someone sets out to kill you, you have to be prepared to prevent him from succeeding. Are you familiar with firearms?"

"Yes. I have a handgun that I keep for self-defense. In the construction trade you can run into guys from the Mafia. One of them tried to muscle me once."

"He did not succeed?"

"I jammed my pistol under his chin and warned him that if he ever tried to mess with me again I would not hesitate to blow his brains out. He was a low-level hood. A punk out to make a name."

"Excellent. I hope you'll never need to resort to your gun while working for us, but if you should, my advice is, do not hesitate to use it. And forget all that sentimental stuff about not shooting out of fear of hitting a woman or a child. Always put yourself first. Your opponent will."

As my lessons continued the next morning I felt as if the calendar had been turned back to my childhood when I studied the complex rules that Moses laid down for Jews in the Torah and in the Judaic oral traditions of the Mishnah. According to the Book of Numbers, Moses sent men to spy out the land of Canaan, to "see the land, what it is, and the people that dwelleth therein, whether they be strong or weak, few or many." Beginning at dawn and working until midnight, David and his guest lecturers introduced me to a considerably more complex Mossad code.

"If you think you hear gunshots," David said, "assume they are."

Ari lectured on the subject of traveling by air. "Don't arrive too early at an airport. Before you choose a seat in a waiting room, look around. Avoid sitting near trash cans, phone booths, vendors' stands, unattended luggage, and packages. They may contain bombs. Never become absorbed in reading a newspaper, magazine, or book in a public place. Such inattention can be an invitation to disaster. Don't pack your valuable papers or other items in luggage that will be checked."

Then he turned to hotels. "Always be inconspicuous. Don't permit strangers to strike up conversations. Inspect your hotel room for concealed cameras and listening devices. Don't conduct business on the phone in your hotel room. Discard nothing in a hotel wastebasket."

The do's and don'ts continued.

"Don't share taxis," David advised.

"Sitting in a public place, choose a spot near the entrance and never turn your back to a window or door," Ari said. "In any location, look for an alternative exit. If someone calls your name, do not answer or look around."

"Avoid discussions of politics, religion, or news events with people you don't know," David added.

Rules of action that seemed endless came down to a simple axiom. Trust no one.

Throughout my third day of training, Wednesday, David offered instruction in the art of deception and concealment, ranging from the use of suitcases with secret compartments to creating hiding places, known as slicks. One of the first things he did in a hotel room, he said, was to locate all the electrical outlets in walls. "The spaces behind them are excellent for hiding small documents or a roll of microfilm."

Late Wednesday night, David handed me my new passport, an exact copy of my own but minus evidence of visits to Israel.

"This sure looks real to me," I said admiringly.

David smiled slyly. "It had better."

He also gave me a Canadian passport. The photograph was mine. The name, however, was that of Howard Mackenzie.

"This goes with it," David said, presenting a briefcase.

Opening it, I found a bundle of business cards, a daily record and phone book filled with authentic-looking notations, a checkbook, letterhead, and envelopes bearing the rue Sanguinet address and a telephone number, a microfilm camera like the one I had been taught to use, and two rolls of film—everything that one might expect to find in Howard Mackenzie's briefcase.

"What happens if somebody dials the phone number on these cards?" I asked, holding up one of them.

"Someone will answer it and take a message. When you call the messages will be relayed to you. But you must never use that number except to collect messages. If you have one to leave, you use a different number. You'll find it in the address book under the M's, for Moses. *Abraham Moses.*"

"Isn't that a little obvious, even dangerous?"

"Not at all. If you look him up in the Montreal phone book, you'll find Mr. Moses listed at this address. You will also find him in directories in London, Rome, and Athens. They will have different addresses and numbers, of course. You will also find a number in your book under the name Samson. It is to be used *only* in case of an emergency. Call Samson's number and you'll set off alarm bells."

"Does Mr. Moses accept collect calls?"

"Always a joke, eh, Hershel? The Moses address is also to be used if you wish to send us something through the mail."

From the briefcase I drew a dark blue folder labeled *Howard Mackenzie.*

"That contains Mackenzie's legend," David said. "It provides all the details concerning Mackenzie's life. He too is in the construction business. Most of the facts of his life parallel your own, except that Mackenzie is Canadian and a gentile. You'll note that his religion is listed as 'Christian.' Arabs are not Americans. A U.S. passport does not list its bearer's religion. Visas for travel to the nations of Islam require it. We've found that Christianity is a wide tent. Memorize Mackenzie's legend. Make it a part of you. Then burn that folder."

I closed the briefcase. "When does Howard Mackenzie get his first assignment?"

"Mackenzie is a backup identity. He's a throwaway, in case you find that being yourself would be unwise or unhealthy. Become Mackenzie only if necessary. He exists only if you bring him to life. After you've completed your first task, destroy all of this material. As you undertake other work you will be provided other identities. Your first task on behalf of the Institute will be undertaken in your own name, however."

"And what will that be?"

"You picked it yourself when you put in that bid for the job in Saudi Arabia. We couldn't have selected a better one."

"What if the bid is turned down?"

David grinned. "I can tell you that it has been accepted. According to my latest information, the notification is in the mail."

"How in hell do you know that?"

"Never mind that. You'll probably find it waiting for you when you get back to your office. Let Mr. Moses know when you will be leaving for Saudi Arabia and call him again when you have finished. He'll advise you as to when and where your debriefing will be held."

"Is that it? Are we finished here?"

"One last point," he said. "It's unpleasant but necessary. I'm sure you'll understand. It may sound a little melodramatic."

"Shoot."

"Should anything—God forbid—go wrong, if you get caught, we will deny you. You'll be on your own. We will, of course, do all that we can to get you out, one way or another. We pride ourselves on that. But we will tell the world that we never heard of you. If you find this unacceptable, you can walk out the door now and no one will blame you."

"You're wrong, David," I said. "I would blame myself."

4

Beginner's Luck

 Few, if any, countries in the world were more difficult for a non-Muslim to enter than Saudi Arabia in the summer of 1974.

First I needed a Saudi sponsor. For someone like me, going for business, the invitation had to be extended by a Saudi firm or a foreign company with a Saudi government contract. In my case the sponsor was a Paris-based French corporation with a Saudi partner, which in turn had asked me to submit a bid for work on a petrochemical complex near Riyadh.

As David had warned, obtaining an entry visa required the applicant to state one's religion. At the Saudi consulate in New York City I followed David's advice and wrote in "Christian."

Examining the form, a clerk asked, "What denomination are you, please?"

Despite all the hours of training and lectures in the house in Montreal, here was something that David and his guest experts had not anticipated. Did the Saudi Arabia government keep a list of approved and disapproved Christian denominations? Might the Baptists be banned? Would an Episcopalian, like a Jew, be looked on as persona non grata?

My mind raced. Then an image came into my head of the pages in Sunday newspapers listing church services. One that had always intrigued me stood out. I blurted, "Ethical Culture."

After a moment in which the clerk's face crinkled with a look of puzzlement, he asked, "Is that Protestant?"

"Yes, it is," I said, hoping they had no idea what Ethical Culture was.

After studying letters from the French company verifying the purpose of my trip, the clerk stamped the visa, enabling me to book a flight on the next Wednesday via a Saudia Airline nonstop from New York to Riyadh.

Although I had gained some knowledge of the Arab world on business-related visits to the Middle East, I had not experienced the fullness of Islam that my reading on the subject said I should expect in Saudi Arabia, the land of Islam's most holy cities, Medina and Mecca, from which non-Muslims were barred.

Forged from nomadic bedouin tribes by Abdul Aziz ibn Saud in the 1920s, the monarchy had subsisted on revenues provided by the pilgrims to the holy cities until the discovery of oil before the Second World War. Developed by the Arabian American Oil Company (Aramco), the petroleum industry swiftly replaced the religious pilgrims as the country's economic mainstay, though the influx of "infidels" put a strain on the kingdom's Muslim fundamentalism.

King ibn Saud died in 1953 and was succeeded by his big-spending, politically ambitious eldest son, Saud, who controlled a country of about two million people scattered across territory the size of India. He came to power at a time when the leading voice in Arabia belonged to President Nasser of Egypt. Barely a day passed without Nasser lashing out at extravagances of Saudi princes in general and Saud in particular. Embarrassed and worried, sheikhs and princes forced King Saud to relinquish his power to his younger brother, Crown Prince Faisal.

A worldly and experienced diplomat, he brought to the throne a passionate opposition to both communism and Zionism that pitted him at the same time against the pro-Soviet policies of Nasser. Believing that the answer to the problems of the region lay in the traditional and religious element in Arabism, he sought an alliance within the Arab and Muslim worlds, culminating in the creation of the Islamic Front.

He said, "What is called progressiveness in the world today and what reformers are calling for, be it social, human, or economic progress, is all embodied in the Islamic religion and laws."

Faisal resisted urgings of other Arab leaders to employ oil as a weapon to force the West, especially the United States, to drop its implacable support of Israel and pursue a more evenhanded foreign policy in the Mideast. However, in the aftermath of the 1973 Yom Kippur War, he did an about-face and retaliated against supporters of Israel by employing what the world called "the oil weapon." Following the lead of Libya and Abu Dhabi, he ordered an embargo on Saudi oil shipments to the United States, followed by drastic cuts in production by Arab oil-producing countries that raised petroleum prices 70 percent.

Like all Americans I had felt the bite of the embargo in my wallet. Forced to wait in long lines at gas stations, I had felt my anger against the Arab world increase minute by minute. But now, as I prepared for my dual-purpose trip to Saudi Arabia, I knew that I had to set aside personal feelings.

As a result of the use of the oil weapon, diplomats on all sides gathered for a peace conference under the auspices of the United Nations to arrange an Israeli pullback from the Suez Canal and to establish a UN peacekeeping force in the Sinai. And separate negotiations had culminated in a disengagement agreement between Israel and Syria on June 5, 1974. It created a buffer zone in the strategically important Golan Heights. The United States, meanwhile, dipped into its pockets for aid packages—$350 million in grants and credits for Israel, $250 million for Egypt, $207 million for Jordan, and $100 million for Syria. With announcement of this largesse, the United States and Saudi Arabia agreed to wide-ranging economic and military cooperation that Secretary of State Henry Kissinger called "a milestone in our relations with Saudi Arabia and with Arab countries in general." The icing on the cake was an announcement of a Middle East tour by President Nixon, set to begin June 10, three weeks prior to my journey to Saudi Arabia.

I followed daily news accounts of the Nixon trip avidly, especially stories related to his three days of conferences with King Faisal, held at Jidda on the Persian Gulf. On the eve of my departure for Saudi Arabia I found Faisal's rhetoric more than a little disconcerting.

The Saudi ruler warned Nixon, "There will never be a real and lasting peace in the area unless Jerusalem is liberated and returned to Arab sovereignty, unless liberation of all occupied Arab territories is achieved, and unless the Arab people of Palestine regain their rights and return to their homes and the right of self-determination."

Upon his return to the White House, Nixon saw "hope" for peace in the region. "Where there was hostility for America there is now friendship," he said. As the possessor of one-third of the oil reserves in the world and a mainstay of America's petroleum supply, Saudi Arabia was central to Nixon's strategy. Noting the promise of military aid to Saudi Arabia, he pledged a new "partnership" in which Saudi Arabia would be "strong and secure."

Although I was eager for the day when I would travel to this intriguing and increasingly significant country, I also dreaded it. Pondering my secret purpose, I grew more and more doubtful. But in these moments of wavering will I reminded myself of my original intent in bidding for the Saudi contract. Plain and simple, it was a real money-maker, I reasoned. Calling off the trip would be a bad business decision. Being there, how could I not carry out the other task, which was potentially more important and for which I had volunteered and been trained?

Having been in the Mideast as a consultant or subcontractor for European associates who held contracts, I prepared for the journey by packing items that experience had taught me to take. I included in my luggage my Swiss army knife, flashlight and extra batteries, several caps, a canteen for water, sun lotion and bug spray, soap, toilet paper, and two pairs of canvas, foam-soled shoes. Into the toe of one I tucked my microfilm camera.

When the fateful morning arrived I journeyed from my hometown in an airport limousine with several other travelers. One by one, they got out at their respective terminals, leaving me alone and looking out the window, anxiously reading signs marking turnoffs from a cobweb of roads, each of the white-lettering-on-green rectangles listing terminals of the airlines of the world that operated to and from Kennedy Airport.

"There it is," I said to the driver urgently. "Saudia."

The driver answered with an edge of impatience. "I can read, sir," he said as the limo swerved to the right.

Fishing the passport that had never been touched by the hand of an Israeli immigration officer and my plane ticket from my jacket pocket, I approached the check-in desk with a surge of anxiety. Did my nervousness show in my face? Might the young man behind the counter see right through me? Would he recognize right away that I was a spy? Was it possible that some Saudi agent knew all about my meetings with my handler? Had the word been passed to be on the lookout for an Israeli agent posing as a businessman and claiming adherence to Ethical Culture?

If so, the young man gave no sign. "Have a pleasant trip, sir," he said, returning my passport and ticket. "The passenger waiting area is just up the stairs," he added with a smile.

Beyond the windows of the waiting room loomed the green-and-white Saudia Boeing 747 that with all its mighty thrust and high speed would still require sixteen hours to complete its non-stop journey. Remembering my lessons in how to behave in an airport waiting room, I did my best to avoid attracting attention to myself. I picked a seat safely distant from trash receptacles and other places where a bomb might be concealed, glanced frequently from my newspaper, and took note of everyone sitting near me.

Because of the length of the flight I had tossed aside my usual reticence regarding extravagance while traveling on company funds and had booked a first-class window seat. Hopes that the aisle seat would remain unoccupied promptly vanished in the form of a portly man wearing a blue pin-striped suit and the traditional Saudi headdress.

To my dismay he immediately made it clear that he wanted to talk. He introduced himself and, eliciting that this was my first visit to Riyadh, assured me that I would find it a thrilling and enlightening experience. He then provided a historical sketch of the city, naming sites I must not miss—the museum; Masmak Fortress in Old Riyadh; the ruins of Dir'alyah dating to the fifteenth century; and the marketplace, souk al-Bathnaa.

Mercifully, he asked little about me and fell asleep after dinner, leaving me in peace.

Still wondering if my traveling companion was what he had seemed to be—a businessman like me—or a spy with instructions to keep an eye on me, I arrived at Riyadh on Thursday afternoon. Because it was the onset of the Muslim holy day, I observed from my taxi a stream of luxury automobiles—Mercedeses, Rolls-Royces, Cadillacs—filled with wealthy families heading out of the city as New Yorkers fled their concrete canyons for open spaces on weekends. They passed my cab blowing horns and blinking lights as if they were in a madcap chase in an old Laurel and Hardy comedy. Veering from side to side, they sped past the rude houses of the local poor, Palestinians and other Arabs imported to perform manual labor. Beyond the clusters of these wretched buildings stretched a reddish desert emptiness.

Although Riyadh had been the capital of Saudi Arabia since

1932, it had been eclipsed by the more amenable and decidedly cooler Red Sea city of Jidda. But as my taxi sped into the city, I noted evidence all around me that under King Faisal's appreciation of the power beneath the sands, Riyadh was making a great leap forward and upward. With construction projects blossoming everywhere, I expected that in a very short time the former oasis would become a sprawling, modern metropolis complete with freeways and deluxe hotels.

On previous trips to Arab countries I had learned that checking into a hotel was not the same thing as pulling off an interstate and stopping at a Holiday Inn. The difference appeared in the look you got. At a Holiday Inn the stranger received a broad welcoming smile. At the Abalkhail Hotel in the center of Riyadh the looks that greeted me seemed to be daggers of suspicion.

With shoulders back and arms swinging, my eyes fixed on the studious gaze of a desk clerk who knew a foreigner when he saw one, I presented my passport and said, "You have a reservation for me, I trust."

Producing a registration form and a pen, he said, "I will need to retain your passport. It is a security requirement. If everything is in order you may pick it up in the morning."

What if everything were not in order? Might I expect a knock on the door in the middle of the night? Would I face men with guns? If they found out I was a spy, would I be allowed to place a phone call to the American embassy? Could I become an "international incident"?

During my lessons in espionage I had asked David whether I ought to register my presence in Saudi Arabia with the American Embassy.

David had looked at me aghast. "Hell no," he blurted. "That is the worst thing you could do. You would only draw attention to yourself. They will immediately regard you as an individual who *expects* to get into trouble."

"What if I *do* get in trouble?"

"Don't think about it," he said with a groan. "Thinking can make it so."

Ascending in an elevator, I pictured angry cables burning up secured lines between Washington and Tel Aviv with demands for an explanation for Howard Schack having been arrested in Riyadh and accused of spying for Israel. Tel Aviv would deny everything, of course. David had made himself quite clear on that.

"This is your room," said the bellboy, pushing open a door.

Overtipping him, I thought of many other places where I would have preferred to be at the moment. As I dropped onto the king-size bed, I muttered, "What the hell am I doing here?"

The cautioning voices of David, Ari, and my other trainers answered. "Be alert to the slightest hole in the ceiling, the mirrors on the walls. There may be cameras."

"Look for bugs. And I don't mean the kind that crawl on the floor!"

"Assume at all times that you are being observed."

I found nothing to indicate I was being watched but acted as if something were hidden to observe and record my every movement. After what seemed to be only a few minutes of sleep I was jolted awake at dawn by the blaring call to morning prayer that seemed to emanate from every minaret in every corner of the capital city of the richest nation of Islam.

Because Friday was a Muslim holy day when no business could be transacted, I had planned to spend the entire day alone in the hotel getting over jet lag. I began with breakfast. Entering the hotel's small dining room, I discovered only one other customer, a Westerner.

I approached his table. "Do you mind if I take this seat?" I asked. "Frankly, I hate eating alone."

"Not at all," he replied. "I'm delighted to have company."

He was short, with a sinewy build and the sun-leathered skin and blond hair bleached almost white that marked him as a man who worked outdoors. The stranger introduced himself as Carl Morgan, a supervising engineer for an Aramco refinery in the Eastern Province. "I'm working in a hellhole called Dammam," he said, sipping coffee. "Have you ever been there?"

"This is my first visit to Saudi Arabia," I said, looking at the menu and discovering to my delight that it offered eggs, any style.

"A friendly word of advice to a newcomer, if I may," Carl said, plucking the menu from my hands. "Stick to Nescafé coffee and the pita bread in this dump. If you really must have a cooked breakfast, go to the Caravan Stop Restaurant in the Al-Khozama Hotel on Olaya Street. They have a Palestinian chef who learned how to cook in a decent hotel in Gaza before the Israelis took it over in the 1967 war. Now he lives for when he can go back to a liberated Palestine and open his own restaurant. *Enshallah*. That means 'God willing.' "

"I know," I said as a waiter appeared to take my order.

"Ah! It's your first time in Saudi," Carl said, "but you have been to the Middle East before!"

"From time to time," I said. "On business."

"You're an oil man?"

"Construction is my line."

"Then you must be here for the big new French job just south of here. Quite a project, I hear. Very hush-hush."

As I gave the waiter my order for coffee and bread, a man's voice blared through the hotel like a foghorn. Wearing a short, brown, monkish robe, flowing white headdress, and floppy sandals, the man poked his head into the dining room to trumpet another call to prayer.

"Looks like you'll have to wait for your breakfast," Carl said as workers, including our waiter, dutifully left the dining room. Carl looked around the empty room. "At times like this," he said, "I always feel like a heathen. That guy with the loud voice is called a mutaw. He's like a religious policeman. Did you see the look that he gave us? It said what he was thinking of us. Infidels!"

In the course of our conversation Carl made an offer I could not refuse. "How'd you like to visit my company's facilities?" he asked. "It's a short hop by plane to Dammam. That's in the Eastern Province on the Persian Gulf."

Because I had nothing to do concerning my own work until Monday, I agreed to go with him the next day, Saturday.

"The flight leaves at ten o'clock," he said, "but we'd better be there at seven. They don't take reservations, so it's a matter of who gets there first. And we should allow some extra time in case we have to do some dickering over baksheesh."

Having had some experience in doing business in the Middle East, I needed no translation. Baksheesh was a bribe. From Casablanca to Cairo it was the bedrock of commerce in the Arab world. For Americans in the private sector trying to do business in the region, the custom of under-the-table payments, kickbacks, and the official corruption presented a double-edged sword. Although nothing could be achieved without providing for baksheesh, an unrealistic and idealistic Congress of the United States insisted on writing international trade laws that prohibited it. This created a situation in which Americans who had no choice but to go along with local customs or lose out on business abroad were turned into criminals.

Getting aboard the flight to Dammam required both Carl and me to come up with twenty American dollars for the ticket clerk, in addition to the fare. Five dollars slipped to another official excused us from inspection of our luggage. While Carl had several valises, my baggage was a canvas carryall containing shirts and a change of underwear.

"The only reason they have inspections," Carl explained as we hurried toward the plane, "is so those bastards can get their palms greased. They only require it of foreigners."

During a three-quarter-hour flight, I looked out the window toward a vast stretch of desert known as the Rub' al Khali, or the Empty Quarter, a region so fierce that even the nomadic bedouin had been reluctant to cross it—until the finding of oil.

Before that historic discovery Dammam had been nothing but a dot in the sands, so meaningless that it had been unworthy of being recorded on maps. The same had been true of nearby Al-khobar and Dhahran, with which Americans were to become quite familiar in the 1991 Persian Gulf War. With the discovery of oil, the three places on the Gulf became the sites of sprawling refineries. Tiny ports that had served fishermen and quaint little merchant boats, called dhows, turned into gigantic facilities for oceangoing supertankers brimming with petroleum bound for the oil-hungry, industrialized West.

After a tour of Carl's refinery that produced nothing that I had not seen in dozens of refineries just like it, the sun began setting, a big red balloon hovering above the rim of the world. As I entered Carl's office, his staff, a mixture of Arabs and Westerners, were leaving their desks, their day's work done. Engineers and technical personnel, they resided nearby in two-room mobile homes. Oblivious to me with my carryall bag, they hurried out while Carl searched his pocket for the keys to his office.

"We have a security force," he explained in a tone that implied that in the Arab world no one could be trusted, "but I never leave my office without locking it. It's a losing cause. Security is lax. I'd bet you next week's wages that those guys who are so eager to get out of here for the day have left stuff all over their desks. I yell at them, I remind them of the rules concerning sensitive materials, but they look at me as if I were the man in the moon."

The phrase "sensitive materials" reverberated in my head. Could this be true? Might I be *that* lucky? Or was this a trap?

What Carl and I talked about in the following half hour I do not recall. My thoughts centered on what he had said and on what plausible reason I might invent to leave the office in order to find out if the abandoned desks in the adjoining room might prove to be littered with items of interest.

Presently, I turned to the most logical excuse I could think of to absent myself. "Excuse me, Carl," I said. "Would you tell me where to find the men's room?" I hoped he would not insist on escorting me.

"Out the door and straight ahead," he said, bending over his desk, engrossed in catching up on paperwork that had accumulated while he visited Riyadh. "It's at the far end of the office."

Closing the door behind me and sweeping my eyes over the long room, I could not believe what I saw. I gaped in amazement at a sea of desktops covered with architectural drawings, floor plans, blueprints, and documents.

Walking slowly and with my heart beating so loudly that I was certain Carl must have heard it, I scanned everything. As I reached the last row of desks, I struck what seemed to me to be paydirt. On top of a heap of papers lay a detailed summary of work that Carl had not shown me. Every page had been stamped with the word CLASSIFIED. This struck me as odd. Nothing I had seen on my tour had appeared worthy of such a designation. Had I seen everything?

Reading quickly in the dim light, I found that Carl's petroleum project disguised facilities for manufacturing jet fuel as an ordinary automotive gasoline refinery. If observed from the ground, as I had seen the unit, or spied on from a reconnaissance airplane or satellite, the section would appear quite innocent, as it had to me. The plans that I held in my shaking hands proved otherwise. The spiral binder pinpointed pumping stations, every oil pipe line, port facilities, roads, the locations of water wells, and topographical maps.

Between the covers of one book, I had discovered the heart and soul of Carl's work. So significant was the information that I feared I had fallen into a trap. I expected to be seized at any moment. But when the offices remained quiet and no one rushed out of hiding to grab me, I ripped out the key pages, rolled them into a tight cylinder, and shoved the markedly thinner binder under a pile of documents.

Wrapping the stolen sheets in a page from a wall calendar, I darted breathlessly into the men's room. Removing my jacket, I tucked the rolled pages into a sleeve. Leaving the men's room, I carried the jacket draped over my arm.

As I returned to his office, Carl, busy answering a stack of interoffice memos, gave me a cursory glance. When I felt certain he was not looking my way I shoved the papers from the sleeve into my bag.

Having gotten away with the material, I faced the challenge of concealing it in my hotel room for a few days and then smuggling it out of the country. I needed a hiding place—a slick. For practice after my training in Montreal I had fashioned several in my office at home. But finding a slick in unfamiliar surroundings proved much more challenging.

I sat on my bed that night in what can only be described generously as a fleabag hotel on King Saud Street opposite the railway station. Gazing at the clothes closet, I noted that the rods for hanging clothing appeared to be metal. I examined them and found that they consisted of adjustable, telescoping aluminum tubes. Pulling them apart, I decided that they were ideal for concealing the papers.

Rolling them even tighter and stuffing them into the slick, I experienced no twinge of conscience. I felt only a concern about being caught. Nor did I hold guilty thoughts concerning the man from whose office I had taken the material. In Carl's easy manner and quick smile I had detected a type of individual who was all too common in international construction: a man on the make. Though I knew only a few Arab phrases I had learned one that seemed to fit him exactly, "muka ab shaytan," meaning "a devil three times over." He had struck me as an opportunist who would have no qualms or guilt in cheating his firm as a freelance dealer in pilfered products to anyone looking for a sweet deal, no questions asked. Consequently, I felt no regrets that he had fallen victim to my maraudings.

But my bravado turned to fear as I lay in bed and dwelt on the possibility that my good fortune in Carl's office might not have been luck at all, but a setup. Going downstairs to keep an appointment with him for Sunday morning breakfast, I expected to be greeted by security men come to arrest me.

Instead I found him alone, smiling, affable in his oily way, and clearly enjoying his role as tour guide. "I have cleared my schedule for the day," he said. "There's not much else to see, but there is an interesting museum and some good archaeological sites."

"I'm not one for looking at dusty ruins," I said, "but I've always had an idea that it would be fun, even romantic, to go sailing on the Persian Gulf. Do you think it could be arranged?"

Ordinary sightseeing was not exactly my intent.

Carl said with a wink, "With a little haggling, anything is possible. I know just the man and the boat, if you can put up with the smell of fish."

Bearing a strong resemblance to Spencer Tracy's crusty and stubborn fisherman in the movie *The Old Man and the Sea*, Amir, the English-speaking skipper of a creaking old craft, proved to be a natural tour guide. As we sailed the jagged headlands he regaled us with tales of Arabian brigands when the inlet-dotted eastern shore of eighteenth-century Saudi Arabia had been known as the Pirate Coast. The area had been notorious for raiding merchant ships, until Britain's Royal Navy came in to impose a *pax Britannica* on the Persian Gulf and turn it into a British lake.

While Amir lectured on history I studied the maze of islands, coves, and inlets that seemed to be ideal for harboring small boats whose purpose was war, not fishing. I had brought my Nikon camera. But when I started to snap pictures the old man waved his arms and yelled to me to stop.

"The government doesn't allow pictures," Carl explained.

This meant that I would have to remember all I saw and write it down later.

Back on shore Carl insisted on a walking tour of the town. Recalling that David had told me that even the most commonplace landmarks could prove vital to an intelligence analyst, I made a mental note of locations of the post office, railway station, bus depot, hotels—even the currency exchange offices. That streets of the town were laid out in a grid would help me in preparing a map.

By the time my accommodating host suggested lunch I realized that Carl was basically a lonely man. Although the fly-infested outdoor restaurant on King Aziz Street was disgustingly filthy and the lamb reeked, I was too hungry not to eat. For more than an hour Carl spoke of other places in the Eastern Province that had blossomed into oil boom towns, lacing his discourse with references to projects in Dhahran, Alkhobar, and Hofuf.

A few hours later, with the spoils of my first adventure in espionage retrieved from the slick and stuffed into my bag with my dirty shirts, I paid another five dollars to avert inspection and boarded a plane for the return trip to Riyadh. The only non-Muslim among the hundred or so passengers, I drew curious looks and whispered remarks in a language I could not fully understand. Self-conscious, I recalled the admonition of Rudyard Kipling, "East is East and West is West, and never the twain shall meet."

Clutching the knapsack containing the stolen documents, I also remembered his warning, "A fool lies here who tried to hustle the East."

In my hotel room in Riyadh I worked well past midnight to record everything I had seen. Filling a notebook, I tried to disguise my notes so that they would appear to be nothing more than the scribblings of a particularly detail-minded tourist but crammed with code words that I hoped would refresh my memory when I rewrote the pages. That is what I planned to do when I reached Rome upon completing my legitimate business in Riyadh. I finished packing the notes and the items from Carl's office into the bottom of my carryall. I then covered them with two shirts and filled the bag with materials that I would need for the first of the meetings with my French associates. Undaunted by my aborted photographic experience in Dammam, I placed my Nikon camera atop the contents of the bag.

A driver sent by my hosts picked me up at my hotel on Monday morning. I settled into the rear of an air-conditioned Mercedes sedan. We arrived half an hour later at offices of the Saudi oil ministry, a gleaming white ultramodern building jutting out of the sand southwest of Riyadh on the highway to Jidda. I was greeted by a young man in the uniform of the Royal Saudi Air Force and escorted to a conference room on the second floor where I joined at least a hundred others like me.

Businessmen from the United States and Europe mingled with their Arab counterparts around an enormous scale model of the project that had brought them together. These men dressed in flowing robes and headcoverings of various styles and colors. Joining them in admiring the model, I wondered if I might dare take my Nikon from my bag and snap a picture. But as I mulled over the idea, the meeting was called to order.

As if I were attending a formal dinner, I located my seat at an enormous conference table by finding a place card with my name on it. To my left I found Yusuf B. Haroun, former prime minister of Pakistan and currently chief executive officer of an international development corporation. On my right sat Sheikh Sabah Jamir of the Kuwait Arab Development Fund.

To my surprise the meeting began with the introduction of an unscheduled speaker, Saudi Arabia's minister of petroleum and mineral resources. Before the Yom Kippur War it would have been unlikely that anyone in the world outside of the international oil business could have named him. But since the war and the Arab oil boycott Sheik Ahmed Zaki al-Yamani had become, due in large measure to television news coverage of the oil crisis, one of the most recognizable faces around the globe.

In boning up for my venture into Saudi Arabia I had done some reading concerning him. Born in 1930, a native of Mecca, he was the son of the chief justice of Saudi Arabia and had studied Islamic and civil law at Cairo's King Fahd University. After flirting with both Marxism and the right-wing Moslem Brotherhood, he rejected these extremes and returned to Mecca at the age of nineteen to serve on the staff of the Finance Ministry.

In 1953 he went to the United States, spending three years studying international law at Harvard. He returned home to find a champion in Crown Prince Faisal. Named minister of state without portfolio in 1960, he became the youngest Saudi Arabian ever to hold ministerial rank and one of the very few commoners in Faisal's inner circle. In 1962 he became minister of petroleum and minerals. That job would catapult him to the center of the international stage six years later with his leadership in the formation of the Organization of Arab Petroleum Exporting Countries, OAPEC, later known as OPEC.

An architect of the post–Yom Kippur War oil embargo, he had visited the United States in December 1973, stressing that Arab oil policy was inextricably linked to Israel's occupation of Arab lands. "Stop this unlimited aid to Israel," he told Americans.

During his tour of European capitals, the newspaper the *Guard-*

ian noted, "By all the precedents, Sheik Yamani of Saudi Arabia is the most formidable Eastern emissary to arrive in Europe since the Tartars swept into Russia or the Moslem hordes reached the walls of Vienna in the Middle Ages."

To me he did not look like a fearsome invader. "His great advantage is that he is as much at ease in a trimly tailored Western business suit as in Arabia's flowing *thobe*," said *Time* magazine in a December 17, 1973, profile. "He straddles cultures, enjoying Arabian poetry and folk dancing, but also loving classical music and oilmen's lusty jokes."

A tall, strongly built man with a Vandyke beard and wearing the traditional garb of his native land, he spoke without notes, addressing us informally, as if we were old friends.

In reviewing events since the war and the oil embargo he repeated what he had said in Washington and Europe. "We are interested in peace and justice, not in enforcing sanctions." He added that Saudi Arabia's oil policy had nothing to do with the existence of Israel. He continued with a smile, "So many Arab leaders announced that they are prepared to sign a peace treaty with Israel, that the question of the existence of Israel is not an issue. It is not tied to the oil issue in any case."

Following Yamani's remarks, the meeting proceeded through the morning with a general discussion of the project, then broke up into groups for conferences on specific details. With lunch being served as we worked I accumulated stacks of documents, plans, and other materials specific to the jobs with which my company would be concerned in the building of the sprawling power plant represented by the model. Copies of the plans, I presumed, would also be of interest to the other organization I represented. Should there ever be a war between Israel and Saudi Arabia, such drawings and blueprints would provide invaluable guidance to a team of saboteurs or bombardiers of the Israeli Air Force.

The day-long conference ended with a buffet dinner in an adjoining dining room that seemed to be twice the size of the room in which Yamani had addressed us. Immediately, I noted that the model of the project had been moved from the conference room to one side of the dining hall. Taking advantage of the jovial informality, I drew my camera from my carryall and drifted among the guests snapping pictures, expecting at any minute to feel a tap on the shoulder by someone telling me that photos were not permitted and demanding that I surrender film and camera and come along for questioning.

When that did not happen I felt emboldened enough to encourage a group of six guests to pose for a shot around the model of the petrochemical project and its supporting power plant. They gladly complied as I followed the timeless tradition of photographers and implored, "One more, just to be sure."

As they smiled admiringly at the model I tilted the lens slightly downward, cutting them out of the frame, and snapped only the model.

Partaking of the most sumptuous buffet in my experience, I drifted around the room, joining conversations and eavesdropping on others. I wished that I had a hidden tape recorder as these gregarious and proud men chatted about the project that united them and others, gossiped about personalities, and expressed the uniform opinion that the nations of the West must, in their enlightened self-interest, become more sensitive and responsive to the Arab cause.

The day after being grandly introduced to the project we traveled to the construction site itself. Encouraged by my photographic success at the banquet, I took along my camera and discovered, amazingly but happily, that no one challenged me as I exposed roll after roll, ostensibly for "souvenir" pictures of my associates but with the lens slightly averted to record the work that had been done already and landmarks that might be helpful in identifying the site.

After four days it was time to leave.

Packing my suitcases, I mingled the items I had stolen from Carl's office at Dammam with the documents, blueprints, maps, and other papers related to the petrochemical project. I trusted that anyone who might decide to inspect my luggage would not recognize the differences between the refinery in Dammam and the plant at Riyadh that would be immediately apparent to someone like Carl or me. I stuffed into the toes of my shoes the rolls of film containing the photos from the banquet and the Riyadh construction site. I had written notes based on my memory of Sheik Yamani's speech, which I folded and tucked into the pocket of a soiled shirt that itself was wrapped in other clothing needing laundering. My experiences in traveling in countries in which luggage actually was examined had taught me that a customs official never poked around in smelly laundry.

I had never been more than a casual drinker of alcohol. However, as my plane lifted off the ground that afternoon I desperately longed for a tall glass of nerve-numbing Scotch. But, alas, I was flying Saudia Airlines again, so the drink had to be deferred until I cleared Italian customs and immigration at my destination, Leonardo da Vinci International Airport, Rome.

With my luggage retrieved and the Scotch under my belt I found a public phone and dialed the number of Mr. Moses's Rome office.

A cryptic male voice said, "Message, please."

"This is Hershel. The message is, 'The furniture will be ready at the Cavalieri Hilton Hotel in about an hour.'"

The voice replied, "I do not know what you are talking about," and hung up.

This was code. The words signified my message had been understood and that I would be contacted soon.

I opened my luggage in my room in the splendid modern hotel that sat atop Monte Mario and overlooked the city. I was eager to see if I could find any signs that the contents might have been examined, but everything appeared to be untouched, just the way I had packed the papers, plans, and rolls of film.

An hour later, my bedside phone rang. A man asked, "Is Hershel there?"

"Who is speaking?" I said.

"This is Reuven. I represent David in the Rome office. He informed me that you have furniture."

"Yes. I'd like to see you as soon as possible."

"There's a nice buffet at the railway station. Shall we say, six o'clock?"

"How will I recognize you?"

"Don't worry. I'll spot you."

Promptly at six, I observed a young man wearing aviator sunglasses, blue jeans, a green sweater, and sneakers, with a knapsack slung over his shoulder. He zigzagged a path through the noisy, crowded restaurant to my table at the rear.

"You look just like your picture, Hershel," he said with a boyish grin. "Have you seen the famous Trevi Fountain? It is nearby. A short walk."

We stopped to watch a bubbly mob of tourists snapping pictures of the famous statute and flipping coins into the pool of water, an act that was supposed to guarantee their return to Rome. There I handed Reuven my bulging carryall bag.

"Hershel, this is remarkable," he exclaimed as he glanced at the documents inside. "A treasure trove. You've done very well."

"I'll need some of those things back," I said.

"Come to the office," he said. "I'll have copies made while we debrief."

Strolling as casually as tourists, we arrived at the equally thronged Piazza di Spagna with its famous steps, turned into the swanky Via Condotti, and walked to a commercial building on Via del Corso.

"Our firm is on the second floor," Reuven said.

Elegant gold lettering on the door proclaimed FASHIONS DI ROMA.

"It's a legitimate business, by the way," he said, opening the door. "We actually had a profit last year."

With copies made of the material that I would need to take back to my company, we settled down for the debriefing at a large table in a windowless room.

"All of this will be analyzed at the Institute," Reuven said. "It's like putting together a jigsaw puzzle. But the pieces are never in one box. They have to be gathered from many sources. What you've brought with you from Saudi Arabia might turn out to be a part of the puzzle that someone has been looking for."

"So what are you going to do when the puzzle is together?" I asked. "Will you bomb the hell out of these places? Or maybe send a crack team of commandos to blow up the buildings?"

"Ah, my friend," Reuven said, rolling his eyes. "If only things were that simple."

5

"Who's the Man With the Beard?"

I returned home at the end of July 1974, thrilled and elated by the success of my first adventure in spying. However, I could not escape the fact that in less than a year after the victory of the Yom Kippur War, Israel's fortunes had taken a turn for the worse.

Rather than exhibiting defeatism, the Arab nations had demonstrated a confidence and unity never seen before. Through the use of "the oil weapon" they had managed to achieve a shift in the balance of world power in their favor. While some expressions of sympathy for the Arabs that came from the oil-dependent Western nations obviously stemmed from self-interest, others reflected concerns over Israel's occupation of Arab territory and a recognition of the continuing, explosive problem of the Palestinians. Whatever the motivation of these countries, the fact was that Israel had lost friends everywhere.

A few days after my return from Saudi Arabia, Israel lost the most important friend of all. On August 9, 1974, overcome by the disaster of the Watergate scandal, President Nixon resigned. In the words of Golda Meir at a White House meeting in August 1970, Nixon had been "a friend, a great friend in the White House." His dramatic order for military resupply in the Yom Kippur War of 1973 had proved his friendship once more. It remained to be seen whether his successor, Gerald R. Ford, would be as staunch an ally in the face of growing pressures on Washington to mend fences in its relations with an Arab world suddenly awakened to the significance of oil as a political weapon.

I soon learned of the depth of Israeli worries about these developments firsthand. Summoned to Montreal for a meeting with

David, I expected a follow-up to Reuven's debriefing in Rome and, possibly, a critique of my work. This indeed turned out to be David's primary purpose, but as we sat down in the parlor on the second floor of the house on rue Sanguinet, he appeared nervous and hesitant. Wondering if he were summoning courage to tell me something unpleasant, I braced for the worst.

In Rome Reuven had had nothing but praise for my work. But I had no way of knowing if he meant it. Had he followed "standard operating procedures" dictated by an Institute rule book for the handling of well-meaning amateurs? Since our rendezvous in the Eternal City, had experts of the Institute analyzed the product of my venture and found it wanting, even useless? Might my eagerness and enthusiasm have warped my judgment?

By the time I arrived at rue Sanguinet I had conjured so much self-doubt about my mission that the moment I found myself with David in the second-floor parlor I blurted, "What about the material I gave to Reuven? Was it worthwhile?"

David sat silently for a moment, then, leaning forward in his chair, his hands loosely clasped between his lanky legs, his brow crinkled, he said, "Often it is the lot of a spy that he does not know if his work has paid off. You must not expect to be different, Hershel."

"Of course not," I said, "but I do expect some feedback."

"I may not always be able to provide it," he said. "The fact is, I may not know myself. Who can say, or would care to say, that a bit of information picked up in some dusty corner of an Arabian desert reached the ear of the president of the United States by way of a whisper by the Israeli ambassador of facts supplied to him by an agent working for the Institute? How can someone document that a snapshot made from a speeding automobile in Iraq confirmed that a nondescript building in some God-forsaken spot in the sand houses a super-secret radar command installation? Is it possible to certify that an agent's personal assessment of the nature of the royal family of Saudi Arabia has assured the Israeli Cabinet that Saudis are just as interested in blunting the greedy intentions of Arab hotheads as Israel? In ephemeral matters such as these, Hershel, even I can only judge the impact of my work by reading newspapers."

He got up and crossed the room to a window.

"There have been times," he went on, "when realizing that something did *not* happen was my only reward."

He turned, looking at me intently. "You must resign yourself not to expect your work to lead to immediate and spectacular military action." He paused as if to let all this sink in. "Having said all that," he continued as he returned to his chair, "I can tell you that my bosses in Tel Aviv are delighted with the result of your Saudi mission. They are so pleased that I've been authorized to speak with you about taking on special assignments from time to time. How does that idea strike you?"

Although I had never shown much interest in athletics, my reply took the form of a lighthearted sports analogy. "You're asking me to give up my amateur status and turn pro?"

"Something like that," he said dead seriously.

"As you know, my intent was simply to pass on to you folks whatever information I happened to pick up. I understood that this would require a little training. Some of it came in handy, too. But being *assigned*? That's a different kettle of fish."

"Forget that I said '*give* you special assignments.' Let me put it this way. How would you feel about being *requested* to do *specific* work? Work that you could *decline*."

"No questions asked? No hard feelings if I opt out?"

"None whatsoever. You've got too much potential for us to hold a grudge."

"Have you got a *specific request* at the moment?"

"I wanted to discuss the idea with you first. If you agree, there'll be no shortage of projects."

"I will do nothing against the interests of my country!"

"Definitely not."

"There are bound to be times when I just wouldn't be free to drop everything and dash off on a mission. I do have a business to run. And a family to consider. I have to make a living."

"We are willing to pay you."

"I'm not asking for money."

He sank back in his chair and lit a cigarette. "I'm going to bring you in on a matter that you might think is far beyond all the things you and I talked about in this very room. I assume that you have heard of the PLO."

"Of course I have," I said. "They're a bunch of terrorists!"

"That's putting it mildly."

Organized in East Jerusalem in 1964, the Palestine Liberation Organization had become the umbrella group for various guerrilla factions operating against Israel after the 1967 war, but with its base shifted to Damascus. Its most visible figure was its chairman, Yasir Arafat, head of Al Fatah. The biggest of the guerrilla organizations, its purpose was to drive the Jews into the Mediterranean and turn Israel into a homeland for the Arabs.

"We anticipate a move by the Arab nations to give these cutthroats legitimacy," David said. "They will designate the PLO the official representatives on the entire Palestinian question. We expect this to happen at the meeting of the Arab League in Rabat, Morocco, beginning on October 26. It's to be a full-scale diplomatic effort at the United Nations, including a speech to the General Assembly by Arafat. The purpose is to get the UN to give official blessing to the creation of a Palestinian state on the West Bank and in Gaza."

"Surely the United States won't go along with that," I said. "They'll use the veto."

"Unfortunately, there is no veto in the General Assembly," David said, extinguishing his cigarette. "And given the warming of relations between Washington and the Arab governments since last year's war, we are not sure that if there were a veto the United States would use it. Nor are we certain that President Ford can be counted on to be as supportive of us as Nixon."

His pessimism left me distressed and disappointed. I also felt puzzled. "What's all this got to do with me?" I asked rather grumpily.

"We want you to add the PLO to your list of things for which to keep your eyes and ears open," he said. He removed a sheet of paper from his inside coat pocket and passed it to me. "These are the groups that we are interested in."

The list read:

Al Fatah. Largest group. Estimated 6,000 guerrillas and militiamen. Also guards refugee camps in Lebanon and Syria.

Popular Front for the Liberation of Palestine (PFLP). Marxist. Most militant of the groups. Estimated membership: 500. Led by George Habash. Trains and supports other terrorist groups.

PFLP General Command. Radical Marxist breakaway group. About 100 members.

As Saiqua. Sponsored by Syria. Estimated strength: 2,000. Branch of the Pan-Arab Command of the Baath Party.

Arab Liberation Front. About 600 members. Supported by Iraq.

Popular Democratic Front for the Liberation of Palestine. More moderate offshoot of PFLP. About 300 members.

"We want to know everything you hear and see," David said. "We want it all. Even if it's gossip. Nothing regarding the PLO is trivial. Anything that you may report should be given the highest code priority. Frankly, we expect this push for a Palestinian state to be accompanied by terrorist activities that will make everything that has gone before pale in comparison."

"There's a cheery thought," I replied. "Thanks a lot from a fellow who expects to be doing quite a lot of traveling in your part of the world."

David smiled. "A very highly placed official of a European government once said to me, 'Israel is a nice little country in the wrong neighborhood.' I expected him to add, 'Some of my best friends are Jews.' "

"So what do you want me to do?" I asked.

"Where does your business take you next?"

"To Paris for follow-ups on my subcontract with the French outfit. Will I see you there for another debriefing? Perhaps an assignment?"

"If not I, someone else," he said.

As David predicted, the Arab League met for four days in September and demanded that the United Nations put the question of Palestine on the agenda for its annual meeting in New York. In keeping with the changes in international attitudes toward the Arabs the UN not only agreed but invited Arafat to address the General Assembly.

Meanwhile, I arrived in Paris for conferences with my French business associates. At luncheons, cocktail parties, and working dinners I found the main topic of conversation to be the flexing of their muscles by Middle East oil producers. On the eve of my trip, a two-day meeting of OPEC had ended with an agreement to raise taxes and royalties paid by foreign oil companies to the oil producing states. OPEC hiked the tax on a barrel of oil by about thirty-three cents and indexed future prices to accommodate inflation. Earlier, Kuwait and the Japanese-owned Arabian Oil Company had signed a "participation" agreement giving Kuwait 60 percent of the company's shares and assets.

All of these discussions led to one conclusion among the participants. Stability in the commerce of oil depended on stability in the region. The stumbling block was Israel. Nothing could be achieved without the withdrawal of Israel from territories it had occupied in 1967 and in the Yom Kippur War. Although I presumed that none of this would come as a surprise to Israel, I wrote a report stressing the virulence of the anti-Israel feelings that I heard, who expressed them, and what firms they represented.

A considerably more practical result of my meetings was my receipt from the French company that had subcontracted with my firm of a complete set of the blueprints for the Saudi Arabian project. Of course, my French associates had no way of knowing that I intended to have copies made for forwarding to the Institute.

I then arranged a rendezvous with a man called Ari for the purpose of providing an oral briefing and my formal written report on the meetings. This was not the same Ari who had taught me the value of a Swiss army knife as a means of self-defense. We met at the edge of a crowd of tourists admiring the *Mona Lisa* at the Louvre, identifying one another by a copy of the *International Herald Tribune*, folded and stuffed into the left-hand pocket of a coat, and a bit of innocent-sounding dialogue that we had arranged during a brief phone call to the Paris office of Mr. Moses.

I said, "The painting is much smaller than I expected."

Ari replied, "Life is full of surprises, isn't it?"

I answered, "But *Winged Victory* was just what I thought it would be."

We then separated to meet five minutes later at the foot of the grand staircase beneath the famous statue and proceed outside to a park bench.

"You've done well, Hershel," Ari said. "This material will be on its way to the Institute within the hour." He tucked the papers into a pocket. "You may expect a call from David at your office in two weeks."

On a Monday, exactly fourteen days later, my secretary buzzed me on my office intercom. 'A Mr. David on line two," she said. "He says it's personal."

"When can you drop in at the home office?" David asked.

Checking my calendar, I said, "I could be there Thursday."

"That's excellent. If you drive, there's ample parking a block away."

"You mean I don't have to take the train?"

"Always a joke," he said, chuckling. "See you Thursday."

As I drove toward Montreal with the woodlands of northern New York ablaze in autumn colors, I thought back to my adventure in the relentless desert of Saudi Arabia. It seemed as if I had dreamed everything. Glancing at the Norman Rockwell–like American towns tucked along the highway, I found it hard to believe that I had found myself spying in the heart of Arabia.

What David proposed I do next left me flabbergasted.

"I have a new term for you to add to your growing vocabulary of spytalk—'threat study,' " he said as he poured coffee for me in the upstairs parlor of the house on rue Sanguinet. "It's an assessment of the entire spectrum of enemy capabilities. In military terms it covers combat material, force employment doctrine, and force structures—what the generals call 'order of battle.' We obtain that in a myriad of ways, chiefly through technical means. But the best military intelligence is practically useless unless it's accompanied by an understanding of the mind-set of the enemy. A complete intelligence assessment of a potential threat has to include the economic and political environment. And the morale of the people."

"In Vietnam War terms," I said, "they called that 'hearts and minds.' "

"Exactly. We can achieve an understanding of the hearts and minds of our Arab neighbors only through human intelligence. We need a man on the ground who is in a position to be, to use a term of art, proactive. We need somebody uniquely qualified to travel all over the Arab states looking for information, rather than relying on picking it up by chance."

"Precisely what would this fellow be looking for?"

"The Arab mind. Arab intentions. Who are the up-and-comers? What ideas are being kicked around? What plans are on the drawing boards? Which countries and what companies are the Arabs in bed with? Anything and everything that bears on the *future*."

"It seems to me what you want is a Wandering Jew with a crystal ball!"

"A Wandering Jew with appropriate *cover*." He thought for a long moment, rubbing his chin. Then he leaned forward, studying my face. "With a proper beard you might pass for an Arab."

"How many Arabs do you know named Schack?"

"The Arab blood could be on your mother's side. Perhaps she was an Egyptian. Maybe Lebanese. We'll leave that up to the boys in the Central Cover Division. Give them a week or two and they are bound to come back with a legend for Mr. Schack complete with a family tree that goes all the way back to the sons of Ishmael. All I need to get them working is your okay. Of course, they'll need pictures of you with a beard."

I rubbed my jaw. "I've always hated shaving every morning."

With a clap of his hands David bellowed, "Great. Do it. When it's ready, get yourself some passport photos and mail them to the office. When the new passport is ready, we'll meet again."

All my life I had been fastidious about my appearance and always clean-shaven, so I was not surprised that letting my beard grow drew the attention of my family. The product of a generation that watched too many adventure programs on TV, the youngest of my four sons took me aside and asked, "Dad, are you hiding out from somebody?"

"Humor me in my old age," I answered

Anyone else's spouse might have suspected a midlife crisis. I had reached the right age for one, forty-seven. But Ruth had become accustomed to my doing the unexpected, often without warning her. I had done so in the 1950s, dashing off one day to the local airport and signing up for flying lessons with an ex–World War II airman who had left behind his fighter plane and bought the crop duster in which I took to the skies.

A few years later I suggested that we pack ourselves and the kids into the car and spend six weeks exploring the highways and byways of America. Rather than throw up her hands in dismay and denounce me as a dreamer and a nomad, Ruth paid a call on the auto club to collect roadmaps. Regarding her husband's beard she shrugged and asked, "So what else is new?"

By the end of September the whiskers had grown in fully, allowing me to obtain pictures at a passport photo studio at Rockefeller Center and send them to the Home Office in Montreal. By coincidence, I dropped them into a mailbox at Grand Central Terminal on October 6, the first anniversary of the beginning of the Yom Kippur War.

That evening Ruth and I watched TV news coverage of the commemoration of the event in Cairo. A parade of Egypt's military might, it was reviewed by President Anwar Sadat with Yasir Arafat at his side. Like millions of Jews and others, whenever I saw Arafat I felt a visceral disgust.

As I waited to hear from David about the date and place of our next meeting, Arafat reinforced my estimation of him. In an interview with the *New York Times* in Beirut, he said there could be no peace in the Middle East until the United States recognized the right of the Palestinian people to their own state and "stopped the flow of arms to Israel and the economic and political support for Israel's expansive and aggressive ambitions."

He also declared that a Palestinian government in exile would soon be formed as a step toward the establishment of Palestinian sovereignty over the West Bank and Gaza. That arrangement would serve as a nucleus of a future Palestinian state that would absorb Israel.

Should I run across Arafat during my odyssey as Howard Mackenzie, I wondered, what might I do? Would I, to borrow one of David's spytalk terms, blow my cover and punch Arafat in the mouth? Sneak into his bedroom in the night and quietly slit his throat with my Swiss army knife?

I found it easy to imagine such things being carried out by a James Bond. But not by me. I thought it would be infinitely more satisfying to kidnap Arafat and deliver him to Israel to stand trial like Eichmann.

On November 13 Arafat came to New York to address the UN General Assembly. Arriving at Kennedy International Airport from Algeria, he transferred to a U.S. Army helicopter and landed at the UN with all the pomp and circumstance of a genuine head of state. Reflecting the post–Yom Kippur War transformation of world opinion to an accommodation with the Arabs and their oil, the General Assembly adopted resolutions recognizing "Palestinian rights" and admitting the PLO to observer status at the UN. All that David had predicted had come true. The nations of the world appeared to be in a stampede to cozy up to the Arabs.

A few days later, despite this recognition by the UN, four Palestinian terrorists hijacked a British Airways jetliner in Dubai. They forced it to fly to Tunis after a refueling stop in Libya and the murder of a hostage. Among their demands were the freeing of eight Palestinians who had been convicted in Sudan for the slaying of three diplomats in Khartoum in March of 1973; and of five terrorists awaiting trial in Egypt for the December 1973 massacre at the Rome airport. The leader of the group that carried out the hijacking, according to David, was Abu Nidal.

"If you run into him in your travels, be sure to give us a call," he joked as he handed me a new passport bearing the picture of a bearded Howard Mackenzie. "The 'wet job' boys of the Kidon section will be delighted to take it from there."

The suggestion that information provided by me might result in an assassination, even of Abu Nidal, made me shudder.

"Now let's get down to our business," David said almost blithely as he opened a briefcase and removed a bundle of papers. "The fellas in Central Cover have been hard at work." He unfolded a map of the Middle East. "As you can see," he said, "they have proposed quite an ambitious itinerary."

Unnamed people in Israel had provided me with a "wish list" that ran through the letters of the alphabet from A for airports (locations of and plans for) to Z for zinc (the suppliers of).

"Naturally, we are interested in any information we can get our hands on about military installations," David said, "but there is much more that can be helpful. Microwave relays towers, radio and television stations, oil storage depots, docks and bridges. Even open fields that might be suitable for landing strips."

An open-ended itinerary would take Howard Mackenzie on a sandy odyssey of espionage under the cover of drumming up business for his construction firm. In the course of my travels from Rabat, Morocco, at the northwest corner of the African continent, to Muscat, Oman, on the Arabian Sea, I would be a wandering Jew in disguise among approximately 132 million Arabs. Add the non-Arabs of Iran and the Muslim population ranged up to nearly 200 million souls, living in teeming and clogged modern cities such as Cairo or in clusters of tents like the nomadic bedouins, whose life-style had remained the same since Genesis.

David said, "To arrange any trip contact Special World Tours Travel Agency at Rockefeller Center. Present your passport and they will obtain any and all visas, travel documents, and tickets."

He gave me half a dozen credit cards bearing various names.

"Everything will be billed to offices in Geneva. Bogus, of course. Should anyone contact that office, it will provide round-the-clock verification of your papers. The accounts are always paid in full and promptly. The timetable for your travels will be up to you. No need for you to notify the home office. Your travel agency will do that for you. Contact the home office to arrange for a debriefing, or if you feel a crash meeting is required. File written reports by post through Rome."

Where to go first?

In mulling over that decision I immediately ruled out Saudi Arabia. Having just been there, I thought the risk too great that someone might see through my beard and spot a resemblance to the old Howard Schack. The best place to start, I decided, would be in the hustle-and bustle anonymity of Cairo. Historically a meeting ground of East and West and the gateway from Europe to the Middle East, Africa, and Asia, the capital of Egypt had become the political, military, and economic center of gravity of the ongoing contest between the Arabs and Israel.

If anyone sought evidence of the significance of Egypt it presented itself in the figures of Henry Kissinger and President Sadat. Anwar Sadat embodied the rapprochement between America and Egypt following the 1973 war. The Egyptian leader had begun a policy of *infitah*, or "open door," that had produced a flood of American and other Western businessmen into Egypt. With so many Western faces at every turn, I figured, mine would not be a standout.

The next question was when?

I faced immediate pressing business affecting my own company throughout October and well into November of 1974, to be followed by the holidays of December, which the Schack family had always enjoyed spending together. That meant I could not begin my trip until January 1975.

Because I had previously transacted business in Egypt I knew that it was not a good idea to arrive without having paved the way. The custom was to arrange a series of conferences with the government ministries empowered to grant contracts. This process began with phone calls or letters requesting appointments with Egyptian trade and commercial officials in New York. They would then arrange for meetings in Cairo.

It was not easy telling Ruth that I would be going to Egypt. "I don't think that is a very good idea," she said sternly. "The Middle East is much too dangerous. Kissinger says there could be another war."

Indeed, the secretary of state had been issuing some rather gloomy warnings. On September 28 he told the UN General Assembly that "the shadow of war remains" over the Middle East, especially as a result of the strains being put on the world economy by Arab oil policy.

On the other hand, Sheik Yamani had told reporters in Washington on October 2 that the oil crisis could be alleviated only upon a solution of the Arab-Israeli conflict. If Israel did not pull out of the West Bank and Gaza, he said, "this would produce a war." He added, "Any solution that will stop the fighting is in the hands of the American government."

Having followed news accounts of the recent hijacking of the British Airways plane, Ruth also envisioned my being taken hostage by terrorists. "I don't think you appreciate the danger that these terrorists pose," she said. "If you did, you wouldn't be thinking of flying off to the Middle East right now."

As I listened to her heartfelt plea I recalled my tutorial by David on the likes of Yasir Arafat and Abu Nidal. I had to bite my tongue to keep from blurting out that I knew quite a lot about Arab terrorism. Instead, I sought to reassure her that if I found myself in a tight spot I would find some way to get word to her.

On the very eve of my departure for Cairo, Kissinger made matters worse by telling *Business Week* magazine that the United States might use military force "to prevent the strangulation of the industrialized world" by the Arab oil producers. The remarks set off a blizzard of angry reaction. Iranian Premier Amir Abbas Hoveida warned that use of force against oil-producing states by one superpower would bring about a military intervention by the other, the Soviet Union. Following up, the USSR's news agency, Tass, referred to "gunboat diplomacy and intimidation," while the

Soviet Communist Party's newspaper, *Pravda*, ranted darkly about "military blackmail."

As if all this saber-rattling were not enough, the terrorism that Ruth feared erupted two days before I planned to leave. On January 19 three Palestinian Arabs trying for the second time in a week to attack an Israeli airliner shot it out with French police at Orly airport in Paris. They took hostages and held them in an airport washroom for a full day before being allowed to leave France and go to Iraq. In the gun battle, twenty people had been wounded.

While this dramatic event did not cause me to cancel my trip to Egypt, it did persuade me to take precautions against my being caught in a terrorist situation. The week before my departure I paid a visit to a gun store and bought an ankle holster for my pistol. Although international terrorism had arrived on the scene, and airplane hijackings had been a fact of life since the 1960s, airport security had not kept pace. As a result, I had no problem boarding a Pan American jetliner at JFK with a gun. In the future, however, as security tightened in most international airports, I could not carry the weapon on me. It had to be put in a suitcase and stowed in the luggage bays, hardly a convenient location in the event of a hijacking. Ultimately, I elected not to take my gun on trips. I reasoned that if a time came when I felt I needed one I would be able to buy a weapon on the black market.

The last time I had set foot on Egyptian soil, president Gamal Abdel Nasser had been president of the largest and most important of the Arab states. With a population of 45 million, or roughly one-fourth of the "Arab nation," Egypt ranked in many ways as the most advanced of the Arab states, yet it was one of the poorest in terms of per capita income.

When I went to Cairo in 1969, Nasser had been president for fifteen tempestuous years that saw Egypt's estrangement from the United States; the 1956 attack on Egypt by Britain, France, and Israel; the nationalization of the Suez Canal; the 1967 war with Israel in which Egypt lost control of the Sinai peninsula; and an avid courting by Nasser of the Soviet Union. Hoping for a "great leap forward," he extracted from the Soviets what the United States had balked at doing—the building of the High Dam on the Nile at Aswân. This gigantic project was intended to catapult

Egypt into a new world of prosperity. But little had changed at the time of Nasser's death at the age of fifty-two in 1970.

Riding in a taxi from Cairo airport in January 1974, I could not miss the presence of Nasser's successor, Anwar Sadat. Giant portraits of him gazed at me from roadside billboards along the entire route from the airport at Heliopolis to the heart of Cairo.

Probably no one had been more surprised that Sadat had inherited Nasser's power than Sadat himself. Looking at his looming pictures, I recalled that only three years earlier he had been Nasser's vice president, described to me by business associates as lackluster and a lightweight. Yet it had been Sadat who launched the Yom Kippur War and managed to persuade Egyptians that overwhelming military defeat had been a gigantic political victory, forcing the United States to take a second look at its pro-Israel policy and to pay more attention to the Arab cause. Moreover, in 1972 he had unveiled a bold change in Egyptian foreign policy that astonished the entire world. He kicked out the Russian "advisers" who had been invited in by Nasser.

Six years earlier when I had checked into Shepheard's Hotel I had encountered Russians at every turn. In January 1975 I found the lobby of the famous old hotel on the Corniche El Nil thronged by Americans and Western Europeans. Located in central Cairo, called Garden City, Shepheard's had been a hallmark of Western colonialism. Described in the 1940s by *Time* magazine as "the most famous rendezvous of the white man in the Orient," it had had to be rebuilt in the 1950s following riots that targeted symbols of Western domination.

Wrote the *Time* correspondent, "Along the broad, tree-lined avenues of modern Cairo streamed a mob from the Arabian Nights world of fetid, twisting back streets and blind alleys—peasants in flowing robes, licorice-water peddlers still carrying their brass-trimmed demijohns, and barefoot newsboys in black skull caps."

Up in flames went Shepheard's renowned terrace, the Long Bar, the high-ceilinged dining room, and its 350 antique bedrooms, torched by mobs that also vented their anti-West ire on the British Turf Club, Greppi's pastry shop, the ten-story Bahri office building, department stores, Barclay's Bank, the Parisiana Restaurant, the Ritz Café, and offices of British Airways and Trans-World Airlines.

Two decades later as I settled into Shepheard's the hotel appeared to be its old self again. The West was back in favor. In their conversation between sips of their strong coffee and puffs of water pipes, Egyptians denounced Moscow for going back on a promise to replace all the arms they had lost in the Yom Kippur War.

A few days before I departed for Cairo Sadat himself had complained. "There has been no Soviet replenishment and no fundamental arms received up to this moment," he said, whereas the United States had "not only compensated Israel for her losses, but has also provided her with new sophisticated weapons."

Adding insult to injury, the Soviet Union had also refused to reschedule four billion dollars in debt as the Egyptian government had requested.

As a result, the only country more unpopular than the Soviet Union in Egypt at the moment of my arrival was Israel. When I presented myself at the Ministry of Economy, which had the responsibility for approving all the international construction projects in the country, the animosity toward the Jewish state took precedence over everything else.

Studying my business card, a ministry official in a crisp khaki uniform asked, "Has your firm transacted business in or on behalf of Israel?"

By pure chance, it had not. Now, thanks to luck, I did not have to worry about the Arab blacklist of companies that did business in Israel. Hundreds of firms that had done so joined a list of condemned businesses compiled by the Arab Boycott Office. Established after the first Arab-Israel war in 1948 as a way of "continuing the Arab struggle against Israel," the organization was based in Damascus and met every six months to review policy.

"My company has not done any work for Israel," I said to the ministry clerk.

"Here is a listing of firms with whom it is not permitted to transact business of any kind in Egypt," the official said, handing me a many-paged booklet. "They have Israeli connections. If your firm wishes to obtain contracts from the Egyptian government you may not deal with these firms in any form."

From a drawer of his desk he drew another list. "These companies will be added to those others effective with a February meeting of the Arab Boycott Office."

Assuming that the Institute already possessed the first list, I wondered if it possessed the new one. Remembering that David had advised me to presume nothing, I slipped the list into my pocket with the intention of mailing it to my Home Base in Rome as soon as possible.

Apparently satisfied that I and my firm met the criteria for doing business in Egypt, the official escorted me into a room of long tables topped by piles of paper.

"Each of these stacks is a project for which the government of Egypt is soliciting construction bids from primary contractors and from subcontractors," he said, walking between the tables. "I invite you to take your time to look through them and to help yourself to the specifications of any that may be of interest to you. You will also find instructions regarding how to submit a bid or bids."

I had planned to spend at least a week in Cairo establishing myself and laying groundwork for subsequent trips by scattering business cards like rose petals. Yet here, in a single visit, I had been left alone in a room that appeared to be an intelligence agent's fondest dream come true. It appeared to be a repeat of the amazing luck of Carl Morgan's offices. As baseball star Yogi Berra had put it, "It was déjà vu all over again."

Before me lay an inviting smorgasbord of plans. Some were for civilian projects. Others had a military nature. But all of them represented a rebuilding effort that might have a decisive impact on the outcome of another war. A new wharf at Port Said was intended for commercial purposes. It would require little work to turn it to military purposes. Widening a stretch of the Delta Road between Alexandria and Tanta and improvements of the Ismailia-Canal Road would facilitate movement of military convoys. Expansion of the parking tarmacs of Cairo International Airport would benefit the Egyptian air force. Nile-dredging at Gerza, improving the outdoor lighting system of the High Dam at Aswân, and dozens of other civil projects also bolstered the military.

Because the limited capacity of my briefcase prevented me from scooping up all of the plans, I took only those that seemed the most significant, choosing on the basis of my personal experience that the thickness of written specifications invariably correlated to somebody's estimate of the importance of a project. Occasionally, the heft of a plan turned out to be more of a reflection of the specification writer's inflated ego than the significance of the work.

I was satisfied with my selection but frustrated at not being able to take one of everything. I also wondered if I might have stumbled into a trap set up by the Egyptian espionage agency, Mukhabarat el-Amma, or the dreaded secret police, Mahabes el-Aam. I beat a hasty exit from the room and the Ministry of Economy.

With my stuffed briefcase clutched in my sweating right hand I fought an urge to break into a run. Proceeding westward along Sheikh Rihan Street, I turned left at the Geological Museum and westerly again in a straight line to my hotel. Frequently glancing back to look for followers, I concluded that if I felt even the slightest suspicion that I was being watched my only recourse was to dash for the American Embassy, a block south, and make a clean breast of things.

Only when I closed the door of my room on the third floor of Shepheard's did I breathe a sigh of relief and achieve sufficient control of my shaking hands to slip the addendum to the boycott list into an envelope addressed to the Rome home office. Hours after a sleepless night when I expected each minute to bring a banging on my door by men of the GIA, I finally felt calm enough to consider venturing out again.

Although I no longer expected to be arrested as a spy, I could not shake off the idea that during my absence my room might be searched. Indeed, the likelihood of my possessions being investigated in my absence had been drilled into my head by David and his "faculty" during my training. The only sure way of avoiding the discovery of possibly incriminating material, they said, was to leave nothing behind. If that proved impossible, I had been told, the best course of action was to devise a means that would reveal whether left-behind items had been touched.

I did not wish to spend a day in Cairo carrying around the weighty briefcase filled with the items that I had taken from the Ministry of Economy, even though I had a plausible explanation for possessing them. I decided to leave them in the room in such a manner that would immediately signal if they had been disturbed while I was out. Placing the closed briefcase atop a table, I positioned it so that its handle hung over the left side and the zipper pull faced the wall.

Admiring my work and feeling quite clever, I realized that someone would, indeed, enter the room and probably disturb the briefcase—a maid with a dustcloth.

After some thought, I emptied the briefcase, then assembled the contents with every third document facedown. I assumed that anyone examining them would inevitably disturb the sequence. I then placed the refilled and closed briefcase atop a table as before, handle over the side, zipper pull toward the wall.

Stepping into the glare of morning sunlight and looking like a tourist with my camera slung over my shoulder, I asked the hotel doorman to signal a taxi to take me to a post office. As the cab fought through crowded streets, I noticed that members of the Egyptian military seemed to be everywhere and that they all carried weapons. Knowing that as a result of the recent war the Israeli army stood on the east bank of the Suez Canal, not so many miles away from Cairo, I understood why the Egyptian government deemed it necessary to keep troops on the alert. But as an American accustomed to seeing troops only in patriotic parades I felt uneasy.

Like soldiers the world over they proudly wore insignia that designated their units. Of course, they were meaningless to me, but in noting their infinite variety I wondered if I might find a book to enlighten me on the subject of uniform markings, not only those of Egypt but of all Arab armed forces. Because I knew from my own brief army experience that military commanders needed to know an enemy's "order of battle," I felt that any data that I could provide the Institute on individual military units would prove valuable.

Returning to Shepheard's to rest a bit prior to lunch, I found my briefcase undisturbed by either spies or the maid. If she had dusted, she did so around it.

Because my next appointment was not until the next day I spent the afternoon as a tourist at the Cairo Museum taking in the wonders of the King Tut artifacts and an endless array of dust-covered mummy cases. Whiling away the time, I wondered what professional spies did with their leisure hours.

Arising bright and early the next morning, I set out by cab for what I considered by far the most promising and important of Mackenzie's appointments. Scheduled for nine o'clock, it was a meeting with General Abn Badawy. The commander of the Egyptian equivalent of the U.S. Army Corps of Engineers, he had been an adjutant to the minister of war, General Ismail Ali, during the Yom Kippur War. Now his job was the rebuilding of everything the war had destroyed. A heavyset man with a Tom Dewey–style mustache, he greeted me with considerably more cheeriness than I had expected from a military man who knew that his triumphant enemy had been dug in along the east side of the Suez Canal for a year. In fact, he brimmed with optimism.

"You have come at an auspicious and opportune time," he said as we sat in his spacious office in the War Ministry. "There is going to be much work to do in rebuilding our country and our military. When the diplomats have finished their work and the Israeli invaders have gone back home, we shall proceed with the modernization of both. In this undertaking, of course, we look forward to the assistance of experts such as yourself. I cannot adequately express to you how happy I am that President Sadat has given the boot to the damned Russians. Total incompetents. I can tell you that having seen their bumbling I do not understand why the Soviet Union has not collapsed."

Although I welcomed these sentiments as boding well for relations between Egypt and the United States, my enthusiasm for the general quickly evaporated as he launched a scathing denunciation of Israel that competed in virulent racism with all that I remembered of the Nazis. But as I listened to his diatribe, I had the satisfaction of knowing I would be reporting everything he said to the Institute, along with information regarding the rebuilding projects that fell within his domain.

The task that he proceeded to describe seemed daunting in the extreme. At the time of the cease-fire on October 24, 1973, Israeli forces had occupied an area of a thousand square miles *inside* Egypt. The brief war had rained ruin, from Mediterranean ports, hit by Israeli naval raids, to the port of Adabiah on the Gulf of Suez that had been surrounded by the Israeli army.

"There is more than enough work for everyone," he said as he swept a hand over a map. "Roads. Bridges. Storage sheds. Hangars. Command bunkers. Missile sites. Seaport facilities. You name it."

Recalling the banquet of documents at the Ministry of Economy, I asked, "Is there a list of projects that you might permit me to take along, so as to study and submit proposals?"

"I understand that your specialty is the construction of large buildings."

"From foundation to roof," I boasted.

"Say no more," he said, crossing the room to a row of steel file cabinets. "I have just the thing."

Returning to his desk, he handed me a three-inch-thick book. "Not since the building of the pyramids," he declared, "has there been such an ambitious undertaking."

Casually flipping through the book, I had to agree with him, but I also wondered why a country with so many people who were so often in need of the basic amenities of life would squander so much money on the accoutrements of warfare. But, I supposed, a similar question probably had been asked by the poor of ancient Egypt as they watched pyramids being built.

I already had my answer. The general had given it in his bitter denunciation of Israel. It came down to one word: hate. And hatred could only mean another war.

During that week, I found such hatred expressed everywhere I roamed in the city of Cairo. Overwhelmed by the experience, I wanted nothing more than to leave the city as soon as possible.

In a call to Rome from a public phone at the Central Telephone and Telegraph Office on Sharia Ramses Street, I said to the young woman who answered, "This is Hershel. I expect to be in town on Friday, in case anyone would care to have a look at my new line of goods."

"You know you are always welcome, Hershel," she said. "Call us as soon as you arrive."

As I waited for my Olympic Airways flight to be announced at Terminal One of the airport, I looked out windows of the waiting room and noted tarmacs littered with military aircraft. Like the insignia on uniforms of soldiers that I had seen in the city, the different markings on the wings and tails of the planes told me nothing. But I knew they would have meaning to someone at the Institute whose job included keeping track of the dispersement of the Egyptian air force's planes. I drew pictures of the insignia on a copy of the *International Herald Tribune*.

Waiting to board my flight, I thought about what my visit to Cairo had accomplished and felt quite pleased and proud. But none of the items that I had gathered from the two ministries seemed quite as significant as what I had learned about the festering hatred for Israel that dwelt in the "hearts and minds" of the Egyptians.

Thinking about it, I feared that the Yom Kippur War had not been the last between Israel and her Arab neighbors. Getting on the plane for Italy, I felt more determined than ever to be sure that Israel would never be on the losing side.

Comfortably ensconced at Rome's Cavalieri Hilton, I phoned the home office and found myself talking to a youthful-sounding handler. Calling himself Yehuda, he indicated a decidedly more upscale place for our rendezvous than my meeting with Reuven at the railway station. He suggested St. Peter's Square.

"Ten o'clock tomorrow morning, east side of the Egyptian obelisk," he said with what seemed to me to be a delightfully whimsical touch of irony.

He showed up on the dot. Short and slender as a reed, he wore a gray sweatshirt, jeans, and scruffy sneakers. Toting a rucksack, he looked like one of the scores of teenage Italian students streaming behind a priest and a pair of nuns on their way across the square toward the basilica.

Sidling up to me, he whispered, "Your new beard becomes you, Hershel." From a pocket he produced one of the pictures that I had had made at Rockefeller Center, showing it to me as evidence that he could be trusted. "There's a park nearby where we can talk."

"I have some things for you," I said, patting the briefcase containing the items I had taken from the Ministry of Economy, the thick book handed to me by the general, and my drawings of the insignia of the planes at the airport.

"Not here, please," he said.

Seated on a park bench while he transferred the material to his rucksack, I explained what they were and how I had obtained them.

"I couldn't believe how easy it was," I said. "In fact, I thought I was being set up. Pretty silly, don't you think?"

"A helping of paranoia is always a healthy thing," he said.

"I also sent an item by mail. Did you get it?"

"The moment we received it we forwarded it to the Institute. Very interesting stuff." He zipped his bag and arose abruptly. "I believe you will see the effect," he said, walking away. "Soon."

Whether as a direct result of my providing the Institute with the boycott lists or simply by coincidence, some details of their contents became public on February 25, released in New York by the Anti-Defamation League of B'nai B'rith and substantiated by the U.S. Department of State, followed in several days by the Arab Boycott Office disclosing the entire roster.

Along with its partial roll of boycotted companies, the ADL accused two U.S. agencies and six private companies of violating civil rights laws by discriminating against Jews "as they make a wild scramble for a piece of the Arabs' new wealth."

One of the U.S. government agencies was the Army Corps of Engineers. Its spokesman said, "The Arabs make the rules and it would be unwise to send a Jew out there."

As a Wandering Jew making plans to go "out there" again, I found no encouragement in his words.

6

The Wandering Jew

 As if the Middle East were not suffering enough from the madness of individuals, the region was shaken on March 25, 1975, by the assassination of Saudi Arabia's King Faisal.

On hearing the initial bulletin on the radio in my office I jumped to the conclusion that he had been killed by a political enemy. But after a few minutes a follow-up bulletin stated that the murder had been carried out by his deranged thirty-one-year-old nephew, Prince Faisal ibn Musad Abdel Azziz. He had approached the monarch during a reception at Faisal's palace marking the birth of the prophet Muhammad, drawn a .38-caliber pistol, and fired several shots. The king died of head wounds at a hospital.

The funeral drew many world dignitaries, including Anwar Sadat, Hafiz al-Assad of Syria, Hourai Boumédienne of Algeria, Ali Bhutto of Pakistan, King Hussein of Jordan, and Vice President Nelson Rockefeller, demonstrating the flourishing concerns of the United States about its standing in the Middle East. Greeting the mourners were the king's brother and designated successor, Crown Prince Khaled, and a younger brother, Prince Fahd. But because Khaled was in poor health and had little taste for politics, it was the latter who truly inherited the power.

At my next meeting with my handler I asked David for the Israeli point of view on the dramatic events in Saudi Arabia.

"It doesn't really matter who is in charge," he said. "We see no reason to expect Fahd to be any friendlier to Israel than Faisal had been. We expect the Saudis to continue their anti-Israel policies and to carry on as the chief financiers in the Arab world. The Saudis remain a prime target of the Institute, so feel free to continue your efforts there, Hershel. They are very much appreciated in Tel Aviv."

"I'm glad to hear it," I said.

"As a matter of fact, that was my primary reason for calling you to this meeting. The home office has decided to make your lot a little easier. You have been bringing back excellent intelligence of a military nature. It's obvious that you have a sense for what's important and what is not. I've been instructed to make those senses even sharper."

"Am I about to sit through one of your famous lectures?" I said in jest.

He smiled. "It's more in the line of a home study course."

Opening a fat leather carryall, he began removing paperbound books, pamphlets, and spiral-bound documents, piling them on a table.

"I hope you have a good safe in your office," he said as the stack grew. "This material is for your eyes only. After you have absorbed the contents, destroy everything."

The challenge seemed daunting. He had set before me a small reference library on mankind's genius for destruction. The reading list ranged from airborne weapons systems to particular types of trucks used by the Iraqi army. One book dealt solely with the subject of Iraqi armored personnel carriers, running nearly one hundred pages and containing photos of each type. Another was a thick treatise on towed and self-propelled antiaircraft guns of Soviet manufacture. Other volumes took the form of the sales catalogs of international arms merchants.

Picking randomly among the items, I wondered if humanity could ever fulfill the prophesy of Isaiah, "They shall beat their swords into plowshares, and their spears into pruning hooks; nation shall not lift up sword against nation, neither shall they learn war anymore." What might Isaiah say, I wondered, if he appeared in that room at that moment and saw the extent to which mankind had gone since his day to perfect the weapons of war?

My expression must have looked rather dour. David reached out and squeezed my shoulder.

"I know that's a lot to swallow," he said brightly. "But nobody's going to give you a quiz. The home office just thought this information might make your job a little easier."

"It certainly will," I said. "I was only thinking about the terrible waste that all these armaments represent, especially in a part of the world where so much ought to be done to help the people. And I don't mean only in the Arab countries. Imagine how much better off Israel would be if it did not have to pour so much money into defending itself."

"I'm sure I don't have to remind you that Israel did not start this confrontation. Believe me, no one would be happier than I if peace broke out and the Institute were dismantled tomorrow. Perhaps one day it will happen. Meanwhile, we must deal with the world as it is. That means we must gather intelligence. Preparedness is the best defense. Know thou thy enemy. That's the job you are helping us perform. Preventive intelligence. Some of this material that I've given you has been obtained at a steep price. Each of these books, every report lying in front of you, is the result of the work of countless men and women just like you. They were smart people with wide-open eyes and keenly attuned ears. Who knows, Hershel? In your travels you might come up with a bit of intelligence that will put an end to all this insanity. Or if not the end of it, perhaps the beginning of the end."

As if I did not have enough to study, David dug into his bag and drew out another document.

"The fellows in the threat assessment section thought this might be useful," he said, handing me a spiral-bound book. "It's a report that has just been completed on the political situation in the so-called confrontation states."

Concealing the report in a newspaper, I read it on the train going back to New York. It began with a concise introductory overview that started with the Arab countries farthest removed from Israel—Morocco, Algeria, Tunisia, and Libya—and concluded with Israel's most immediate neighbors, Syria, Lebanon, Jordan, Saudi Arabia, and Egypt. It even reached down and across the Red Sea to the Sudan.

Whoever wrote the book could have had a future as a compiler of travel guides. Accompanying an analysis of each country was a description of its geography and a brief review of its history. The picture presented was of countries that seemed so intent on their own ancient rivalries and self-interest that it should have been impossible for them to find any common cause. What could possibly tie the tiny, rich Gulf states of Kuwait, Bahrain, Oman, and the Emirates to the sprawling and poor giant Egypt? What could link an aggressive Syria to standoffish and xenophobic Saudi Arabia?

What drew the Kingdom of Jordan to lockstep with Iraq and the People's Republic of Yemen, the first Marxist state in the Mideast? And what, Islam aside, welded these Arab states into an uneasy affiliation with Persian Iran? The answer: Israel.

To support this conclusion the author of the analysis quoted a communiqué that had been issued after a conference between King Hussein of Jordan and King Faisal of Saudi Arabia in which Faisal expressed his conviction that it was his duty, and the duty of other Arab states, to support the confrontation states against Israel.

The analysis went on to assert that implacable opposition to the Jewish state in the midst of Islam inevitably led to resentment against the chief supporter of Israel, the United States. Yet even this seething animosity did not coalesce into a unified policy toward America until after the Yom Kippur War, when oil-producing states imposed their oil embargo.

"Without the awakening to the power inherent in controlling the lifeblood of the West," the writer stated, "it is unlikely that the United States would have acted so dramatically in seeking to mend fences with the Arabs. Had the Arabs not turned off the petroleum faucet we would not be witnessing the 'shuttle diplomacy' of Secretary of State Kissinger."

As the train approached Grand Central Terminal, I tucked the report into my briefcase. I agreed with the author's view that Israel should never again rely on the unquestioning and unhesitating support of the United States. This left me depressed. But it also renewed my determination to do all within my power to provide Israel with everything I could get my hands on that might be useful in meeting the challenge presented by the confrontation states.

As it happened, my first journey after returning from my meeting with David in Montreal took me to non-Arab Iran. I arrived at the moment that its ruler, Shah Mohammad Reza Pahlavi, declared in an interview published in the Cairo newspaper *Al-Ahram* that Iran would not participate in any new war against Israel. "Of course Iran is not thinking of participating in the fighting," he said. "But our sentiment will be on your [the Arabs'] side."

Secretary of State Henry Kissinger interpreted the comment as indicative of "trends in the Moslem world toward the direction of greater solidarity."

I viewed the Shah's statement and Kissinger's response as proof that fears of another oil embargo had tipped the balance of power in the Middle East from Israel toward the oil-producing countries. And in that exclusive club no country, with the possible exception of Saudi Arabia, ranked higher than Iran.

Additional evidence of the willingness of the United States to tread lightly came with the announcement by Iran that it had contracted with Rockwell International of Anaheim, California, to build a communications intelligence base capable of intercepting military and civilian communications throughout the Persian Gulf area. Under terms of the deal Rockwell would recruit former employees of the U.S. National Security Agency, our most secret spy agency, located at Fort Meade, Maryland, and its air force component, the Air Force Security Service. At the same time Rear Admiral Robert J Hanks informed a congressional committee that the United States planned to sell Iran three diesel-powered submarines. Built in 1951, the subs would permit the Iranian navy to operate outside the waters of the Persian Gulf.

Both of these developments seemed to me to pose a future threat to Israeli security and therefore were worthy of my investigation. Fortunately, I had a contact in the government of Iran who would not be suspicious if I were to show up in Tehran to get a piece of the action in the communications intelligence project. I also intended to poke around for information on the submarine deal, assuming that the delivery of the vessels would require submarine pens and building facilities for the personnel who would work in them, as well as housing. I knew Iran to be deeply engaged in numerous other projects, both civilian and military, paid for out of Iran's booming oil industry.

Boarding an Iran Air jet, I found it teeming with American businessmen who treated the plane as if it were a magic carpet carrying them to a land of treasures. Each understood that no country in the Middle East offered quite the opportunity to make a killing as Iran. Virtually any proposal seemed to find its way into reality. Tehran was awash with development schemes promulgated by sycophants and courtiers with access to the ear of the Shah or his underlings who approached their tasks with the greediness of unscrupulous carpet merchants. No proposal, no matter how farfetched, fell on deaf ears, as long as it promised ample baksheesh to grease the ways. It made no difference whether the project involved hardware for the Shah's already massive military establishment or equipment for an ambitious program to eradicate illiteracy.

My contact in this thriving international bazaar was a former dealer in Persian rugs who claimed to be a distant cousin of the Shah, Mannachar Turun. He recognized that he could amass a fortune quicker by tapping the country's oil-fueled building boom than in haggling over rugs. He had employed formidable business acumen and the personality of a likable rogue to set up one of the largest contracting companies in Iran. He maintained offices in Tehran, Geneva, and Paris. I had dealt with him a few years earlier through associates of mine in Paris.

With an enormous girth squeezed into a Savile Row suit he looked like Sidney Greenstreet in *Casablanca*. Waddling across a lushly carpeted office, across the street, appropriately, from the National Carpet Museum, he boomed, "Welcome to Iran. How can we do business?"

With such a character one did not beat around the bush.

"What's the scoop on this intelligence communications station?" I asked. "The word is there is going to be plenty of work to go around. If so, I'd like to be sure my company in on the 'A' list."

"Consider it done," he said. "When the specifications are ready you shall be provided with all the proper tender documents. At that time we can discuss arrangements that will be mutually beneficial."

"How soon will that be?"

"Patience. These things take time. A few months at the most. All good things come to those who wait. All in due course."

"Is there nothing you can show me now?"

"I have in my possession a draft of the contract."

"May I see it? Better yet, might I have a copy to take with me? I prefer to be a jump ahead of the competition. As to the arrangement between us, I believe I can guarantee you a more than generous participation."

Beady eyes glinted from the deep recesses of his pumpkinlike face. "There will be millions to be made," he said. "You have not wasted your time in coming to see me. Once again it is a case of the early bird catching the worm, no?"

"I also have information concerning the possibility of new submarines being added to the Iranian navy. Three of them, I believe. Surely there will be a need for pens and for servicing facilities. My company specializes in just that kind of work. Any idea where they will be located?"

"Bandar Abbās," he said, turning to a map of Iran behind his desk and stabbing a stubby thumb on a spot on the north shore of the Strait of Hormuz between the Persian Gulf and the Gulf of Oman. "You are correct. There will be new facilities required. Again, when the details are available they will be forwarded to you so that you may do the necessary financial calculations."

"I would like to get a head start," I said, making a sour face. "I am really interested in this submarine project. What are the chances of my going down to Bandar Abbās and having a tour of an area that I've never visited?"

He threw up his thick but beautifully manicured hands in a gesture of futility. "The navy has declared it off limits."

"I have been told," I said, cracking a smile, "that in Iran nothing is off limits to Mannachar Turun."

A laugh rumbled through his big body, shaking rolls of fat like Jell-O.

"What a slick one you are. You have the clever tongue of the devil himself," he said, reaching for a telephone. He spoke into it in Farsi. It was Greek to me, but when he put down the phone he had a broad grin. "I have arranged for you to have a pass and a plane to take you. You go tomorrow. Dress for heat."

The small harbor city had been founded by Shah Abbās in 1662 and had never lost its significance as a trading port and guardian of the narrow body of water linking the Persian Gulf with the rest of the world. As early in 1515, the Portuguese trader Alfonso of Albuquerque recognized its strategic importance by building a fort on the island of Hormuz.

When the pilot of the small Iranian air force plane flew over the island he pointed out the fort for my benefit. But what troubled me as I looked down was a pattern of concrete rectangles and long buildings that attested to modern defensive works—a missile base. Grabbing my camera, I began shooting pictures.

"You must not," the pilot said. "Photography is not allowed in this region. You will have to give me the film."

"But I was only getting a shot of the fort," I said with an innocent-looking and pleading expression. "This film has pictures that I took all over Iran. They are strictly souvenirs of my visit to your wonderful country. If you take the film I will have nothing to show my children of my trip. I promise I won't take any more pictures without asking your permission. By the way, may I take one of you?"

By now he had to concern himself with speaking over the radio to the control tower. "Yes, yes. Okay. Okay," he said.

In addition to one picture of the fort I had managed to snap six of the missile base, confident that the photographic experts at the Institute would have means to enlarge them. However, my pledge to my pilot and escort dashed my hopes for taking pictures of the naval base itself. The best I could do for the Institute was provide sketches from memory, drawn in my hotel room in the front and endpapers of an English-Farsi dictionary.

Bandar Abbās lay just across the Strait of Hormuz from other countries that I wished to visit. Therefore, I decided not to return to Tehran but go directly to Dubai, crossing by ferry. This trip permitted me to snap pictures of the Iranian navy base without worrying about an eagle-eyed escort threatening to confiscate my film. It also allowed photography of the port of Dubai, a veritable parking lot for supertankers as they filled their holds with the lifeblood of the West.

One of the nations that formed what some students of the Middle East called "the El Dorado States," Dubai belonged to a handful of small states and city-states that lay embedded in the eastern coast of the Arabian peninsula like pearls in a necklace. They included Bahrain, Qatar, the United Arab Emirates, and Kuwait. From Dubai I moved southward to Oman and then north again to Bahrain and Qatar and onward to Kuwait, snapping several rolls of film showing oil fields, highways, and construction projects.

Farthest north and resting like a walnut between the jaws of the nutcracker of Iran and Iraq, Kuwait stood above an underground black sea and was ruled by one family. In no way a military threat to Israel, it had taken on considerable importance in the region with the establishment of the Arab Development Fund, which provided financial backing for numerous projects in the Arab world. It also held within its borders an enormous concentration of Palestinians who had come there after the wars of 1948 and 1967, seeking either refuge or employment.

My purpose in calling at the offices of the Arab Development

Fund was not entirely for the possible benefit of Israel in having an updated list of projects being bankrolled by the Kuwaitis. I also planned to go home with a list of projects that might produce contracts for my firm.

Packing my suitcases for a flight from Kuwait City to Cyprus and on to Rome, I stuffed the list and several canisters of film into unwashed and smelly socks, which filled the toes of three pairs of shoes.

"If you keep up this volume of work," said my handler as he shoved the socks into his pockets at a café on the Via Venneto, "the Institute may have to put in a request for a supplemental budget just to cover the costs of processing your films."

"If things are that tight," I said, "I can take them to my corner drugstore for processing. It makes double copies at no extra charge."

Three months after my whirlwind tour Mannachar Turun proved himself a man of his word by delivering all that he had promised. A complete set of specifications for the Iranian intelligence communications base arrived at my offices. The submarine project details followed a month later.

After photocopying them I mailed the originals back to him in Tehran and copies to Mr. Moses in Montreal. Along with the originals I enclosed a letter expressing regrets that I would not be committing my firm to either project after all.

At our next meeting in the house on rue Sanguinet David scratched his head and asked, "How in blazes did you manage to get them?"

"Simple," I replied with a shrug. "I asked."

"Wonderful," he exclaimed, clapping his hands. "I once tried that technique with a woman. But all I got was a slap in the face."

While he laughed at his joke the door opened and we were joined by a ramrod-stiff, gray-haired man who crossed the room with a slight limp in his right leg.

"You are the agent called Hershel," he said, sitting at the center of a long couch and extending the favored leg. "I have been told that your work has gotten off to an auspicious start. Please accept my congratulations."

"Thank you," I said, bowing my head a little and wondering who this stately figure might be and what he had to do with me, if anything.

Although I had never regarded myself as an expert in what Sherlock Holmes had called "the art of deduction," I had in my years as the manager of a large business developed an ability to read people. Deciding that a man of his years had to have seen military service, I presumed that the gimpy leg represented a war wound received either in the 1948 War of Independence or the Six-Day War of 1967. His age and a European accent ruled out his being a sabra, a native-born Israeli. That he was Jewish and a ranking officer of the Mossad was obvious. Were he not he could not have simply walked in on David and me.

"The general is visiting us as part of an inspection tour of Institute home bases in the Western Hemisphere," David said. "He has read your reports. He insisted on meeting you."

Noting the deference with which David treated the man, I had to conclude that such respect had to have been earned in some truly extraordinary way.

"I am always interested in meeting a man who is prepared to set aside personal safety in the cause of his country," the general said. "But to sit down and talk with one who does so for a nation that is not his by virtue of birth is unusual." He paused and added, "Even though the Law of Return allows all the Jews of the world to claim Israel as a homeland, that kind of idealism is rare."

"Yes, I'm an American, and I always will be," I said. "I have no intention of invoking the Law of Return. But I decided that I could no longer sit on the sidelines while others deny that opportunity to Jews who see Israel as their homeland. Frankly, I don't like to see anyone being pushed around."

"You will be up against a formidable foe. For the Arabs the struggle goes far beyond a matter of who possesses the land that is now claimed by Israel. For them it is a religious war. And it is one which reaches beyond the Middle East. It's a crusade on behalf of Islam. They cry, 'We are fighting for Islam.' Anyone not believing in Islam is the enemy. To them Israel and America are the Great Satan. You are an American working for Israel. That puts you in double jeopardy. You are the infidel. My only advice to you, Hershel, is be careful."

The meeting ended as abruptly as it began. The general rose with difficulty. Wincing in pain and limping out the door, he left me to choose whether Israel's troubles with its neighbors were rooted in a dispute over geography or, as the general believed, in a historic clash in which the faithful of Islam could envision only one outcome, victory for the legions of Allah.

"The general is quite a fellow," David said. "As a matter of Institute policy I can't tell you his real name. Suffice to say, he's a hero of Israel. He's also one of the non-Muslim world's leading experts on Islam. He truly believes that the Muslims are engaged in a holy war and that any negotiating with them is futile. To borrow a phrase that we all heard so often about the war in Vietnam, he's a hawk. He also speaks as an expert on what can happen to an Israeli agent who falls into the hands of the Arabs."

"Is that how he got the bad leg?"

"It's the visible souvenir of the years he spent in one of their prisons," David said. "And nothing has changed. You should hear the stories that have been told by Israelis who were freed from Syrian imprisonment last June in an exchange of POWs from the Yom Kippur War."

I had read newspaper accounts. Israeli pilots who had been shot down over Syria had told journalists they had been treated harshly during the first four months of detention and that their captors had subjected them to mistreatment. A flier who had parachuted safely after his plane was hit by Syrian antiaircraft fire reported that his interrogators had crushed his leg during the very first day of questioning. Another pilot described how his navigator had been shot by a Syrian pilot as he floated earthward near Damascus. Others testified to having been whipped, blinded with spotlights, and beaten on the soles of their feet and on their hands and backs.

While Syria responded with claims that Israel had maltreated Syrians who had been taken prisoner, Israeli Defense Minister Shimon Peres told Parliament of at least five Israeli prisoners who had been maimed by Syrians and two who had died, apparently after torture. He charged that Syrians did not hesitate to use every kind of pressure, including electric shocks applied to sensitive regions of the body, extraction of fingernails, blows to all parts of the body, and torture by blows on open wounds. The Knesset promptly adopted a resolution using language suitable for the Bible, expressing "agitation and wrath."

I preferred to believe that if any prisoner of war from Syria had suffered at the hands of Israeli captors it had been the act of an aberrant individual.

In preparation for venturing into the lands of Islam I had tried to educate myself regarding the most important aspect of the lives of their peoples, their religion. Of course, I knew that I could never gain complete knowledge of so complex a faith, but I felt that I had developed some understanding.

I had learned that the faithful of Islam were enjoined to prayer, fasting, and almsgiving. I knew that I must expect that the men with whom I conducted business had to demonstrate their faith five times a day by kneeling and bowing to Mecca, reciting the phrase *Allahu akbar* (God is the most great). They also carried an obligation to fast during the holy month of Ramadan and to make a pilgrimage (*hajj*) to the Sacred Mosque at Mecca.

In the process of absorbing as much as possible about the religion I did not assume that everyone who claimed to be a follower of Islam would live up to all of its requirements, just as I had never expected to find total adherence to Judaism among Jews and the teachings of Jesus among Christians. Each of these religions demanded that its followers worship the "one true God." Yet many put the things of the world ahead of God. As a businessman I had never found a shortage of people who were eager to put making money ahead of any deity.

Consequently, when I went to the Middle East I felt that I had nothing to fear from the true children of Allah. The ones to look out for would be those who gave only lip service to Islam. My argument was not with Muslims but with the governments that happened to rule them and venal men who sought to destroy a people who wished Muslims and their religion no harm and who had suffered enough.

7

The Ships of Latakia

 Nothing in leaving on a trip thrilled me as much as coming home. After a jaunt halfway around the world, there could be no sweeter sound to me than the joyful voices of my children when I came through the front door.

I had become a seasoned traveler long before I began working for Israel. Business affairs had led me to far corners of the globe. Vacations had included family treks to Mexico, canoe trips all over the United States, roughing it with Ruth in the Canadian Rockies in a travel trailer, and glittering nights on the town in Europe.

At the end of all these trips, if asked, and often without being asked, I had delighted in providing full details of the event without having to weigh my words. To avoid revealing the true nature of my journeys to the Middle East, I had to learn the art of omission.

But something else had happened to me during my first two adventures for the Institute. Previously, after coming home from a trip I had been content to settle into old routines. I used to look forward to getting back to my office, making and taking phone calls, boning up on the details of my company's newest project, holding meetings, arguing with suppliers about suddenly inflated costs, haranguing trucking firms about missed delivery dates, and handling all the other problems that went along with running a company with far-flung interests. Suddenly, none of it seemed to matter quite as much.

My attention often wandered at meetings, carrying me back to Carl Morgan's men's room and my hurried stuffing of secrets into a sleeve, cajoling people into posing for "souvenir" pictures but sneaking photographs of a model of a development project behind them, turning a hotel room closet into a hiding place, pillaging documents from the Ministry of Economy in Cairo, and suppressing anger while I, a Jew, albeit a disguised one, listened to racist garbage from an Egyptian general with inflated dreams of the destruction of Israel, despite the fact that his army had been left in ruins for the second time in seven years.

The pessimism about peace for Israel that I had felt in the Cairo airport was reinforced when Secretary of State Kissinger announced suspension of his latest efforts to achieve disengagement of Israeli and Egyptian troops in the Sinai peninsula. Declaring that the differences between both sides "on a number of key issues have proven irreconcilable," he said it was "a sad day for America, which has invested much hope and faith, and we know it is a sad day also for Israel which needs and wants peace so badly."

The focus of the difficulty centered on Egypt's demand that Israel withdraw from the strategic Mitla and Gidi passes and the Abu Rudeis oil field of the Sinai peninsula, and Israel's refusal to do so without a pledge from Anwar Sadat that Egypt would cease its belligerency.

Having so recently witnessed the depth of animosity toward Israel by government officials and ordinary Egyptians, I saw no reason to expect a dramatic shift in that sentiment. Indeed, the Egyptian foreign minister, Ismail Fahmy, charged that Israel was entirely to blame for the collapse of Kissinger's peace mission. He also warned that no accord could be reached in 1975 that did not deal with "the rights of the Palestinians."

From Damascus, the PLO happily greeted this view, as did Syria. Through its government radio, the secretary-general of the ruling Syrian Arab Socialist Union Party, Fawzi Kayyali, declared Sadat's position to be "very wise" and a "service to Arab unity." Further demonstrating the close ties between Syria and the PLO, the Palestine National Assembly's Central Committee said that it was accepting a proposal by President Hafiz al-Assad to form joint political and military commands with Syria.

Immediately, a high-ranking member of the PLO declared, "If the Israelis attack a Palestinian camp anywhere, this will be regarded as an attack on Syria and there will be a response."

Avidly following these events in newspapers and on TV news, I decided that I had to resume my travels in the Middle East as soon as possible. Because Damascus was so much in the news, I felt I had an obligation to go to the "flash point," as Kissinger called it.

In the Yom Kippur War the Syrians had suffered a disastrous defeat. They had seen 3,500 of their soldiers killed, 370 taken prisoner, and 1,150 top-of-the-line tanks destroyed or captured. Strategically, they had lost the crucial Golan Heights, described by one Israeli soldier as "the eyes of Israel" because possession of the high ground on the Israeli-Syrian border gave Israel an early-warning system and prevented Syrian gunners from raining artillery onto Israeli settlements.

Recognizing how little I knew about Syria, I launched an intensive course of study by accumulating all the books I could find. To avoid the possibility of questions should I suddenly show up in the local library looking for books, I gathered my reading matter from stores in New York City.

Not wishing to prompt queries at home, I kept the volumes in a cabinet in my office, studying them with the door closed. My secretary told all visitors that I was not to be disturbed. I did the same regarding maps, buying them in the city and stashing them in the office, then studying them in secrecy.

Although I did not plan to do so I began what would become an ever-expanding archive requiring several file cabinets. Each required a code known only to me, whose presence I explained to my secretary and others as containing personal papers and other items for a book I intended to write as a legacy for my family.

"It will be what's known as an 'ethical will,' " I said, pointing to Jewish tradition. I noted that Jacob had gathered his children about him to teach them how they should conduct their lives after he was gone, and Moses had instructed the Children of Israel how they were to comport themselves after his death.

I am certain that this rather unusual undertaking and the locked cabinets were accepted as my growing a beard had been received: a symbol of Howard Schack's deepening midlife crisis. Indeed, I sometimes asked myself if I might be in the throes of what some people called "male menopause." In September 1975 I would be two years shy of fifty, the most sobering landmark in a man's life. He suddenly awakens to having emerged on the downward curve of life with fewer years left on earth than he has already enjoyed. I had reached the moment when a man looks at the figure in his shaving mirror and asks, "Dad, what are you doing in there?"

Even through my beard I could discern my father in myself, almost hearing his voice, demanding, "Kid, just what the hell do you think you're doing? You've got a company to run. The company I started. And you've got a family to take care of."

By the time of my birth in 1927 Joseph Schack had turned a small glass repair shop into a building construction enterprise. He was well on his way to becoming a builder whose work orders would include the Rockland County residences or getaways of Helen Hayes, Maxwell Anderson, Adolph Zucker, Paulette Goddard, and "the little tramp" of silent movies, Charlie Chaplin, as well as the famed painter Edward Hopper.

After the company passed into my hands I had engineered its growth into a major concern with contracts and clients in most of the world. Thanks to good planning, the firm's success made it possible for me to sit in my locked office and work out a plan for espionage in the country that was the most adamant of the enemies of Israel—the Syrian Arab Republic.

In my reading on the country I had come across a quotation by a tenth-century traveler. He wrote, "Syria is a land of blessing, abounding in fruits and peopled by holy men." Then the area had encompassed the Mediterranean Arab world—Jordan, Lebanon, Israel/Palestine, and Syria. At the eastern tip of the Mediterranean, it had flourished as an important Phoenician trading post and later played a vital role in the empires of Rome, Persia, Egypt, and Babylon.

With the dismantling of the Ottoman Turkish empire during World War I, the Western Powers handed Syria to the French with the understanding that the Syrians would be granted independence. It was a hollow pledge. Syrians had to wait for sovereignty until 1946. Then came years of internal struggle by political rivals and wars with Israel, leading, at last, to a military takeover in 1970 of the government in Damascus by General Hafiz al-Assad, a ruthless dictator whose personal ambitions and hatred of Israel drove him to spend two-thirds of the country's budget on the military.

Appreciating the historic and continuing relationship of the French with the Syrians, I decided that my best route to getting into the country would be through the French firm that had asked my company to bid for a subcontract on the petrochemical project which took me to Riyadh in 1974. Accordingly, I contacted the firm's new representative in New York, Charles Renault.

Because I did not know him I proposed an exploratory meeting over lunch at the Colony restaurant. I figured that taking him to the elegant and expensive eatery in Manhattan would underscore in his mind that I intended to have a serious discussion about doing business in Syria, though I had no intention of doing business with the most virulent of Israel's enemies. Should the Syrians offer contracts, I intended to submit bids that would be so inflated, even by Middle East standards, that my company would find itself out of contention. My only purpose in going was espionage.

As I waited for Renault to arrive at the Colony, I savored a moment that approximated, at last, the romantic image of spying that had been fostered by novelists and screenwriters. I did not have on the crisp white dinner jacket with a red rose boutonniere of a James Bond. I wore a plain business suit. Nevertheless, I basked in the moment, in the proximity of the super-rich and famous who dined in the Colony's exquisitely elegant setting, and in my secret.

Renault fit right in. He was impeccably clothed in a gray suit with stiff French cuffs extending from his coat sleeves in precisely the length expected of a gentleman. He looked as suave and debonair as his smooth voice on the telephone had suggested. Slender and tall, he crossed the opulent dining room with an air of worldly élan, a combination of Charles Boyer, Maurice Chevalier, and Yves Montand. I stood to greet him and suddenly felt that if this were a scene in one of their movies, I had been cast as the matinee idol's rumpled and curmudgeonly uncle.

Although Renault lunched with the savoir faire of a French screen idol, he quickly demonstrated his credentials as the New York representative of one of France's most prosperous construction companies. As we ate, he asked me about my recent visit to Saudi Arabia and discussed details of other Middle East projects in which my company had subcontracted with his over the years.

"Regarding Syria, your timing is excellent," he said as a waiter rolled a dessert trolley to our table and we both declined to be seduced by its tempting glories. "Only last week our Paris office received a notification that the Syrian army and Armed Forces Headquarters plan to build a new telephone cable system and ground communications network for the military. It will include the total revamping of the system at Damascus airport."

As he paused to sip champagne, I could see that he was enjoying himself, as gossips always do, but whatever pleasure he may have felt could not have exceeded the delight I experienced while I sipped coffee and thought ahead to sending a report on his table talk to Tel Aviv.

"The communications system that they have in place was only a few years old," he went on, "but apparently Israelis destroyed it in the first hours of the war. I gather that each of these installations was entirely above ground. They were easy targets."

I pictured Israeli jets swooping out of the Syrian skies and hammering the installations.

"Like sitting ducks, eh?" I said with a grin.

"Exactly. The error will not be repeated. The new system is to be constructed entirely underground. The person in charge of the project is a Major General M. S. Awad. Do you know him?"

"I have never done business in Syria."

"The project is being financed by the Soviets but will not be built by them," he continued. "General Awad insists on this. Apparently, he has had several disastrous experiences that have turned him off on Soviet engineering. That's good for us, *non?*"

"*Oui,*" I said, lifting my cup in a toast. "Here's to Russkie incompetence."

Throughout my life I had regarded "incompetent" as the worst adjective I could apply to a person. It ranked right up there in my vocabulary, or should I say "down," with unforgivable sins. Unfortunately, the word applied to much of the work that I found being done in the Middle East.

"I confess I do not understand the Syrians," continued my luncheon companion. "Here is a country blessed with a magnificent Mediterranean coastline that easily could be turned into a vacation paradise. With proper planning and execution, the entire region might become a Middle East equivalent of the resorts in the south of France. Yet the northeastern area of al-Jezirah remains undeveloped, an utter waste of a golden opportunity. If given a chance the city of Aleppo on the Mediterranean could become another Beirut. If the Syrians built dams and other water projects, the agricultural areas could be another California. Frankly, I should much prefer to be building hotels and dams than underground military command posts."

"Why don't you tell that to President Assad?"

Though I said it jokingly, Renault's eyes widened in horror.

"Just kidding," I said, picking up the bill.

"Of course, as long as there is an Israeli state," he said, "I suppose the Arab nations feel they have no choice but to arm themselves. What a pity!"

"Do you mean a pity that Arabs arm or that Israel exists?"

He studied me closely for a reaction. "Excuse me, Howard, but are you Jewish? If you are, or if your company is doing business in Israel, you can give up hope of doing business in Syria. They don't deal with Jews."

"If I were a Jew," I answered, forcing a chuckle to mask the anger raging through me, "would I be sitting here with you talking about going to Syria?"

"Of course, my firm will be delighted to assist you," he said, lighting a small cigar, "but I am not always up to date on the latest info out of Syria. I recommend that you pay a call on our Paris headquarters for a briefing."

"I was hoping I could do so," I said.

"The man to see is Marcel Deverre. He's an old hand in the games that are played in the Middle East and our resident expert on the Syrians. I'll telex him to expect you."

As our waiter collected my American Express card and my guest savored his cigar, I wondered if Renault hated Jews on a personal basis or simply blamed them because the Middle East conflict kept him from building resort hotels in Aleppo.

Driving back to Rockland County, I went over everything that he had told me. When I reached my office the report was so well organized that I rushed inside in the way a man feeling a formidable call of nature dashes for a men's room. Closing my office door, I told my secretary that I could not be disturbed for at least an hour. But I wrote so quickly that I completed the task in ten minutes.

For the first time in a message I began with the codeword "Umbra." This signified that the message contained what the sender considered to be vital new information. To alert the receiver of the envelope to the urgency of the contents, I typed in the lower left corner of the envelope: "Attention: Mr. Courier." In mailing such material to home base, Institute regulations required that I randomly select a street-corner mailbox.

With the "Umbra" message tucked in my pocket, I used my private telephone to call the special travel agency in the city to arrange the journey to Syria. However, my request would not be as simple and straightforward as Howard Mackenzie's journey to Egypt. I wanted the option of arriving in Syria as Howard Mackenzie. But I felt that I had no choice but to go to Paris as myself. This would require booking a flight from New York to France as Howard Schack and then some means of getting Howard Mackenzie from there to Damascus. How this trick could be achieved, I left in the hands of the experts at the agency.

Although I wanted to go as soon as possible, I specified no exact departure date. I left it to the agency to sift through airline schedules, which were unlikely to be as flexible in getting Mackenzie to Damascus as my hop across the Atlantic to Paris. A date for my departure *from* Syria lay outside my control. I understood that Mackenzie could be in the country only as long as the government permitted, as stipulated in a visitor's visa.

To my astonishment, getting answers to these puzzles took only two days. "We have your itinerary and your travel documents ready," said a young woman with a chipper voice over the phone in my office. "Can you come in tomorrow and pick them up?"

"I'll be there this afternoon."

I was handed a bulky brown envelope in which I found an itinerary that would take Howard Schack to Paris on June 1, 1976. A round-trip Pan Am ticket left the return date open. Mackenzie's tickets had him departing Paris two days later, allowing Howard Schack a full day to meet with his French business associates. Howard Mackenzie would then fly via Air France to Beirut, Lebanon, and onward via Middle East Airlines to Damascus. He would arrive on a Saturday morning and spend the limit of the full week permitted by the Syrian entry visa that the travel agency had affixed in the Mackenzie passport. I assumed the visa was an Institute forgery.

With the tickets I found an envelope. Addressed to Herschel, it contained a message from Colonel Langatzky:

> Especially interested in photos of Soviet ships in ports of Latakia and Tartus. If available, deliver by hand to Rome. Good hunting, bon voyage, shalom! Shred this note. Mike.

That the travel agency had been able to so quickly resolve the problem of getting me to Paris and Mackenzie to Syria, in effect made it possible for Howard Schack to be in two places at once.

This sleight of hand did not surprise me as much as finding the message from Langatzky. I had expected the travel agency to alert the home office to my plans and that someone might contact me. But the swiftness of both events—and a message from Langatzky rather than my usual handler, David—led me to speculate that a long-distance, time-consuming communication between the travel agency and Langatzky might not have been necessary.

Driving across the George Washington Bridge on my way back to Rockland County and my office, I wondered if Langatzky were in New York and, if so, why he sent a written assignment rather than calling me in for a meeting.

We had not seen one another since he introduced me to David. After more than a year, I thought it odd that he would not want to see me. In that period I had provided a lot of data that in my view demonstrated that Langatzky's selection of me as an agent had been more than justified.

Colonel Langatzky and David had assured me the Institute did not carry out espionage against the United States. They had taken scrupulous care to train me outside the country, and had made sure that all my debriefings took place on foreign soil. However, I felt that Langatzky's not seizing an opportunity to see me was being scrupulous in the extreme.

Frankly, I felt a little hurt.

But as I pondered the situation, I envisioned numerous reasons to explain why Langatzky had not contacted me in person. First, my deduction that he was in New York appeared to be hasty. The message from him had been typed and could have been dictated over the phone or telexed from anywhere in the world. Furthermore, he was a high-ranking Mossad officer. In the lingo of the trade, he probably was "running" numerous agents. Or, I supposed, he might have had a personal code of conduct that did not permit socializing with his agents, even if only to give them a "well done" and a pat on the back.

Finally, a sinister scenario took shape in my very active imagination. In it, he feared that I might be under surveillance and that if he met me he would find himself in jeopardy. Consequently, from the moment I left the bridge to the instant I pulled into my company's parking lot I kept looking into rearview mirrors to see if someone were tailing me.

In retrospect I found the notion ridiculous. Were anyone conducting a surveillance of me it would be a task assigned to someone who was not about to be spotted by a rank amateur named Howard Schack, as a woman on a train with a Bloomingdale's tote had demonstrated so convincingly.

Arriving home that evening, I faced the prospect of having to inform my family that I was about to leave them for another business trip. Although I had no intention of telling them that my destination was Damascus, I knew they would rail against another journey so soon, even to Paris. But even worse than lying to them again loomed the possibility that my wife might decide that a trip to *Paris*, by rights, ought to include *her*.

But it was my eldest son who objected to my going. "I don't see why you have to go to these places when you could do it by phone," he said.

Of course, he was right. "Some things are too important to handle on the phone. Face-to-face contact is required."

While this certainly was true, everyone in my family knew that I employed people who were as able as I in dealing with important individuals, and had done so frequently. There had been numerous instances in which I had left highly sensitive negotiations in the hands of subordinates for purely personal motives. The truth was that my firm had become so well organized and the employees so competent that I felt no compunctions in absenting myself for weeks at a time to travel with the family.

Had my son chosen to mention these facts I would have found myself in an untenable situation. Fortunately, he dropped the subject, relieving me of the unpleasant necessity of concocting yet another lie.

A few days later I landed in Paris and proceeded directly to a telephone to contact the offices of my French associates in order to arrange an appointment with Marcel Deverre. Put through to him by his secretary, I spoke to a man with a booming voice that evoked a mental picture of a towering, athletic, and sun-bronzed stereotype of a French legionnaire.

The following morning I arrived at his office in a sumptuous duplex edifice on the Champs-Élysées halfway between the Arc de Triomphe and the Louvre. There I found a portly, balding, past-middle-aged gentleman with the bearing of a diplomat rather than a soldier.

"Your destination is Syria," he exclaimed. "What a country. Of all the nations of the Near East that I have had the pleasure to get to know I found it to be the most fascinating. I have an abiding interest in antiquities, you see. In that, Syria is without par. The Omayyed Mosque in Damascus. The ancient city of Ugarit near the port of Latakia. The island of Arwad in the port of Tartus, with fortifications going back to the Phoenicians. I do hope your business will not be so encompassing as to keep you from a little sightseeing."

"I will be on a tight schedule," I replied. "My visa is for a week only."

"What bureaucratic nonsense. I shall give you the name of an official who will overcome this absurdity. He is an old friend of mine from my days as a military attaché in Damascus, a wonderful gentleman by the name of General Awad."

"Renault mentioned him," I said. "I understand he's the one in charge of Syria's major military rebuilding program."

"That is why he is precisely the person to open all doors. I used to tease him unmercifully. I called him the 'Open Sesame' to all of Syria."

My conference with Deverre went a full hour longer than the half hour designated for my visit. I soaked up all he had to offer in the way of enlightenment and advice, from characterizations of Syrian officials to the amenable hotels where a Westerner might obtain a decent bottle of wine to go along with dinner.

Unfortunately, Deverre's graciousness in offering to smooth my way in Syria could throw a monkey wrench into my travel plans. I had been booked as Howard Mackenzie. However, Deverre would be alerting General Awad to expect Howard Schack.

This meant that I could look forward to the prospect of being Mackenzie on the flight to Damascus and at my hotel but having to become Schack again when dealing with Awad. I felt like the man in the poem by Hughes Mearns:

> As I was going up the star
> I met a man who wasn't there.
> He wasn't there again today.
> I wish, I wish he'd stay away.

Having established Howard Schack's presence in the City of Lights, I checked out of my picturesque Rive Gauche hotel two days later. As I did, I declared loudly to the desk clerk that I was heading for an auto excursion through the French provinces. Instead, I headed for Orly airport and an Air France flight under the name Howard Mackenzie to a place in which Howard Mackenzie and Howard Schack would appear and disappear, depending on circumstances.

Boarding the jetliner, I felt that I was literally fulfilling Moses' command to the people of Israel in Deuteronomy to take their journey unto the great Euphrates. Into my mind as I stopped briefly at Beirut airport sprang scriptural images of cedars of Lebanon being cut down and hauled to Jerusalem to adorn Solomon's Temple.

The coastal cities of Tyre and Sidon that had sounded so romantic and faraway when I read of them in the Torah as a boy could still be found on the map of modern Lebanon. If I had the time, I might go to the ancient site of Byblos, believed to be where the word "Bible" came from, to the ruins of Baalbek, or to an especially notable remnant of a Crusader castle at Sidon.

If history did not matter, Beirut offered all the luxuries of a modern city that seemed more West than East, less Arabic than French. Lebanon had been carved out of the Ottoman Empire after World War I and mandated to France until independence after the Second World War. Consequently, its coastal capital city of gleaming white high-rises had blossomed and flourished with a Gallic flare. It had become a major trading and banking center and won itself a reputation as the Paris of the Middle East.

Alas, the situation proved short-lived.

Situated north of Israel and between the Jewish state and Syria, Lebanon found itself in a political tug of war between a population that was half Christian and half Muslim with Arab factions in a constant struggle for supremacy. At the same time it was caught in the crossfire of fighting surrounding an influx of Palestinians. The PLO had been driven out of Jordan and envisioned creating guerrilla bases in Lebanon for launching attacks on Israel.

I remained in Beirut only long enough to change planes for the continuation of my journey to Damascus. Yet being in such a cosmopolitan and romantic city with its warring factions made me realize that my impulsive reaction to the Yom Kippur War had led me into a historic struggle. My adventures in Saudi Arabia and

Egypt had been like a game of hide-and-seek. On both occasions I had been on the lookout for anything easily picked up. But going to Syria was different. This was *intentional* espionage.

Sitting alert and on guard in Beirut's splendidly modern airport, I followed rules of readiness that had been drilled into me by David in the safe house in Montreal. I waited for my flight to Damascus with the sober understanding that I had crossed a line. What I had done in Saudi Arabia and Egypt had been for the benefit of Israel. This journey to Syria was not going to be a piece of cake. I was more nervous than I had ever been.

The trip was a hop, really. Less than an hour after "wheels up" I stood before a Syrian immigration officer.

"What is the purpose of your visit?" he asked in flawless English.

"Business," I said, figuring the less I said, the better.

"What is the nature of the business?" he asked.

"I'm here to solicit construction work from the government," I said forcefully. "I have an appointment with General Awad."

Mentioning the name did the trick. Apparently General Awad was indeed an Open Sesame. The official handed me my passport without further delay and a few minutes later I was in the back of a Mercedes taxi. The German sedan seemed ubiquitous in Arab countries.

Having experienced Arab taxi drivers' passion for speeding, I braced myself for a breakneck pace. But the middle-aged driver proved an exception, proceeding sanely and affording me a chance to observe terrain that had taken a beating from the Israeli air force in the Yom Kippur War.

Although I found no evidence of it in 1975, a year and half after the Yom Kippur War, I knew that the city of Damascus had come perilously close to being captured by the rapidly advancing Israeli ground forces. But wise heads had prevailed, persuading decision-makers in the Israeli war cabinet that to occupy an Arab city of a population of more than a million would prove to be a costly proposition for years to come, possibly turning Syria into an Israeli Vietnam. Faced with a similar opportunity in the 1991 Persian Gulf War to push into Iraq and take Baghdad, the United States would show the same prudence.

Traveling the thirty-five kilometers from the airport into Damascus, I could not fail to appreciate who ruled the country. Huge roadside portraits of Hafiz al-Assad stared at me at frequent intervals, as Sadat's had done in Cairo.

"He is a good man," muttered my driver with a nod at each of the images of Assad zipping past my window.

Rather than attack Assad's capital on the ground, Israelis had concentrated on pinpoint air assaults on military targets and the headquarters of the Syrian General Staff in the city. Beyond Damascus they had ranged across the countryside and along the Mediterranean coast, plastering vital ports, such as the ones of which Colonel Langatzky had expressed interest in my obtaining photographs: Latakia and Tartus.

My taxi arrived at my hotel, the Omar al Khayyam, located on Saahat al-Chouhada (Martyrs' Square) in the heart of Damascus. I had no idea whether I would be able to journey to the seaports. Indeed, I did not know if I might be permitted to leave Damascus at all. As in every Arab nation, except tourist-dependent Egypt, the extent of my travels in outlying areas would depend upon government approval; in this case, I presumed, General Awad's.

Deverre had assured me that I would encounter no difficulties in soliciting projects, but the Syrians had not taken the lead of Egypt by purging the Russian presence in the aftermath of the war. Whether a Western contractor would find a welcome in the corridors of power in Damascus remained to be seen.

Calling General Awad's office, I identified myself to his aide as Howard Schack, wondering fleetingly if the hotel room phone were tapped and if so what the listener would make of a man named Schack placing a call from a room registered in the name of Howard Mackenzie.

When General Awad spoke I expected to hear the heavily Arabic-accented English that had become familiar to me. Instead, he sounded as if he had used the language of William Shakespeare, John Milton, and the Oxford English Dictionary all his life. I later discovered that he had studied English literature at Cambridge University and had gone through a special course for Mideast army officers at Sandhurst, Britain's West Point.

"I have been waiting for you to ring me up," he said. "Any friend of Mr. Deverre is a friend of mine. Can you come to see me tomorrow at ten? Or do you prefer a day or two for rest?"

"Tomorrow is fine, General. I've come to your country to do business, not to rest. Just tell me how to get to your office."

"Do not worry, sir. I shall send my car to collect you at half past nine precisely."

Into my mind leapt a scenario in which his driver asked the desk clerk for Howard Schack, only to be informed that no such individual had registered in that name.

"Thank you for the generous offer," I said, scrambling to come up with an alternative, "but I have a previous appointment and might not be back at the hotel. Might your driver pick me up elsewhere?"

"Anywhere you like."

I flipped open a street map of Damascus that I had bought in Cairo and jabbed a finger on a black dot on Port Said Avenue, not far from my hotel.

"I'll be at the Commercial Bank of Syria," I said, reading the fine print adjacent to the dot. "Would it be convenient for your man to come there at half past nine? I'll be in front. How will I recognize your car?"

"There will be no problem. It is a black Mercedes with a pair of flags on the front fenders, the Syrian and my command flag. Meanwhile, I shall be looking forward to seeing you."

Exactly at nine-thirty the next morning the gleaming black Mercedes limousine drew up in front of the bank. As I approached, a young army officer leapt out and snapped a salute. "At your service, sir," he said, holding out a hand and inviting me into the rear seat. "I am Captain Hammed Azziz, aide to General Awad."

Proceeding with the speed of an Arabian taxi, we followed broad Choukri Kouwati Avenue to the outskirts of Damascus, arriving half an hour later at the headquarters building of a nameless army base. Following the captain down four flights of stairs, I came to an anteroom with reinforced concrete ceilings and walls that my practiced eye discerned to be at least four feet thick. Obviously, the Syrians had learned a lesson in seeing aboveground facilities destroyed in the Yom Kippur War.

I found General Awad to be all that Deverre's description had led me to expect. In crisp khakis and with a flourishing mustache, he looked like a figure out of time, a throwback to Syria's French-colonial past.

A gracious host and military in bearing and tone, he spent most of an hour discussing Syria's needs. Citing plans for army and air force construction, he demonstrated a deep appreciation of the details of each and an acute understanding of the specifications, anticipating most of my questions.

While everything he revealed amounted to an intelligence officer's treasure, he confined himself to projects in and around the capital. Mindful of Langatzky's request for data concerning the seaports of Latakia and Tartus, I decided to press my luck.

"Naturally, my firm is interested in getting involved in these projects you have outlined for me," I said, "but I'm a little worried about the logistics of bringing in necessary equipment and supplies. According to my latest information, which I admit is not very up to date, your port facilities sustained quite a bit of damage in the recent war."

"Do not fret about this," Awad replied, waving a hand. "The ports have been completely repaired and are fully operational. But you shall see for yourself! At your convenience, a driver and a member of my staff will be placed at your disposal to take you to Latakia for a personal inspection of the facilities. It is not far, a few hours by car. You can go up and back in a day. When would you care to go?"

"I'm a man who believes there's no time like the present."

"That proves you are a true American," he said with a laugh. "I have spent some time in your country. Everyone is always in a hurry." He pressed a button on an intercom. "I like Americans," he continued. "That is why I believe it is such a tragedy that the United States government has chosen to throw in its lot with Israel rather than solicit the friendship of the Arab states."

The office door swung open and Captain Azziz stepped in, saluting smartly.

"Hammed, you are to escort Mr. Schack to Latakia," the general said crisply. "He is interested in a tour of historic sites and the port. Show him everything. Take my personal car."

Emboldened further by the general's felicitous attitude, I blurted, "Might I be permitted to make photographs?"

The general paused, thinking hard, then shrugged. "If it will be helpful to you, why not?"

The ancient and strategic seaport opposite the eastern tip of Cyprus was located about 150 miles by air from Damascus. The overland journey was more than 200 miles over a route that took us northward, paralleling mountains of eastern Lebanon. Turning west at the town of Hims, we crossed the Litani River and drove into rich agricultural land, directly to the coast.

Throughout the journey the captain proved to be not only an affable traveling companion but somewhat of an expert on the region. He regaled me with the local history and folklore. But as we neared Latakia itself he turned to vivid descriptions of the Israeli naval raids on the city in the 1973 war. No one in Arab countries referred to it as the Yom Kippur War, a fact that I had to keep constantly in my mind whenever I found myself drawn into a discussion of the subject.

Although Captain Azziz skipped what must have seemed to him to be embarrassing details, I knew that the attack on Latakia had begun at a few minutes before midnight of October 6. The battle involved a double-pronged assault by Israeli missile ships engaging Syrian navy torpedo and missile boats. When it ended after twenty-five minutes, the first naval missile battle in history had resulted in a devastating Israeli victory that destroyed a Syrian torpedo boat, a minesweeper, and three missile boats—the backbone of the small Syrian navy. In the naval warfare of which Latakia had been a part, combined Egyptian and Syrian losses had totaled nineteen, including ten missile boats, while Israel lost not one ship.

As we rode through Latakia, Azziz waxed poetic about it, noting that it was easily the most cosmopolitan city in Syria and the least conservative religiously and culturally, as all busy seaports usually are. That Latakia ranked high among important Mediterranean ports became immediately apparent. Tied up at docks or at anchor offshore, oceangoing freighters of all sizes and shapes bore flags of nations from throughout the world. Whatever damage had been inflicted in 1973 had been erased.

Photographing everything that I could without being obvious I memorized the locations, dimensions, and capacities of docks and towering steel cranes used in the port's loading and unloading operations. Later I recorded them in a small notebook along with the names and other identifying markings of the dozen or so ships that I had seen tied up in the port.

Two freighters especially attracted my attention because they flew the flag of the Soviet Union and because their superstructures bristled with antennas. As I copied their names, painted in Cyrillic characters, I wished that I had studied the language of my Russian ancestors so that I would know the names that I was jotting down. But I consoled myself concerning my linguistic shortcomings with the certain knowledge that Israel's population consisted of thousands of people with Russian roots who could translate them.

As it turned out, the first Israeli to look at my jottings deciphered my copied letters of the Russian alphabet immediately. Calling himself Aaron, he debriefed me in a hotel room off Piazza del Poppolo in Rome two days after my arrival from Syria. "These are not ordinary Soviet cargo ships," he said excitedly as he read my notes. "They are the *Caucacus* and the *Yuri Gagarin*."

"They're important?" I said.

"You have no idea!"

"No, I don't, " I said impatiently. "Perhaps you could tell me about them."

"They are meant to appear to be freighters, hardly worth a second look," he went on. "But, they are loaded with the Soviet Union's most sophisticated electronic equipment. The sole mission of these innocuous-looking ships is to spy on Israel. They are floating Elint gatherers. Elint means—"

"Electronic intelligence," I interjected.

"Excuse me. I didn't intend to condescend. Between them they can monitor every radio and telephone message in, from, and to Israel. Their mission is to listen in on every phone call. The tapes are then helicoptered to the USSR. They also monitor all the communications of Lod airport, civilian as well as military. The *Gagarin* also has uplink capability with Soviet spy satellites. There is at least one more ship that we know of, *The Crimea*. Perhaps when you were in Latakia, *Crimea* was on station in the Mediterranean, eavesdropping."

This revelation came as a personal shock. Because my wife and I had relatives in Israel, we often called them. That these familial conversations might have been listened to by Russian spies had never occurred to me. Of course, prior to my becoming an Israeli agent anything I said to relatives could only have bored such an eavesdropper. Assuming that everything Aaron had said about the spy ships were true, I now would have to be on guard constantly during any phone conversations with our cousins in Israel in the event that somehow someone might pass on to Arab intelligence services that the Howard Schack chatting with relatives in Israel might be the same Howard Schack working for Mossad.

Despite this chilling realization of the vulnerability of myself, and everyone else on earth, to the eyes and ears of the world's intelligence networks, I left Syria with no need to use the Mackenzie passport as a means of escape. I felt excited and proud. My first deliberate attempt to seek information, rather than simply grab whatever chance brought within reach, had been a resounding success—in Aaron's phrase, "a coup."

Returning to my role as the head of my construction company, I plunged into duties that once upon a time had seemed dull and routine.

Hardly had I sat behind my desk, than I began thinking of what I might do next and where I might go in pursuit of my efforts on behalf of Israel. Yet I knew that I could not do so. I had my family to think about. Family tradition required the Schacks to go on vacation. Almost always a trip lasting several weeks, our travels began as soon as possible after a family get-together and cookout on the Fourth of July. For the summer of 1976, America's Bicentennial, Ruth had arranged a patriotic odyssey to national shrines: Valley Forge, Gettysburg, Civil War battlefields of Maryland and Virginia, Colonial Williamsburg, and Washington, D.C.

Unfortunately, as we looked forward to our gala backyard Independence Day and the trip, our plans were suddenly eclipsed by an act of Arab terrorism that began thousands of miles away but struck with horror and outrage into the hearts of Jews and all decent people everywhere.

On Saturday, June 27, four PLO terrorists hijacked Air France flight 139 shortly after it left Athens on a flight from Tel Aviv to Paris. The identification of the Air France flight number left Ruth and me stunned. Returning from a visit to Israel a year earlier, I had taken flight 139.

Slipping through lax security at Athens airport, the Arabs came aboard the plane with guns and hand grenades. Brandishing the weapons, they forced the jet to land at Benghazi, Libya, for refueling. Proceeding to Entebbe, Uganda, they joined other PLO members and units of the Ugandan army in holding the flight's 256 passengers and 12 crew members hostage. Having done so, they demanded the release of 53 convicted terrorists being held in prisons in Israel, West Germany, Kenya, Switzerland, and France.

The tense and astonishing events of the following days have been published in great detail elsewhere. The opening of negotiations by Israel was actually a ruse to gain time until the hostages could be rescued by Israeli special forces in a daring raid on Entebbe carried out with a secrecy unparalleled in the history of Israel.

Two years after Entebbe I picked up a paperback book, *The Mossad*, by Dennis Eisenberg, Uri Dan, and Eli Landau. When I came to a passage in a chapter entitled "Invisible Spies," dealing with the Entebbe rescue, my eyes were riveted to page 243.

"In the eastern Mediterranean, just beyond the range of the naked human eye," it began, "lies a fleet of three nondescript-looking Soviet vessels."

The book proceeded to describe two of the ships that I had spotted at Latakia and the one I had not seen, the *Crimea*.

When the Entebbe rescue operation was being planned, the authors continued, "orders went out to everybody concerned: 'Keep your mouth shut—and your radio off!' Had the Russians picked up advance warning of the operation, they could have radioed it to Entebbe—with obvious results."

Only the exertion of my willpower kept me from showing the book to Ruth and telling her that I had seen and photographed two of those ships weeks before the Air France hijacking and the subsequent miracle at Entebbe. I can only surmise my spotting the Russian spy ships in a Syrian port a couple of weeks before the raid on Entebbe had contributed to its success. The truth lies in Institute archives.

I like to think it did.

8

Footprints in the Sand

 In addressing the United Nations after Entebbe, Israel's representative, Chaim Herzog, declared, "It has fallen to the lot of my small country, embattled as we are, facing the problems which we do, to demonstrate to the world that there is an alternative to surrender to terrorism and blackmail. It is now for the nations of the world, regardless of political differences which may divide them, to unite against this common enemy which recognizes no authority, no borders, respects no sovereignty, ignores all basic human decencies, and places no limits on human bestiality."

Entebbe prompted Herzog's somber challenge to a world that showed little will to confront PLO terrorism. The event forced me to realize that if I continued working on behalf of that small, embattled country, I faced greatly heightened dangers. Throughout my adventures in Saudi Arabia, Egypt, and Syria, I had always been aware that being caught would not be pleasant. That I might wind up in the hands of terrorists had never been a serious concern.

After Entebbe I had to accept the possibility that I easily could become a hostage, exposing my family to an ordeal that had the potential for being far more disastrous than if I found myself arrested by an Arab government. Nations could be expected to play by international law and diplomatic customs. Terrorists could not. Were I to be grabbed by a PLO terrorist group and my captors discovered that I was an Israeli agent I could look forward to a bullet in the head. Was that a risk I ought to assume? Had I not done enough for Israel already?

While I wrestled with these questions, the summer of 1976 flew by in a blur of patriotic excursions. Autumn propelled me back to my responsibilities as the owner of a thriving, demanding business.

Then winter rushed in, bringing the excitement of the holidays. Hearing nothing from the Institute in all this time, I began to believe that nameless, faceless men in Tel Aviv and my home office in Montreal had decided that "Hershel" had outlived his usefulness. Did they feel my cover was no longer effective?

Believing that my avocation as a spy was finished, I prepared to leave my office late on a bitterly cold December afternoon. Looking out the window I saw a low, scudding, slate-gray sky and pictured myself snowbound for the weekend. Like singer-songwriter Judy Collins in her hit song "Both Sides Now," I had looked at clouds for some time. She had gazed at them and saw "flows of angel hair and ice cream castles in the air." As a boy studying the sky I had detected a boy's things: fighter planes in dogfights and battleships with their big guns ablaze. But with the sting of a stiff winter wind in my face, I recognized clouds for what they were—a promise of snow.

As I opened the office door to leave, the telephone rang. Because my secretary had already left for the weekend, I was alone in the offices.

A man's voice said, "As soon as possible, go to the phone booth at the corner. Wait. Someone will call you."

Feeling a rush of excitement, I hurried to the location and stood in the cold wind waiting for the call. It came a few minutes later.

"Come to the Windjammer restaurant in the town of Nyack," a man said.

I recognized the voice of David.

"When?" I asked.

"As soon as possible," he said.

"I'm on my way now," I said.

The Institute had not forgotten me!

When I arrived in Nyack fifteen minutes later light snow had already dusted a village that now resembled a Currier and Ives rendering of nineteenth-century America. Several miles east of my company's location, the town boasted splendid Victorian mansions, some with large, well-kept lawns that swept down the hillside to the wintry-gray Hudson River.

Other areas were not so charming. The Windjammer, a bar and restaurant, stood in one of them. I turned into a parking lot at its rear and found David waiting. Bundled into a sheepskin-lined windbreaker, he leaned against the side of a gray van that had seen better days.

Pulling up beside it, I rolled down my window. "Have you been waiting long?" I asked.

"Let's go for a ride," he said. "There's someone I want you to meet. We'll use your car. Okay?"

"Of course."

"Drive around for a while," he said, getting into the car, "then go to the big mall in Nanuet."

Although I itched to know what was going on and wondered about whom I would be meeting, I knew David well enough to appreciate that he would reveal everything in his own time. If he felt the need for taking precautions I was not about to question him.

Presently we arrived at the mall. "It's the red Chevrolet," David said, nodding at the car.

A tall youth leaned against it, coatless and hatless despite the snow.

"There's your new handler," David said.

"He's a kid," I exclaimed.

"He's on the young side," David answered, "but he's damned good."

"How come I'm getting a new handler?" I blurted. "Why break up a good team?"

"Ours is not to reason why," he said. "But I can tell you that the change has nothing to do with you. I've been reassigned to the embassy in Washington. I am to be a deputy in the press office."

"I had no idea you were a journalist."

"There's a lot about my checkered past that you don't know."

"Will I never see you again?"

"Never say 'never,' Hershel."

"What's my new handler's name?"

"His work name is Jonathan."

"King Saul's son and David's friend."

"You know your Scripture, Hershel."

With my car parked behind the red Chevy David got out and Jonathan took his place beside me in my car.

"I'd heard of your work, Hershel," he said, "but only when I read your file did I realize just how much you've achieved. It's a privilege to be working with you."

"Is this meeting just a howdy-do? Or do you come as David's replacement bearing an assignment for me?"

"David told me that you were a no-nonsense guy. Yes, I have a proposal. I'll tell you about it while you drive."

We both watched David depart in the Chevy.

"Shall I drive to anywhere special?" I asked.

"I've never been to Rockland County. You can take me on a tour. When we're done, you can deliver me to the van in Nyack."

With the snow growing heavier and showing every sign of becoming worse I did not fancy an aimless drive along country roads that could become impassable very quickly. Explaining the situation, I persuaded Jonathan to select at random a roadside diner or fast-food emporium. I figured that if we were caught in a Rockland Country blizzard we could ride it out in a comfortably warm place where there was food and drink.

We ended up in Spring Valley's Red Eagle Diner on Route 59, the county's main thoroughfare. Jonathan said, "I've been ordered to ask you to help us set up a safe house in Montreal."

"What about rue Sanguinet? Are you shutting it down?"

"Not at all," he said, nibbling a drumstick. "We just need another place. But we require a front man to rent the house. Our hope is that you'll take on the job."

"I haven't a clue about renting houses in Montreal. I know next to nothing about the city."

"We've tentatively chosen two locations in Old Montreal. If you agree to help us out, you'll make the final decision. If neither of the two we've proposed suits you, feel free to pick a house of your own. Within reason financially, of course. We want you to be comfortable in the place."

"Hold on a minute. What's this house got to do with me?"

"There's a man we'd like you to help us debrief. I can tell you that he is a Lebanese Christian who has a construction firm in Sidon. He has indicated that he is willing to provide us with information regarding the location of PLO training bases in the Bekaa Valley in Lebanon. I can't get into more of the particulars at the moment because we can't be sure he won't change his mind. We'll know in about a week. If it's a 'go' situation he will be in

Montreal the week after next. We have to be ready for him. I know this is unfair, but I need to know right now if you're on board. If you agree, you'll go to Montreal tomorrow."

"*Tomorrow?* Have you noticed that we're in a blizzard? I'll be lucky if my street is plowed by next week."

"It's not a blizzard," he said, dabbing his lips with a paper napkin. "It's a fairly intense squall associated with a fast-moving cold front. The snow should be over soon, about two inches maximum. The forecast for tomorrow is fair and cold."

"What are you? A weatherman?"

"Hardly. While I was waiting for you and David to show up at the mall I listened to the radio. When it comes to collecting intelligence, you can't beat the radio. Did you know that when the Japanese attacked Pearl Harbor, their planes homed in on Honolulu radio stations? If the station I heard is right—and I have no reason to doubt it—you'll have no trouble from the elements in going to Montreal; that is, if you accept the proposition."

"You knew I would accept. Otherwise you wouldn't have gone to the trouble of asking."

"You're right," he said, handing me a large manila clasp envelope. "This contains all the information you need to get the job done. You'll find a list of furniture rental companies, the numbers to call to get the utilities turned on, and the contact for getting a phone installed. There's also a shopping list of groceries and other things for you to get."

Opening the envelope, I found evidence of just how confident the Institute had been that I would take on the task. Clipped to a multipage list of tasks was an Air Canada first-class ticket in my name to Montreal with departure the next day.

"You'll notice that the return flight date is not booked," Jonathan said. "That's to give you time to do what has to be done without being under a deadline. But we hope you can button this up in a couple of days. As soon as we find out if this guy is going to be available, we will let you know when to go back to Montreal for his debriefing."

"I'm still not clear as to why I have to be there."

"We'll be looking for lots of details from this guy. He says he'll be bringing plans of camps, including blueprints. With your expertise, you're in a unique position to evaluate whatever he gives us, on the spot."

"That's very flattering, but I find it hard to believe that there's nobody that you could bring from the Institute with the necessary qualifications. There's got to be more to this than my sizing this guy up. Level with me, Jonathan."

"David told me you were a cautious customer," he said with a chuckle. "I'm not holding back. It's just that I like to take things one step at a time."

"I appreciate that. But I've always been a person who looks beyond tomorrow. Step one is the safe house. What's the second?"

"If this man is legitimate we will want more out of him than a one-shot contact."

"Ah, the plot thickens!"

"We hope that he'll continue to feed us information on just what's going on among the Palestinians in southern Lebanon. If he becomes an ongoing source, we'd like you to keep in touch with him. You know, include him in your travel plans whenever you're in the vicinity. Drop in on him in Beirut or wherever. Maybe he will introduce you to his PLO contacts."

"How can you be sure he's not a double agent?"

"We're pretty sure he isn't."

"*Pretty* sure? That's encouraging."

"Nothing in life ever gets beyond pretty sure."

"So what's this guy's motives?"

"He's afraid the PLO is going to try to force a partition of Lebanon. From his point of view as a Christian, Israel is the only hope for checkmating such a move. Incidentally, our long-range threat-analysis section agrees that since Jordan gave the PLO the heave-ho, Arafat's crowd and their Lebanese allies have set their greedy eyes on southern Lebanon. They plan to set up a permanent base for attacks on Israel. Our visitor also appears to have a personal score to settle. His wife's youngest brother was an officer in the Christian militia. He was killed during a clash between his unit and Palestinians a few months ago. The man we will be meeting is not in this for money."

A beam of sunlight fell across his face. "You see?" he said, looking out the window. "The radio was right. The snow is stopping. You'll have clear flying weather."

"How do I let you know that I've set everything up?"

"Telephone the rue Sanguinet number and say, 'Paul is ready for the delivery of the furniture.' Then give the address of the house that you've selected. But reverse the house number. If it's 1-2-3, for instance, make it 3-2-1."

"Suppose the house I rent is number 2-2-2?"

His face crinkled momentarily with puzzlement, then burst into a grin.

"I heard you were a joker, Hershel," he said, shaking a chicken wing in the direction of my nose. "But nobody warned me that your sense of humor could be so cruel!"

The first two addresses suggested to me turned out to be on quiet streets. I felt that we needed a busy area in which no one would stand out. I found just such a place off rue Notre-Dame between rue St. Pierre and rue McGill. A townhouse with two rooms and a kitchen on the ground floor and two bedrooms above, the place required little in the way of furniture. This was promptly delivered by a firm chosen at random from the phone book. Discovering that the utilities were already on, I needed only to phone to have them listed in the name of Howard Mackenzie and billed to the home office. A call to the phone company brought the promise that an installer would come around in two days, giving me a full day in which to stock the modern but tiny kitchen with supplies, primarily items to suit a Middle East taste— lamb, rice, and tea.

Using my new phone, I left the required message with an operator at rue Sanguinet and waited.

Jonathan arrived within an hour, pronounced my choice and my work "outstanding and expeditious," and sent me back home to await word on whether I would be returning to meet our mysterious Lebanese.

Four days later the call came directly to my office from Jonathan.

"The deal is off," he said, his voice choked with emotion.

"All that work was for nothing? What happened? Did the guy get cold feet?"

"Our prospective partner," Jonathan said after a deep sigh, "has met an untimely death."

"What? Was it an accident?"

"He ran into a soft-nosed bullet to the back of the head in his car parked in an alleyway at the back of his sister's house in the Christian Quarter in Beirut."

As I put down the phone my thoughts skipped to the house in

Montreal. I had left there a refrigerator stocked with lamb and a cupboard with a box of rice and packets of tea to provide a home for the nameless, faceless man with a story to tell about terrorists in his homeland.

Had that been the cause of his becoming a murder victim in a Beirut back alley? Somewhere, somehow, had his plan to meet with the agents of Israel been discovered and his fate sealed? Or had his contact with Israel been unrelated to the murder? Might it have been a coincidence?

Certainly, there was ample reason to suppose that the murder could have stemmed from other motives. Recently, long-simmering animosities and rivalries between the country's Christians and Muslims had bubbled into warfare. The dominance of Christians was being challenged by a swelling population of followers of Islam, demanding recognition in all aspects of Lebanese life. These internal stresses worsened in the context of the East-West contest throughout the Middle East. In Lebanon, Muslims joined with their brothers elsewhere in looking to the Soviet Union while Lebanese Christians turned to the United States and Israel. This burgeoning civil war also created opportunities for people to settle personal scores. Might a grudge have been the motive behind the brutal murder of our potential informant?

While I could not dismiss the idea that he died because of his contact with Israel and, by extension, with me, I did not know—and probably never would know—why the man had been murdered. But no matter what provoked the killing, I thought as I sat in the quiet security of my office, the tragedy served to drive home to me a dark fact of Middle Eastern life that always had been in my mind, namely, that I ventured into a region of the world in which human life was often held cheap.

I could just as easily meet death at the hands of a street robber in Beirut as from an assassin. Although there was a risk of falling into the hands of PLO aircraft hijackers, the crash of an airliner whose fuel intake lines had clogged with desert sand seemed far more likely.

I also reasoned as I contemplated the vagaries of life and death that the day was bound to come when I ran into the Grim Reaper, so why worry about it? Besides, I thought, the inevitable encounter seemed far more likely to result from my fondness for rich food and fast driving than random violence on a Middle East street, or a New York one, or at the hand of an assassin or headline-seeking terrorist.

In mulling the implications of the death of the man who never got the chance to enjoy the amenities of my safe house, I recalled a pertinent parable of the English writer Somerset Maugham, which the American novelist John O'Hara had inscribed at the beginning of his book *Appointment in Samarra.*

DEATH SPEAKS

There was a merchant in Bagdad who sent his servant to market to buy provisions and in a little while the servant came back, white and trembling, and said, Master, just now when I was in the market-place I was jostled by a woman in the crowd and when I turned I saw it was Death that jostled me. She looked at me and made a threatening gesture; now, lend me your horse and I will ride away from this city and avoid my fate. I will go to Samarra and there Death will not find me. The merchant lent him his horse, and the servant mounted it, and he dug his spurs in its flanks and as fast as he could gallop he went. Then the merchant went down to the market-place and he saw me standing in the crowd and he came to me and said, Why did you make a threatening gesture to my servant when you saw him this morning? That was not a threatening gesture, I said, it was only a start of surprise. I was astonished to see him in Bagdad, for I had an appointment with him tonight in Samarra.

If an untimely and violent death were to be in the cards for me in Samarra or elsewhere, I figured, would it not be far more meaningful and satisfying were it to happen in pursuit of a good cause?

Although I was often scared to death, I found a challenge in my secret life. If in my middle age as I left my footprints in the sands of Arabia I bumped into the Angel of Death coming the other way, so be it. My kids were grown and well equipped to cope with life.

Rather than feel daunted by the murder of a man in Beirut, I looked forward to my next journey and began making plans to go

in March 1977, the earliest date that personal and business obliga-
tions permitted. The primary destination, I decided, would be a
nation that I had visited only briefly—Kuwait.

In my readings on Arabia in the book I had purchased on that
first trip to Montreal, I had become fascinated by the tiny oil-rich
city-state on the Persian Gulf. In many ways it seemed dramatically different from other Arab countries. Basking in the riches of
petroleum, the Kuwaitis saw the advantages of spreading around
enormous wealth, tearing down mud-walled hovels and building a
gleaming and modern port and capital of cement and steel, Kuwait
City. Money also had been pumped into education, not just for the
ruling elite but for the general population, including females.
Resources became available to other Arab countries through the
establishment of the Kuwait Fund for Arab Development. Among
the projects that I had found in the planning stages on my previous
visit had been expansion of the port of Beirut, modernization of
railways in the Sudan, and the upgrading of agriculture in Tunisia.

By going back to Kuwait I hoped to learn how these projects
might have progressed. I also wished to update my list of ventures
being financed by the Kuwaitis. The announcement to the Institute's travel agency in New York City of my intention to visit
Kuwait resounded well with my new handler. Jonathan wasted no
time in contacting me.

"Can we get together?" he asked in a phone call to my office a
few days later. "I have a shopping list for you. I'd like to meet with
you as soon as your schedule permits in that charming house you
recently acquired. I'll be accompanied by an old friend of yours, by
the way."

To my surprise and pleasure the "old friend" who greeted me in
the cozy parlor of the safe house turned out to be Colonel
Langatzky. I had not seen him since he introduced me to David in
Washington Square Park in the spring of 1974. Although he
looked as fit as he had two years earlier, he seemed unusually
anxious as we sat in a pair of cheap but comfortable armchairs.

"Before Jonathan gets down to the nitty-gritty of what we are
interested in concerning your trip to Kuwait," he said, leaning
forward intently, "I want to bring you up to speed on how we
view the new administration in Washington and how we expect
the election of Jimmy Carter as president to affect the dynamics of
the Middle East. In a nutshell, we believe that there is going to be a

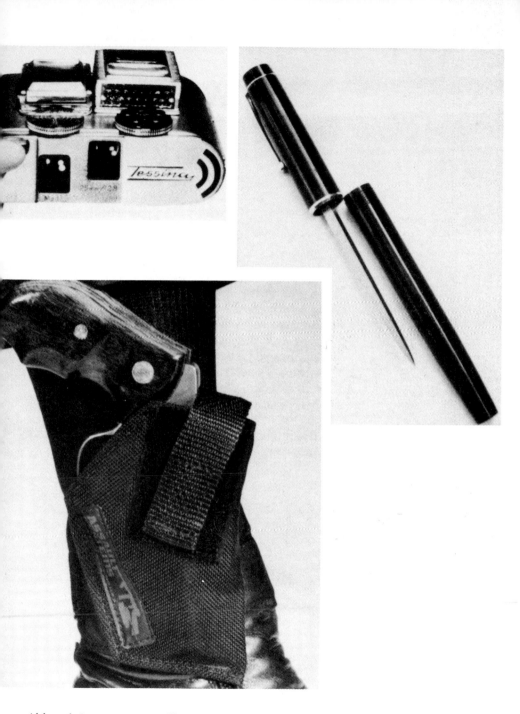

Although I never saw myself as a James Bond, my work for Israel's Institute for Intelligence and Special Operations, known as Mossad, resulted in a training course in the equipment of espionage agents. The gadgets included a microfilm camera and a stiletto disguised as a ballpoint pen. Until terrorists forced airport security to be tightened in the 1980s, I only carried a pistol in an ankle holster. Ultimately, I relied on my Swiss army knife for self-defense.

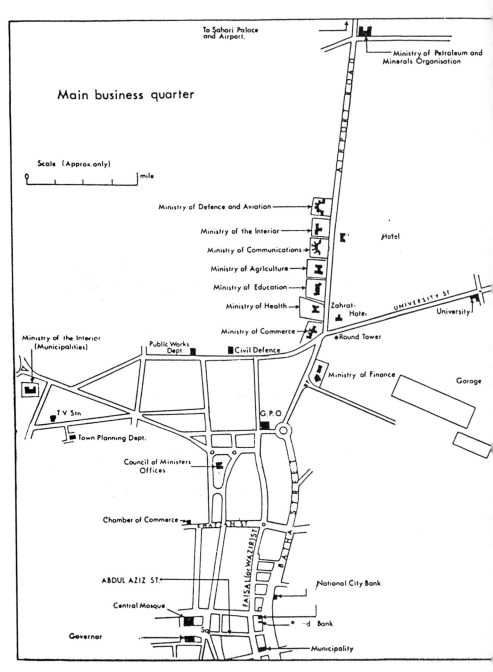

Main business quarter

To Ṣahari Palace and Airport.

Ministry of Petroleum and Minerals Organisation

Scale (Approx.only)

0 ⊢——————————⊣ mile

Ministry of Defence and Aviation

Ministry of the Interior

Ministry of Communications

Ministry of Agriculture

Ministry of Education

Ministry of Health

Hotel

Zahrat. Hotel

Ministry of Commerce

Ministry of the Interior (Municipalities)

Public Works Dept.

Civil Defence

UNIVERSITY ST

University

Round Tower

Ministry of Finance

Garage

T.V Stn

G.P.O.

Town Planning Dept.

Council of Ministers Offices

Chamber of Commerce

FAISAL or WAZIR ST

RAT AN ST

BATHA

ABDUL AZIZ ST.

Central Mosque

National City Bank

-d Bank

Governor

Sq

Municipality

Collecting intelligence information for Israel did not always require snapping secret photos. I found a great deal of significant information available for the asking. This map of central Riyadh, the capital of Saudi Arabia, denotes the locations of government offices, the public works department, the television station (invariably a potentially vital military target) and the civil defense headquarters.

Because the Institute's intelligence analysts were always interested in a potential enemy's internal transportation system, my handlers regularly requested such information. Of interest to strategic planners was a militarily-important highway that cut through Saudi mountains.

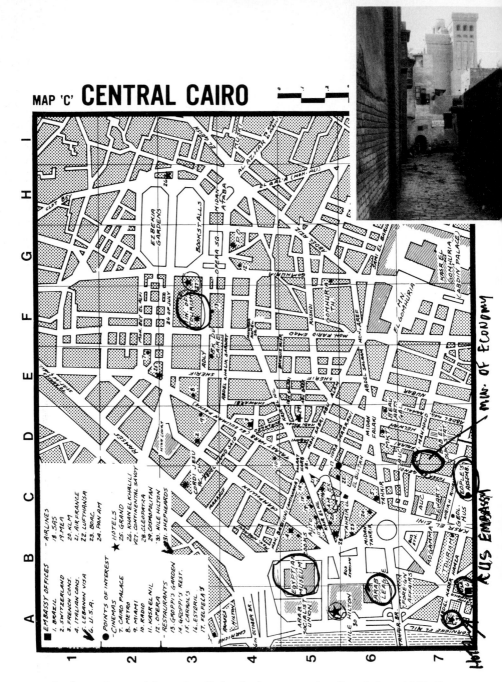

MAP 'C' **CENTRAL CAIRO**

As the major participant in all the Arab wars against Israel since 1948, Egypt ranked high on my list of nations to be visited in carrying out my intelligence activities for Israel. But as I gathered materials at the Ministry of Economy related to new Egyptian military projects, I feared that I had fallen into a trap. If so, my only hope was to run for safety in the nearby American embassy (map). After a nervous night at my hotel, Shepheard's, I realized I was not about to be arrested. I pretended to be a harmless tourist by exploring the old Jewish Quarter of the city (*inset*).

In November 1977, Egyptian President Anwar Sadat, President Jimmy Carter and Israeli Prime Minister Menachem Begin signed the Camp David Accords (*top*). I welcomed the peace that the agreement signalled between Israel and Egypt. Despite the smiling portraits of Sadat which I found all over Cairo the following year (*center*), I discovered that Egyptians resented the peace pact with Israel. The depth of anti-Sadat feeling exploded during my visit to Cairo in 1980. Sadat was assassinated. By chance, the day before the attack, I had photographed the reviewing stand (*bottom*) where Sadat would pay the penalty for making peace.

(*Top*) My photographing workers taking soil samples at this air force base in Iraq was a ruse to permit me to snap shots of aircraft, hangars, runways and other objects.

(*Center*) Soviet-built SAMs (surface-to-air missiles) in storage at the Iraqi air base at Al-Falluja.

(*Bottom*) The Iraqi military escort who drove me around the air base believed I was taking his picture. What I really wanted to photograph was the row of white concrete anti-tank barriers outside a munitions assembly complex.

Secretly photographed, fueling piers under construction on the Red Sea near Jidda, Saudi Arabia, were designed to service warships of several Arab countries.

A prime target of Operation Desert Storm bombers was the Al-Mussaib power plant located 72 kilometers south of Baghdad. When I photographed it a few years before the war it was capable of generating 1,280,000 kilowatts of power. With giant facilities such as this, Israeli intelligence could only wonder why Iraq felt the need to build nuclear power stations. The world soon found out that Saddam Hussein intended to make nuclear weapons.

An installation similar to this project near Basra was installed under the luxury hotel in the heart of Baghdad that housed news correspondents covering the Gulf War. Another was concealed beneath a civilian air raid shelter that was hit by U.S. forces during Operation Desert Storm.

When I obtained blueprints and photographs of a major project at Osiraq, Iraq, I was told it was an electricity generating plant. I immediately recognized a nuclear research facility capable of producing material for nuclear weapons. The plans called for erecting the core of the reactor below ground, as in this photo. As a result of my information, Israeli air force pilots knew exactly what to look for when they attacked the plant and destroyed it in June 1981.

considerable tilt toward the Arabs. Let's face it, Carter is no Nixon. In terms of the world balance of power that man was a hard-nosed realist. Carter looks like he's going to be a misty-eyed idealist, especially on the Palestinian question. I don't say that he is going to abandon Israel. But I do feel that we can no longer count on the United States the way we used to. In that context, friends like you, Hershel, become even more crucial to the security of Israel. We require your particularly acute eyes and ears more than ever before. You also appear to have a keen sense for choosing the right place at the right time. This visit to Kuwait, for instance."

"That's flattering," I interjected, "but my choice of Kuwait was pure curiosity, believe me."

"Whatever the reason for your choice, whether curiosity, chance, or divine inspiration, it's propitious."

"Through highly reliable diplomatic sources," Jonathan said, "we have received information that Kuwait is about to conclude a deal with the Soviet Union for the purchase of SAM-7 surface-to-air missiles. We expect an announcement by Defense Minister Sheik Saad Abdullah Sabah as early as next month. They are dickering, also, for tanks and artillery. Naturally, we have a keen interest in finding out how and where this equipment is to be deployed."

"I'll see what I can do," I said.

"The report may not be true," Langatzky said. "But like all good firemen, we in Israel must respond to every alarm with the assumption that some will be false."

The Institute had been right in providing Langatzky and Jonathan with the basis for their worries about the Carter administration. This fact became apparent to me within days of my return from Montreal. On March 19 President Carter told a town hall meeting in Clinton, Massachusetts, that he believed that a prerequisite for a lasting Middle East peace was "to deal with the Palestinian problem."

He concluded his remarks by saying, "There has to be a homeland for the Palestinian refugees who suffered for many, many years." He added that "some provision has got to be made for the Palestinians, in the framework of the nation of Jordan or by some other means."

Implicit in the comment was the possibility that the United States would support the creation of an independent Palestinian state on the West Bank, an idea that was anathema to the Israelis because it might open the door to control of the new state by the PLO. If so, they would have no need to take control of southern Lebanon, as feared by the young Christian Lebanese patriot who died as the result of a soft-nosed bullet in Beirut.

As to Jonathan's information on Kuwait's seeking weapons from the Soviet Union, verification seemed to me to be a tough order to fill. I could not, after all, come right out and ask some Kuwaiti official if it were true that his government was talking to the Russians about acquiring SAM missiles.

Arriving in Kuwait, I would follow my customary pattern of introducing myself to the appropriate officials as an earnest, non-ideological American businessman out to make a buck, then wait and see what happened. On the day after my arrival I phoned the Ministry of Defense and got an appointment for the next day to see the chief of engineering for the air force, Colonel Abdullah Al-Hilalli.

Possibly because Kuwaitis had nurtured no historic animosity toward Westerners, I found the handsome young colonel with his crisp uniform and sporty Errol Flynn mustache to be considerably more open and friendly than the Arab officials with whom I had dealt in Egypt, Saudi Arabia, and other countries.

"Schack. The name sounds German," he said. "Your background is German?"

"My background," I said with a shrug, "is business."

As he laughed, I noticed a picture of him on a wall behind his desk. Rakish and daring-looking, he stood beside a vintage pre–World War II biplane of the type used by 1930s American barnstormers, aerial circus performers, and wing walkers trying to drum up public enthusiasm for aviation.

"That is quite a vintage aircraft," I said, nodding at the picture. "When I was young and learning how to fly I would have enjoyed taking up a beauty like that."

"I own this plane," he exclaimed, jumping up behind his desk. "I hangar it at an air base that we are in the process of expanding. It's nearby. Ali al-Salem! You must find time in your schedule to let me take you up."

"That would be terrific," I said.

My enthusiasm stemmed from the prospect of seeing the air base rather than the offer of a joy ride above the desert in an airplane that seemed to be an oversized version of the paper-and-balsa-wood models that I had built, flown, and crashed when I was a boy.

"I'm free whenever it is convenient for you," I said.

"There is no such thing as an inconvenient time when it comes to flying," he declared, clapping his hands with all the delighted anticipation that I had known during my flirtation with aviation. "Tomorrow?"

"Tomorrow is fine with me."

"I shall pick you up at your hotel at ten in the morning." Now rubbing his hands with glee, he resumed his chair. "With that settled, how may I assist you today?"

"As I'm sure you have already assumed, I've come to your country to explore the possibility of obtaining contracts or sub-contracted jobs for my construction company."

"We have many."

"I know, but I will be frank with you, Colonel. This is not simply what we in America call a 'fishing expedition.' I'm here to follow up on a rumor that I picked up from an associate whom I am not at liberty to name. He said he had heard on reliable authority that a deal is in the works for your government to obtain updated air defense systems from the Soviet Union."

The colonel's brown eyes went wide.

"If what my source told me is accurate," I said, "this will require building a series of bases. Am I right?"

"You are a man of the world, obviously," he said, folding his hands on his desk. "A practical man. So you will appreciate that I am unable to speak to this rumor in terms of confirming the information."

"Naturally. I did not expect you to. But as you said, I am a practical person. I have not succeeded in building a thriving business by failing to follow up on things I hear, no matter how farfetched they may seem. My intent is not to go away with a signed contract today. I came to Kuwait to let it be known that should there come to pass a situation in which contracts are to be let, I'd like my company to have a piece of the pie. In my country we have a saying: 'The squeaky wheel gets the grease.'"

"I like your directness, Mr. Schack," he said, relaxing and tilting back in his chair. "While I cannot promise you anything at this time, you may rest assured that I have made note of your squeaky wheel. Therefore, do not be surprised if soon you will have an opportunity about getting it greased."

His words struck me as a kind of wink confirming the information that Langatzky had given me. I felt confident that the missiles and tanks would be delivered to Kuwait from the USSR. Assuming that this was all the confirmation that I would be getting at the moment, I pressed the colonel no further.

When I saw him the next morning, he looked jaunty and eager in a blue flying suit. With his black mustache and toothy grin he was the image of Clark Gable in a 1930s movie about stunt pilots. Wearing blue jeans and a Sears Roebuck tan windbreaker, I felt considerably out of place and awkward.

Only minutes later—the colonel's aide drove as madly as any Cairo cabbie—I stood at the edge of a windy tarmac of a sprawling air base. A small ground crew rolled out a two-seater. Compared to the sleek jet fighter-bombers of the Kuwaiti air force parked nearby, it looked like a Model-T Ford amid a fleet of Indianapolis 500 racing cars.

Climbing into the backseat, I regretted not having brought my camera. I had decided not to press my luck. But as I settled in and the colonel taxied for takeoff, I saw at my side a leather storage pocket crammed with aeronautical charts. Although I was eager to examine them, I chose to wait until the colonel began talking to the control tower for our runway clearance.

As he did so I slipped the first of the maps into my lap and waited for the gunning of the engine in preparation for takeoff. Then, with the boxy, double-winged airplane lumbering down the runway gamely like a fat old goose, I glanced down as if I were simply trying to avoid the wash of the wind in my face and noted that the chart in my lap was in English as well as Arabic. A chart of air routes of the Persian Gulf, it was a map that was routinely available to commercial airlines and consequently of no intelligence value.

Nor did the second map that I drew from the pocket contain anything special. It was another international navigation chart, but confined to overland routes of the entire Middle East. A similar chart could be found in the cockpit of every airliner and cargo plane in the region, including those of Israel's airline, El Al.

Taking out the last of the charts, I saw a third map and recognized that the information was important. In my hands I held a

Kuwait air force chart bearing the coordinates of the base from which we had just taken off and other strategic navigational data related to Kuwait's air defense system and the systems of its neighbors. At that instant the colonel's voice startled me.

Speaking through my headphones, he asked, "How are you doing back there?"

How, he had asked, not *what* was I doing back there, I thought with relief.

"I'm doing fine," I answered, jamming the map into my jacket pocket.

Below the bouncy little airplane I could see the oil fields of Kuwait on the shimmering desert below. Evenly and neatly spaced, the pumping rigs numbered in the hundreds. In contrast, the wellhead pumps seemed like weird desert animals, their heads bobbing for drink. Looking down, I realized that if our ancient biplane were capable of carrying bombs and rockets we could have wrecked havoc. In thinking about the vulnerability of those oil fields, which accounted for an enormous share of the world's petroleum needs, I understood why the Kuwaitis would desire Russian SAM missiles. And I saw, too, why Israel needed to know their locations.

Although I was unable to confirm the Kuwaiti-Soviet missile deal, the Kuwaitis did so themselves a few weeks after I returned to the United States. On April 13, a Kuwait newspaper announced that the minister of defense, Sheik Saad Abdullah Sabah, had signed an agreement in Moscow for SAM-7s and that talks were continuing regarding the acquisition of tanks and artillery from the Soviets.

Whether the map that I had swiped proved useful in any way to Israel I cannot say. Since the day I helped myself to it, Israel and Kuwait have never tangled militarily, though I presume that the chart may have drawn the attention of Israel's air force planners during Iraq's invasion of Kuwait in 1990 when the Ali al-Salem air base fell into Iraqi hands.

During the hundred-hour war known as Operation Desert Storm, like all Americans—indeed, like decent people the world over—I viewed with revulsion the TV news pictures of the fires set by the retreating Iraqis at the hundreds of oil wells that I had seen from Colonel Hilalli's vintage flying machine.

9

I'm Outta Here!

 Barely a month after my return from Kuwait, the voters of Israel took a step that would have a profound effect on the course of events in the Middle East. On May 17, 1977, they gave a plurality of the Knesset, the Israeli parliament, to the right-wing Likud party, headed by Menachem Begin. A tough veteran of the struggle for creation of a Jewish state, he had led a band of Irgun guerrillas who bombed the King David Hotel in Jerusalem.

On June 17 Likud declared in a policy statement that "the Jewish people have an eternal historic right to the land of Israel" and that the government could legally apply Israeli law throughout occupied territories. But it would not do so, the government said, while peace negotiations with the Arabs were in progress.

Begin then made it clear that he would not accept establishment of a Palestinian state on the West Bank. He further declared that the Israeli government would never deal with the PLO, which had become deeply entrenched in the south of Lebanon, as had been feared by the man for whom I had set up a safe house but never met.

With the ascendancy of Begin's Likud hard-liners, I felt an urgent need to get back to the Middle East. Immediately I began mapping an extensive itinerary that would take me across the Arab world, from Morocco to the Emirates. My intention was to gather all the military information I could regarding Arab preparedness should there be a new war. I also wanted to get a sense of the state of mind of the people and the leaders of those countries.

While I certainly did not see myself as an authority, I had come to realize that my handlers wanted me to provide exactly that sort of information. Indeed, I sensed that they took it for granted that I would show up for their debriefings loaded with purloined maps, plans, and other documents. It became clear they also came to our clandestine meetings prepared to plumb for any nuggets of intelligence learned only through observation.

Again and again I gave them a glimpse into the enemy mind that could be measured during table talk at dinners, at afternoon tea, in hotel lobby gossiping, through small talk in a shared taxi, and by eavesdropping. I found I could provide some insights into the attitudes, mood, morale, jealousies, grudges, personal motivations, and all the other human frailties out of which a skilled intelligence analyst might produce a psychological profile of a people.

The ability to absorb these intangibles could not have been taught to me in my crash course in espionage at the house on rue Sanguinet in Montreal. It was an extra that my trainers and handlers had not expected of me. Having discovered that I had such capabilities, they came to value them as highly as the hard intelligence that I continued to produce in abundance.

Typically, a debriefing began with me presenting my handler with whatever materials I had gathered, whether openly and legitimately or by stealth and cunning. I also provided them extensive written reports.

Whenever I could I supplemented the documentation of my discoveries with photographs. This part was not easy. Frequently I found myself at locations of military importance at which the taking of pictures of any kind was prohibited. Quite often I ran into resistance—even hostility—growing out of the traditional Arabic taboo regarding people being photographed.

This meant I had to decide beforehand whether to carry a camera. I could not ignore the very real possibility that if I were caught with a camera in a forbidden zone, an interrogation might result in my being unmasked as an Israeli spy. Such a dire development would extend far beyond my personal peril. I could never forget that if I were to be identified as an agent of the Mossad, Israel itself would be placed in a difficult situation, not only in being caught red-handed at espionage against the Arabs but in using an American citizen at a moment when the United States government was deeply involved in brokering a Middle East peace conference.

I wanted to avoid any situation in which an irate Arab ambassador handed Jimmy Carter's secretary of state a bunch of photographs of a secret military installation snapped illegally by an American citizen on behalf of Israel. I had no wish to become a cause célèbre. The idea that I might be caught was daunting enough in itself.

Yet whenever an opportunity to snap pictures presented itself, I did so. In many cases, they had to be taken on the sly or by means of some ruse. Most of the time I could do this by asking permission to snap "souvenir" shots. On occasion I insisted that I had to take photographs if I were to conduct the construction business that had brought me to a particular location.

Quite often I would sit before something that I wanted to photograph, rest my right leg on my left knee, and casually draw back my pants leg as if I were scratching an itch, then quickly snap a picture. Of course, there was no way to aim and no way of knowing if I was photographing what I wanted or simply getting a patch of earth, the sky, or somebody's backside.

On one occasion when a Saudi Arabian security man spotted me as I clicked off shots of a ground-to-air-missile battery at an air base near Riyadh I adopted the position that the best defense is a good offense.

"How dare you question me?" I demanded. "I have permission to photograph directly from the Crown Prince Fahd. If you don't believe me, telephone His Highness at once. Better yet, I'll call him. Take me to a telephone immediately. What is your name?"

The stunned expression on the man's face left no doubt that he did not look forward to finding Prince Fahd on the other end of a phone line. With profuse apologies and a snappy salute, the officer backed away. Having never met the crown prince, I could only wonder what would have happened if the officer had called my bluff.

I had always reacted to being told "you can't do that" by promptly finding a means to do the forbidden. I therefore decided that I needed a camera that could be concealed on my person yet easy to use. For advice, I turned to my handler Jonathan. I requested a meeting in Montreal.

"There are three possible solutions to your problem," he said after I told him what I had in mind. "One is a wrist camera that looks just like a watch. The film is a disc that holds six pictures. But that could mean frequent changing. The Tessina company makes a 35-millimeter camera with a 25-millimeter lens that's the size of a cigarette pack. It uses standard film, has a built-in noiseless motor that will automatically shoot up to ten times. It works as close as six inches, perfect for document copying. And there's a nifty little number that weighs under four ounces and has an electronic shutter system. Just aim and shoot. And get this. It comes with a gizmo that lets you shoot *around corners*."

"I could use one of those," I said enthusiastically.

"That figures," Jonathan said with a grin. "You pick the one that costs thirty-five hundred dollars. The wrist camera runs to about two hundred."

A week later my secretary buzzed my office intercom. "There is a Mr. Johnson on the line," she said. "He says it's about the order for special equipment."

"The item you requested has been forwarded by our Rome office," said the caller. "The manager will provide you with a full set of instructions."

Recognizing Jonathan's voice, I asked, "Does it come with a warranty?"

"Naturally," he said, chuckling. "And we're throwing in the developing."

The camera arrived by special delivery the following day, a date on which history took a turn that left me and the entire world breathless. At 8:03 P.M., Middle East time, November 19, 1977, an old warrior in the Arab cause, Anwar Sadat, came down the steps from an Egyptian airliner to set foot on a red carpet at Ben-Gurion International Airport to be greeted by another implacable crusader, Menachem Begin. Accompanying him were Foreign Minister Moshe Dayan, General Ariel Sharon, and two former premiers, Yitzhak Shamir and the irrepressible Golda Meir.

Golda asked, "What took you so long to get here?"

The first Arab leader to set foot on Israeli soil since Israel's birth in 1948 told the Jewish parliament and people, "If you want to live with us in this part of the world, in sincerity I tell you that we welcome you among us with all security and safety."

Begin said, "The time of the flight between Cairo and Jerusalem is short. But the distance between them was, until yesterday, quite large. President Sadat passed this great distance with courage, heartfelt courage. We, the Jews, know how to appreciate this courage of heart and know how to assess it with our guest. For with a courageous heart we were created and with a courageous heart we live."

Four years, one month, and eleven days had gone by since the start of the Yom Kippur War, when I heard Sadat boasting on TV of winning an easy military victory over Israel.

As I sat with my family in our home six thousand miles away from Jerusalem to watch this historic event on television, I felt a chill down my back and tears trickling down my cheeks. I wondered if soon I would be able to throw away my new little camera and destroy the locked file cabinets in my office that held the secret records of those forty-nine months and eleven days as a most unlikely spy.

But four months after the euphoria of Sadat's visit to Israel, the frail flame of peace appeared to explode as Israel struck at PLO bases in southern Lebanon. Reacting to indiscriminate raids by Palestinian guerrillas, Israel launched an invasion in March 1978 in an effort to wipe out PLO strongholds. Reaction by Sadat was even-handed. Although he condemned the Israelis, he also deplored PLO actions.

Determined not to be detoured by the PLO, Sadat took his place at a table on the lawn of the White House on March 26 to join Menacham Begin and Jimmy Carter in signing the Camp David Accords. The following year he and Begin shared the Nobel Peace Prize.

These were public manifestations of a new era in Israeli–Egyptian relations. But events just as dramatic had taken place behind closed doors. By secret treaty the two nations agreed to share intelligence information.

In *The Spymasters of Israel*, published in 1980, author Stewart Steven viewed the agreement as a dramatic shift in the balance of power in the Middle East. "In one blinding stroke the Palestinian resistance movement had been weakened to an astonishing degree," he wrote. "Israel, in short, had won one of its greatest battles."

According to Steven, and confirmed a few years later by one of my handlers, when Sadat made his historic visit to Israel he did so with a feeling of personal gratitude to Menachem Begin. In July 1977 Begin had helped abort a plot to kill the Egyptian leader. Informed by an officer of the Institute that Libya's Qaddafi had agreed to back a plan to assassinate Sadat, using Palestinian hit men, Begin ordered the Mossad to pass the file to Sadat.

"Tell Sadat it is with the compliments of the Israeli government." he said. "Let the Egyptians see that we have no quarrel with them."

In a series of dawn raids Sadat's forces rounded up the conspirators. Their addresses in Cairo had been provided by the Institute. Their confessions confirmed the Mossad information regarding the plot. But that did not put an end to conspiracies against the president of Egypt. His signing of the Camp David Accords only served to deepen resentment against him. But now he did not have to worry that he might be on an Israeli assassination list. Rather, he could count on Israel looking out for his well-being.

This time I found myself in Egypt meeting with heads of Egyptian construction companies. These sessions in January 1979 would lead to a conference with President Sadat's brother, the chairman of the Omar and Omar Construction Company. I looked forward to testing the waters of Egyptian public opinion in the light of Sadat's visit to Israel and the signing of the peace treaty with Israel. Huge portraits of him still smiled at me along the route from the airport to the suburb of Giza, site of the pyramids and Mena House, a very famous hotel.

I had chosen the hotel after hearing a story, probably invented by a travel agent, about a tourist who gazed at the Great Pyramid of the Pharaoh Cheops, the five-thousand-year-old sole survivor of the Seven Wonders of the Ancient World.

The tourist asked the guide, "When Cheops was building his monument where did he stay?"

The guide replied, "Why, the Mena House hotel, of course."

As I arrived, I saw what the tour guide meant. Built as a royal lodge in the nineteenth century, Mena House had welcomed countless luminaries. In 1943 it had been the site of the Cairo Conference between President Franklin Roosevelt and British Prime Minister Winston Churchill. Field Marshal Bernard Montgomery had occupied a suite while he commanded Britain's desert army in its battles against the German general Erwin Rommel. The hotel memorialized Montgomery by naming the suite after him. Movie director Cecil B. DeMille and the stars of *The Ten Commandments* had resided there during the making of the epic.

President Carter had also been a Mena House guest during his meetings with Sadat in 1977.

When I stepped into the sprawling deluxe hotel, I felt as if I had rubbed a magic lantern and been swept into the *Tales of the Arabian Nights*. Escorted to a room in a new wing, I could hardly wait to step onto its balcony to look at the Great Pyramid and two of its smaller companions overlooking the Sphinx.

Though I had been to Cairo several times, staying in one of the high-rise hotels in the city or at Shepheard's, I had never so completely realized that I was in Egypt nor experienced the vivid contrast between the opulence of such places as Mena House and the crushing squalor of the ordinary people of Egypt. As I had on so many other occasions, I wondered how much better the lives of the common people might have been if previous governments had realized, as had Sadat apparently, that it made no sense for Egypt to squander its treasury on the machines of war in a futile effort to destroy Israel.

While I believed Sadat deserved praise for his dramatically different foreign policy, I promptly discovered that the Egyptian man in the street and every taxi driver and hotel employee with whom I spoke on the subject disagreed. Their hostile attitude found its most succinct expression in the words of the cabbie who took me to the meeting with Sadat's brother. "Israel no good," he growled, turning down his thumb. "Sadat better stayed home and not went to Israel. Israel no good. Jews no good."

While the bigoted remark rankled, I kept my mouth shut and accepted it as proof of the effectiveness of my masquerade as a gentile businessman from America.

Sadat's troubles also extended to his advisers. He had shaken up his cabinet, dismissing Prime Minister Mustafa Khalil while replacing six other top members, including the boss of the Ministry of Economy. It was in his offices in 1975 I had tested my talents as a fledgling intelligence agent by helping myself to all the plans for new projects that my briefcase could hold.

In the meeting with Sadat's brother I expected no such windfalls. The conference was advertised as a background briefing on Egypt's new role in the Middle East and what the change in policy meant to businessmen in a country whose president seemed determined to address long overdue civilian needs.

Assuming that our host reflected the views of his brother, I listened to him intently. I took notes in my peculiar kind of shorthand, jotting down what he had to say about the current events of the region, from the civil war in the North African country of Chad to the dramatic events then unfolding in Iran.

In ancient times Iran had been known as Persia. The gateway to the Far East, Persia had been invaded again and again but had always retained a fierce determination to be ruled from within. The person who occupied the Peacock Throne in 1979 was the autocratic, ruthless, military-minded, pro-West Reza Shah Pahlavi.

Like the visages of the rulers of Syria and Egypt that had peered at me from roadside billboards in Damascus and Cairo, the Shah's had loomed everywhere I turned in a visit to Tehran. Typically, he wore a military uniform. And like other rulers in the Middle East he had squandered Iran's enormous oil treasures on building a vast arsenal, rather than devoting the riches to meeting the needs of the poor among a population of 51 million people. Those who opposed him felt the wrath of his secret police, the dreaded Savak.

But as I sought business for my company in that seemingly bottomless well of extravagant and inappropriate building projects, I sensed trouble brewing. It stemmed not from the common people but from the most elite members of the population— students and a religious hierarchy, called Mullahs. They yearned for creation of a Muslim state that adhered strictly to the fundamentals of the Koran.

All of this came to a head a few days after my arrival. Under intense pressure from riots and mass demonstrations and lacking support for his regime in the oil-sensitive West, the Shah decided to save his neck and make a run for it. On January 16, 1979, he abandoned his throne and fled the country.

Having driven out the hated Shah, the Iranians welcomed back to Tehran their exiled spiritual leader, the Ayatollah Khomeini. Promptly declaring the establishment of an Islamic republic, they began a bloodletting, executing the head of the Savak and scores of other followers of the Shah, who by then had become a pitiful vagabond looking for refuge and medical attention.

Reaction by President Sadat to the fall of the Shah and the return of Khomeini had been hostile. Because the Shah had been a friend to Egypt during the 1973 war, Sadat did not turn his back on the Iranian ruler in 1979, offering him a safe haven despite the fervent protests of Egypt's own Islamic fundamentalists.

I took detailed and lengthy notes as Sadat's brother discussed the rise to power of a militant Islamic fundamentalism and the chances that it might spread to Egypt. I felt that his words might indicate President Sadat's thinking and, therefore, would possibly prove valuable to analysts at the Institute specializing in Egyptian affairs. I looked forward to typing up my notes in Rome and passing them to my handler.

Arriving in Rome, I found that I had a new handler. Looking even younger than the last one, he called himself Ezekial. Purely out of curiosity, I asked him what had happened to Aaron.

"He got a promotion," Ezekial replied.

"Good for him," I exclaimed. "He seemed especially capable."

"Yes, Aaron always scores 'superior" in the annual reviews."

I found this information interesting. I had not thought about my handlers coming up for yearly evaluations, the way executives of American corporations were rated each year.

"That must be a difficult task for the evaluators," I said, "given the fact that you guys deal in secrets and have to handle amateurs like me."

"They all should be as good as you, believe me. With the great information you brought to Aaron over the past few years how could he not get an outstanding evaluation? I count myself lucky that you have been assigned to me."

Another two years and two other handlers came and went before I returned to Egypt.

Meanwhile, the Khomeini revolution took a dangerous turn on November 4, 1979, as so-called students swarmed their way into the American Embassy and grabbed every American they could find. Over the next 444 days, the fanatical young followers of the aged Ayatollah held them, the world, and President Jimmy Carter hostage.

Given the fate of Americans in Iran, I crossed Iran from my list of countries to visit. Of course, I had plenty of others from which to choose, including the largest and most important of all.

Purely by coincidence I returned to Egypt in October 1981, the twelfth anniversary of the start of the Yom Kippur War. My purpose was not entirely to carry out my work for Israel. Because my previous visit had resulted in business for my company, I had been invited to meet with representatives of several other firms with which mine shared contracts for civilian projects. After our conference we were all to have dinner with Sadat's brother.

The plan proceeded routinely. But on the eve of our meeting with the president's brother I was informed that the dinner had been rescheduled for the following day. I welcomed the news because it allowed time to make advance arrangements at Cairo airport for my departure via Alitalia the day after the meeting. I wanted to check most of my luggage ahead of time, thus avoiding, I hoped, the usual departure crush at the busy and not always very well organized airport.

Getting there proved difficult. The anniversary of the beginning of the 1973 war was being observed that day with a lavish military ceremony that coincided with the conclusion of joint Egyptian–American military exercises. President Sadat was slated to review a parade of military units, a display of armor, and a flyover by the air force at the site of Egypt's memorial to her Unknown Soldier, a shrine in the form of an impressive representation of a pyramid along the road to the airport.

The festivities disrupted the entire city. The customary tangle of traffic in downtown Cairo turned even worse. The route that my taxi had to follow to the airport became a hopeless jumble of cars, trucks, carts, donkey-drawn wagons, and buses, with detours everywhere. To the accompaniment of horns, angry drivers vented their ire on one another. But there was a plus in this chaos. My otherwise heavy-footed cabdriver was compelled to go slowly.

The airport was bedlam. But walking toward the Alitalia counter, I sensed something strange. Out of the corner of my eye I noticed white-uniformed soldiers in what could only be described as a flurry of panicked activity. Rifles usually carried slack at sides were cradled in arms, menacingly, while unholstered pistols bristled in anxious hands. While soldiers ordered people to line up against a wall, I stepped out of the ticket line and walked as swiftly as discretion dictated to a stairway that led up to a second level. There, should the nervous soldiers decide to open up with their guns, I would be safely out of the line of fire.

As I barged into the office of Air Egypt, the only person within looked at me in alarm. "We are closed," he blurted.

"What's all the excitement about?" I asked.

The young man gasped. "Haven't you heard? President Sadat was assassinated."

Because sensational rumors, almost always baseless, were not uncommon in the Middle East, my immediate reaction was to doubt what I had heard.

"No one told me," I muttered.

Recalling the armed men on the floor below us, I thought, "Maybe this guy is right. Maybe it's not a rumor. Maybe Sadat *has* been killed."

The airline man shrugged. "It was going to happen sooner or later. Sadat betrayed Egypt."

"Yes, I suppose so," I said, wondering how I might absent myself quickly, preferably on the first outgoing airplane, no matter what its destination. "Egypt will survive," I said. "*Enshallah.*"

On hearing this ancient expression the clerk's attitude changed from prickly to calm, cool, and businesslike.

"If you have come to inquire about a flight out, I'm sorry, sir," he said, "but the government has ordered that all scheduled departures for Europe are to be canceled until further notice."

"You said 'Europe.' What about other places?"

He responded with a shrug.

A loud noise rose from the floor below ours. Fishing a wad of Egyptian pounds out of my pocket and slapping it on the counter, I said, "Do I take it that there might be something going somewhere besides Europe?"

Pocketing the cash, he smiled nervously. "There *is* an Air Egypt flight to Nigeria that is just boarding."

Once again, Lady Luck seemed to be on my side. I had done business in Abuja, the country's new capital, and counted several Nigerians as friends.

"Nigeria is okay with me," I said, growing more conscious of the riotous noises on the main floor of the terminal.

Pursing his lips, the clerk shook his head. "The plane is full. There is nothing I can do."

Sensing that his words translated into "A little baksheesh, please," that is, "I can get you aboard if you grease my palm," I pulled out a British ten-pound note.

"Maybe there's been a last-minute cancellation?" I said. "Perhaps you have overlooked a vacant seat?"

Palming the money, he sidled away. A moment later he was in front of me again, holding a boarding pass.

"You'll have to hurry, sir," he said. "It's due to leave from gate nine in ten minutes."

Grabbing my bags, I dashed out of the office and down the stairs into the chaos and began shoving my way toward the distant gate.

Handling both international and domestic flights, the Cairo airport also served as an Egyptian air force base. In the best of times I had found it a polyglot beehive of confusion with pushing, shoving, and shouting passengers from all corners of the Middle East and Africa. Each person seemed determined to be first in line, all to the consternation of Americans like me who had been raised to be a little more polite and courteous. "Rudeness never got anyone anywhere," my aphorism-citing, proverbial father had taught me.

"Perhaps not," I thought as I elbowed my way forward, "but if it takes rudeness to get me on that plane, then rude I shall be and the devil take the hindmost."

Barging through the throng like a battering ram, I reached my gate. Bypassing a line of startled passengers, I waved my boarding pass under the nose of an Egypt Air official collecting tickets and shouted, "Official business."

Unchallenged, I scampered across the tarmac to the stairs of an aging Boeing 707. No airliner before or since ever looked more beautiful or welcome as I bounded up the stairs two at a time and ducked inside.

Grabbing the nearest seat and gulping to catch my breath, I looked upon another scene of confusion. The Nigerian passengers were jostling and shouting as they took sides over the news of Sadat's murder. In the midst of this tug-of-war over seating, two valiant but overwhelmed flight attendants did their best to clear the aisle of suitcases and get everyone seated and buckled up for takeoff. The fact that almost all of the passengers were drunk did not help. Nor did being the only white person on the plane make me feel at ease.

As a semblance of order appeared I heard a sound infinitely more arresting of my attention than the voices of the passengers. Having flown hundreds of thousands of miles on all kinds of aircraft, I had no trouble detecting the fact that the engines of this overused and overloaded plane were badly out of tune.

The more the pilot revved them, the worse they sounded and the more convinced I became that we were unlikely to get off the ground. If we did get airborne, I thought, we stood an excellent chance of belly-flopping into the sprawling buildings of the city of Heliopolis. And should the pilot actually avoid an immediate disaster and gain altitude, there were no guarantees that the laboring engines would not give out and drop us like a rock in the vast, trackless expanses of Africa between Cairo and Nairobi.

Weighing the possibilities, I resigned myself to an untimely demise or a miraculous survival, neither of which was in my power to choose. As to my fellow travelers, they roared on in ignorance of the offbeat engines, rebellious against the cabin crew and, I noted thankfully, oblivious to me as I slouched in my window seat with my hat tilted over my face awaiting the verdict of Fate.

About an hour out of Cairo a fight broke out between half a dozen Nigerians, requiring two of the crew from the cockpit to come back to the passenger cabin to break it up. Shortly after calm was restored, the steady voice of the pilot came over the sound system. First in Arabic, then French, then English, he said, "Ladies and gentlemen, we will be making an unscheduled landing at Fort-Lamy, Chad. This is to carry out a minor repair so as to assure a safe arrival at our destination. On behalf of Air Egypt and the crew, I apologize for the inconvenience."

Although I welcomed the announcement as evidence that the crew of the plane finally had recognized the obvious, I did not look forward to setting down in Chad because I carried a United States passport. A former French colony that had achieved its independence in 1960, Chad was located south of Libya. Activities of Muslim rebels in Chad had led its leaders in December 1980 to invite the Libyan dictator Qaddafi to intervene in a civil war by sending in troops. He did so, but hardly altruistically or out of feelings of Islamic solidarity. His mind was set on grabbing control of the one treasure that set Chad apart from other Arabic countries, its rich sources of uranium, the basic ingredient of the atomic bomb.

By any measure Chad's attitude toward the United States had been unfriendly if not outright hostile. This outlook only hardened under Qaddafi's influence. The same held true regarding Sadat, viewed by Qaddafi as a traitor because he had made peace with Israel. Consequently, I figured that an American who had just been to Egypt to do business with the Sadat government could not expect a warm welcome, even in an emergency landing.

Then there was the problem of whether they would decide to inspect my luggage and find the tools of my other trade.

After a surprisingly smooth landing, the plane taxied to a tarmac quite a long distance from the arrivals terminal. It stopped before a ramshackle building that looked like a barracks. While the engines of the jet were still running, the door of the building opened and armed soldiers rushed toward the plane.

My heart raced. "This is it. The game is up," I thought as the rear door of the plane opened. "They're coming aboard to arrest me."

Expecting to be jerked out of my seat, I watched with amazement as the soldiers barged past me to grab the six Nigerians who had engaged in the airborne fisticuffs.

As they dragged the men off the plane, I wondered what would happen to them. I knew there was never any love lost between the people of Chad and Nigeria. But my concerns quickly returned to my own situation. Might I be the next one arrested and dragged off the plane? As I waited and worried, the plane began to move again. Only then did I realize that the landing in Chad had not been because of concern over the engines but had simply been a ruse by the Air Egypt captain to get the troublemakers off his airplane. Airborne again, I looked through my window at a setting sun that seemed to me to be a wonderful red bulls-eye marking our destination. I thought, "Soon I will be in Nairobi, then onto another plane, and soon after that, home—alive and in one piece."

10

Passports

 With the rise of the Ayatollah Khomeini in Iran, a new danger presented itself in the threat that his zealous followers might attempt to foment Islamic fundamentalist revolutions throughout the area.

This unsettling prospect confronted me as I headed back to Saudi Arabia. As I entered the airport at Riyadh the eyes of security men were peeled for any individual who might prove to be a Tehran-sponsored rabble-rouser, a member of the PLO with murder in mind, a Syrian carrying out orders of the ambitious President Haffiz al-Assad, a battered Lebanese on a martyr's mission, or a fanatic among the Arab world's crazies. Or the security men might be looking for a frequent traveler in a pin-striped suit coming in from Rome who might be a very dangerous modern version of history's most hated traveler, the Wandering Jew: an Israeli agent.

While suspicion had always been a hallmark of traveling in the Middle East, it rarely went beyond rudeness. But in the atmosphere of heightened attentiveness and alertness as I lined up to clear customs and immigration at the airport in Riyadh I sensed an anxiety that might readily turn ugly.

Holding my passport in his right hand, a checker compared the photo in it to the face before him. A technique of passport control officers all over the world, the cold-eyed stare was intended to unnerve anyone who might not be as advertised.

Familiar with the ploy, I peered straight back, smiling.

Lowering his eyes and the document, he licked a finger and slowly flipped the pages, scrutinizing each visa and stamp. "You are quite the traveler," he said.

"It's the nature of my business."

"What is your business?"

"Construction."

He closed the passport. "Moment, please," he said, stepping out of his cubicle and into an office.

With supreme confidence I waited for him to return with or without apologies for delaying my customary mad dash to the taxi line and an inevitable bidding war to get one. As the delay stretched to three minutes and then to five, I became aware of the impatient murmuring of people behind me.

But suddenly they fell silent. Turning around, I found myself flanked by two policemen. Brandishing an M-16 rifle, the one on my right said, "Step away from the window and come with us."

As the other's rifle poked persuasively into my ribs, I followed them to a spartan office whose only decorations were photographic portraits of the Saudi royal family. At a large desk a leathery-faced colonel sat beneath the picture of a dour-looking King Fahd ibn Abdul Aziz-al-Saud.

Under his folded hands lay my passport. "There appears to be a problem," he said, picking it up and leafing through the pages.

"Impossible," I said, frightened. "I can't imagine what it could be. As you can see, I've made several visits to your country using that very passport without any *problem*."

The colonel shrugged. "There will have to be an inquiry. Your visa is not in order. There are different dates in Arabic and English."

The passport had not been provided or altered by the Institute. It was my own that they were questioning. Again relying on the belief that the best defense is a good offense, I leaned angrily across his desk, my face in his. "This is outrageous," I said. "I have come here on business involving your government. I have done so many times, as my passport shows. I insist on speaking to your superior officer."

"That may take some time. He is not here."

"May I place a phone call?"

"That is not possible."

"Then I demand to speak to a representative of Pan American Airlines in order to have this situation reported to the official of your government with whom I am doing business."

I paused, both to judge if the colonel were going to believe this bit of bluster and to catch my breath.

"And here's one more thing to contemplate, Colonel," I went on. "Do you want to take the chance of this unfortunate incident appearing to be a hostage-taking?"

This ploy seemed to catch him off guard. "Don't be ridiculous," he exclaimed. "You are not a hostage. This is not Iran. This is not Lebanon. We are not Palestinians. Saudi Arabia does not take hostages."

"Fine. Prove it by allowing me to talk to the Pan Am representative. If you don't, I can guarantee you that my business associates in Europe will take steps that will result in the embarrassment of—"

Turning my eyes to the portrait of the king, I let his imagination take over. As he addressed one of the soldiers in a burst of Arabic, the soldier hurried out. I felt no need for a translation. A young and worried-looking Pan Am man appeared.

"These men have raised questions about my passport," I said calmly. "But this misunderstanding can be corrected if you would be kind enough to make a telephone call for me."

I gave him a phone number. "The party you must ask to speak to," I said, "is General Muhammad Al-Fawzi."

From the corner of my eye I saw the colonel's jaw go slack.

"I assure you that the general will vouch for me," I said.

This was not bravado. I had worked with General Fawzi on several occasions. Holding his hand over the receiver, the Pan Am man told me the general was in Spain, accompanying the king.

"Then call him there," I demanded.

The Pan Am man placed the call and received another number to reach the general.

After a few minutes and another flurry of Arabic, the young airline official muttered, "General Fawzi," and thrust the phone into the colonel's hand.

Bolting up, the officer snapped a salute. I had to will myself not to laugh. Carried on in Arabic, the conversation proved largely one-sided. When it ended, the colonel carefully set down the phone and forced a weak smile.

"General Fawzi has asked me to apologize," he said. "We do regret any inconvenience caused by this . . . *misunderstanding*." He corrected the dates on the passport. "In making amends," he said as he handed it to me, "please accept one of our automobiles to take you to your hotel."

My relief at not having to face the prospect of another kamikaze cabdriver lasted only a few minutes. The colonel's man turned out to be just as much a speed demon as any cabbie in my experience. But in spite of the reckless trip from the airport I could not help but notice dramatic changes since my 1974 visit.

As a result of the explosion in oil revenues throughout the 1970s, the Saudi kingdom had made a gigantic leap forward in its infrastructure. Broad new highways spanned the desert to link expanded seaports to the oil fields. Cities that bristled with new buildings were served by modern airports that had experienced a tenfold increase in passengers. But just as noteworthy as the internal changes was the increase in the number of foreigners in the country. The Saudis were now turning to Western corporations for aid and guidance in the modernization process.

Interested in obtaining a share of that abundant work for my own company, I planned an ambitious tour that would take me first to the Gulf coast, then west to the Red Sea. I wanted to have a look at two wholly new industrial cities, Jubail on the Gulf and Yanbuʿ on the Red Sea. Both had sprung up during the boom decade of the seventies. While I hoped this itinerary would result in new business, I also wanted to bring myself and the Institute up to date on everything that had transpired in the richest of all Arab nations since my last call.

After two days in Riyadh to recover from jet lag, I moved on to the Gulf coast where I used Dhahran as a base for excursions in a rented car to Dammam (my friend Carl's whereabouts were unknown); al-Khobar with its twenty-five-kilometer-long King Fahd Causeway linking Saudi Arabia with Bahrain (on the pretext of tying the laces of my boots I snapped several pictures with the trusty camera Jonathan had provided); Jubail with its busy port of al-Hasa (unruly laces again and half a roll of pictures); and on my way back to Dhahran a look at the port of Ras Tanura, where I did indeed use the special lens that permitted me to shoot around a corner to obtain a picture of a small gunboat.

Having used the last of the film for what I hoped would be good shots of an oil-loading facility, I returned to my car to find a lanky, khaki-clad young man leaning against it, his arms crossed, a smile creasing his deeply tanned face.

Straightening as I approached, he blurted, "What the devil are you doing around here?"

The question ought to have staggered me. But he asked it in such a friendly tone that he left me wondering. And the voice was American.

"You don't remember me, obviously," he said, extending a hand in greeting. "Fred Pawley. I'm with Aramco. We met at that briefing given by Sheik Yamani a few years ago."

Although I had not a glimmer of recognition I grabbed his hand and shook it vigorously, relieved to know that he was not about to arrest me for unauthorized photography.

"Is your company working around here?" he asked.

"I'm on a scouting expedition. Trying to drum up business, as usual."

"Are you putting in a bid on the big new radar system?"

"I'd like to build the supporting buildings," I said, having no idea what he was talking about, "but I haven't been able to locate anyone who can tell me whom I should talk to about it. Perhaps you can."

"As a matter of fact, I can. I happen to know quite a lot about it because Aramco is bankrolling it."

I still had no memory of having met him, but I immediately recognized in him the universal characteristics of someone who would have found work in some exotic corner of the world had he not become an employee of Aramco in Saudi Arabia. I had met adventuresome expatriates like him often. They ranged in age and style from older ex–World Federalists working in the American foreign service to bright-eyed and bushy-tailed idealists of the Peace Corps to men who managed to combine wanderlust with well-paying work. Never had I met one of these footloose Americans who did not embrace a chance to spend time with someone from home.

"Is there a spot where we can talk and I can get a decent meal?" I asked, confident that he would jump at the suggestion.

"There's a hotel nearby," he said enthusiastically. "It's got a restaurant. But the best thing I can say about the place is that it's clean."

As I gnawed overly cooked lamb and ate glutinous rice he talked almost without pause. Peppering me with questions about events in the United States, he expressed great interest in what I thought of the prospects for President Carter being reelected in view of the hostages being held in Iran. Not wanting to appear too eager to get him to talk about the radar project, I humored him. Patience paid off.

"As to this radar thing that interests you," he said, "I think I can be of a little help to you. Would it be useful if you had a set of the plans for the whole layout?"

"It certainly would. Do you have the name of the person that I should see?"

"I can do better 'n that," he said. "For some reason that I have never been able to figure out, because it's not really in my domain, so to speak, I happen to have been sent two sets of plans for the project. I suppose I should hang on to one of them. You're welcome to the spare, if it would be helpful."

"That's very kind of you. Yes, it certainly would be very helpful. It will save me a lot of time and effort tracking down the person in charge. I am on a pretty tight schedule."

On the way to his office he returned to American politics. "What's the story on this guy Reagan?" he asked. "Is there any chance he could wind up being president?"

From his tone I could not discern whether he would welcome or be repelled by the prospect of Reagan in the White House. The last thing I wanted at that moment was to give an answer that would make him change his mind about giving me the radar plans.

"Well, I'm no expert on politics," I said.

"What are you?" he asked. "A Democrat or a Republican?"

Faced with a fifty-fifty chance of a wrong answer and the possibility of not getting the extra set of plans, I recalled the advice of my father, "Never talk politics with a stranger." Then I remembered a scene in one of my favorite movies. In *Casablanca* the Nazi Major Strasser asked the owner of Rick's Place about his politics. Humphrey Bogart as Rick snapped, "I'm a drunkard."

Taking Bogie's cue, I answered, "I'm neither a Democrat nor a Republican. I'm a businessman."

Like Bogart's retort, mine drew a laugh and put an end to talk of politics. More important, within an hour I held in my hands all of the particulars of a sophisticated computer-assisted radar system that encompassed much of the Persian Gulf. Using the microfilm camera that had served me so well since I received it at the house on rue Sanguinet, I spent most of the night photographing the plans as a backup in the event the originals might be confiscated.

Pleased with what I had accomplished on the Gulf coast, I headed west across a thousand miles of desert on a brand new highway toward Jidda. The most important Saudi Arabian port on the Red Sea, it lay a short distance northwest of Mecca, one of the three holy cities of Islam. The others are Medina, also in Saudia Arabia, and Jerusalem. Because Mecca is open only to the faithful, signs directed me and all other non-Muslim travelers to a bypass that ran well out of sight of the city.

I checked into the Red Sea Palace Hotel in Jidda and began a search for bugs, both the electronic and multilegged animated kind. As I did so, I thought about the differences between a Holiday Inn and this typical hotel in Arabia. In a Holiday Inn at home there would have been a Gideon Bible. Here, on the shelf above a wooden clothes rod that would be useless as a slick lay a neatly folded, colorful Islamic prayer rug. And a traveler stopping in Judeo-Christian America might soothe his ragged nerves with a drink at the bar. No such comfort beckoned to me in Islamic Saudi Arabia.

The bathroom offered tiled walls, a marble floor, a shower as well as a tub, and plenty of fresh towels. Everything was clean. But the best attribute of the room turned out to be above my head, a dropped ceiling. Climbing onto the toilet seat, I pushed aside one of the foot-square panels. There was no room for me to hide, should I have to, but I noted that the space would serve nicely for stashing small items. Leaving the bathroom, I found that if I had to get out of the room fast, the window was the only way. Unfortunately, my room was on the third floor and offered no fire escape. I fell asleep almost instantly in a big lumpy bed.

Awakened the next day by the ubiquitous call to prayer that was reliable as an alarm clock but considerably more jolting, I stared bleary-eyed at my surroundings. A plastic-covered, sand-colored couch. Matching armchair. A glass-topped coffee table. Frayed Persian rug on the floor. Or maybe it was Turkish. Or Afghan. The Muslim world was always beautifully carpeted.

Atop a bureau stood my long flashlight, ready to help me cope if there were a power failure. Or to be bashed over the head of anyone intruding in the night with questions about a passport.

A giant mirror reflected a figure in the sweat-soaked king-size bed who bore an uncanny resemblance to Yasir Arafat and wanted nothing more than a hot shower, a close shave, a Coke, and a Big Mac with a large order of fries. Peeking behind the mirror, I assured myself there was no peephole for a camera.

As the last raspy cries of the call to prayer faded, a hot breeze came through the open bedroom window. It carried the aroma of fresh-baked pita bread, reminding me how hungry I was. Because I always enjoyed bread, the smell was tantalizingly delicious. And when I turned over the pita that had been set before me along with a cup of thick brown coffee, I was delighted and surprised to see that it contained raisins, quite an unusual treat. Alas, on closer inspection, I discovered the raisins were thoroughly baked-in sand flies.

Even without an ulterior motive for visiting Jidda I would have found the city fascinating. Once it had been important as the port of entry for pilgrims on their way to Mecca. But the change of fortune for Saudis in the discovery of oil had turned it into a bustling city of commerce. Before the establishment of Riyadh, Jidda had served as the nation's capital. It even earned the title "the Paris of Arabia" and a reputation for being the most interesting and friendly of the kingdom's cities.

Because of this cosmopolitan atmosphere in which tourists had become more common, I felt comfortable in using a camera openly. In the several rolls of film I exposed were a scattering of historical and tourist attractions, from exteriors of the Al-Shaffee Mosque to the colorful and inevitable souk, or market. But the bulk of the pictures consisted of port facilities, government buildings for agencies that had yet to complete their move to Riyadh, and assorted other edifices, roadways, and landmarks that only an intelligence analyst could find compelling.

This hodgepodge of pictures was typical of what the darkroom technicians at the Institute had come to expect from me. Invariably, rolls of film shot with my ordinary camera contained souvenir pictures that the Israeli developers and printers had to separate and promptly return to me so that I would have snapshots to show to my family and friends with each return from a faraway place. Indeed, I purposely filled the first third of each roll of film with these ordinary pictures, reasoning that if the film were developed and examined by someone other than me and the Institute, such a person looking at the early exposures might be convinced that the film contained nothing unusual. Fortunately, I never found myself in such a potentially dangerous situation. Of course, if someone had seized my special camera and studied its contents, my adventures as an avocational espionage agent could have ended then and there, possibly with a bullet in my head.

Having gleaned all that I could in Jidda, I returned to Riyadh to find a message awaiting me at my hotel from my friend the aviator, Colonel Abdullah Al-Halilli. It read:

> What a nice coincidence that we are visiting Saudi Arabia at the same time. We must get together. Call me at my office.

Since I had soared above the Kuwaiti desert with him in his vintage airplane and helped myself to the map containing the coordinates of his air base, I had received several letters from him asking when I would be visiting his country again. Friendly in tone and packed with glowing descriptions of our flying adventure in the old plane, they had offered no information on whether he had discovered that the map was missing, so I felt no qualms in contacting him again. Rather, I hoped that I might pick up bits of information worthy of being relayed to my handler.

I also wanted to find out why he had an office in Riyadh. He offered an explanation without being asked. "I have been assigned here on temporary assignment, a liaison job. I would have been very disappointed if we both left Saudi Arabia without at least saying hello. You shall be my guest for dinner. Tonight I shall take you to the Equestrian Club!"

11

Billionaire Boys' Club

 None of the stories I had heard about the Equestrian Club of Riyadh had fully prepared me for the lengths to which architects, designers, and builders had gone to satisfy its members' desire for opulence. Appearing to rise naturally out of the desert, it was built of reinforced concrete in the shape of a horseshoe. With the unfurling of its many awnings, the effect created was of an enormous bedouin tent.

On several levels, the interior offered connecting staircases and ramps, soaring columns, silken draperies, gold sconces, marble tables that rose and receded with the touch of a button, terraces, lounges (no liquor, of course), enormous rooms spilling into one another, discreet alcoves and chambers where members and guests could while away an evening with cards and billiards. To tone up their muscles they had a choice of courts for tennis and squash, a gymnasium, and a swimming pool. After exercising they could retire to several massage rooms.

I scanned entries in a guest book in an ornate lobby dominated by the emblem of the club, a golden horse set on a malachite pedestal. I found the names of recent guests: King Juan Carlos of Spain; King Hassan of Morocco; Hussein of Jordan; the chancellor of Germany, Helmut Schmidt; the emir of Kuwait; and Britain's Prince Philip. The queen had not been admitted. The Equestrian Club was for men only.

Although the adjective commonly applied to the club was "exclusive," Colonel Halilli fervently denied this was so. "First of all, exclusivity is contrary to the tenets of the Arab world." He blithely passed over the fact that only Saudi males who put up five thousand rials, or fifteen hundred dollars, could be admitted, and then only after a rigorous screening process requiring a unanimous vote by a five-member review board, which also had to approve admission of foreigners. Of course, no Jews could have applied, even if Jews were permitted to reside in the kingdom that stood guard over the sacred mosques of Mecca and Medina.

The club served as an oasis for officials of the Gulf Cooperation Council (GCC), made up of the states of Bahrain, Kuwait, Oman, Qatar, the United Arab Emirates, and Saudi Arabia. It had become the place where oil princes rubbed shoulders with the chief executives of the top corporations of the world. On any evening, billion-dollar deals were sealed with a handshake or the Arab tradition of a kiss on the cheek.

While wealth was certainly a common denominator, educational achievements were valued as well. The membership rolls contained more Ph.D.'s than any business club in the world. They listed 183 doctorates, fifteen of them held by foreigners. But from the very first moment that I set foot on its wall-to-wall oriental carpets, I appreciated that the true bond between these men was neither brains, money, nor status, but power.

To be invited to enter behind the sequestering walls of this most exclusive club in the world was an opportunity that would have enchanted even James Bond. Here at last, I would have access to a most elusive element of intelligence gathering, the unveiled and unguarded mind of the adversary.

On almost any evening an intelligence agent could expect to eavesdrop on Sheik Yamani as he hosted a sumptuous dinner for the leading luminaries of OPEC, listen in while the Saudi minister of finance shot billiards with Prince Abdullah, or be invited to join an after-dinner discussion of oil policy with the very men who established it.

Thanks to Colonel Halilli, I found myself party to riveting conversation by a handful of members and a highly placed Iraqi businessman. The Iraqi spoke openly about the Soviet Union's progress in biochemical warfare and of the Soviets' willingness to share their discoveries with friendly Arab governments. He went on to discuss details of similar biochemical research under way in Iraq.

I believe the information that I gleaned and subsequently forwarded to my handler proved useful to the Israelis in convincing them to develop vaccines and instruments to detect the presence of biochemical agents in the air. The results of the research were visible during Iraq's Scud attacks on Israel during the Gulf War of 1991, as viewers of the television coverage of the attacks will recall. Within seconds after a Scud impacted, Israeli civilian defense officials were able to discern whether the missiles had carried toxic agents.

When I briefed my handler a few days later he could barely contain his excitement. "This is terrific," he exclaimed as we split a bottle of wine in a trattoria near the Galleria Nazionale in Rome. Being an art enthusiast, he had suggested the art museum for our rendezvous. I welcomed the chance to see its treasures, so I arrived early.

"You have no idea how long we have been trying to get a man inside the Equestrian Club," he went on. Then, cracking a devilish smile, he whispered, "What are the chances of your planting a few bugs with transmitters behind a couple of the couches?"

For an instant I let myself enjoy the delightful prospect. But, of course, such a thing would be impossible.

"Slim, huh?" he said as the twinkle went out of his eyes.

"Let's say 'none.' "

"I'm sure you're right, but I had to ask. It's too bad you didn't build the place. You could have planted a few bugs in the walls. So we don't have listening devices. I guess we can't have everything. Thank God we've got you."

"Thank God I have a pretty good memory," I said.

Not being a Saudi, a multimillionaire, or a Ph.D., I could never qualify to be a member of the Equestrian Club, but being introduced to its inner sanctum by Colonel Halilli validated me as a temporary member. To my great delight I found myself being invited back time and time again, not only by the colonel but by a widening circle of his friends and associates to whom he introduced me.

Although I garnered a great deal of information during these evenings and compiled a substantial amount of data regarding the thinking of those whom I met, I also confirmed an axiom of human behavior. In analyzing the men of the Equestrian Club I thought I could hear my father whispering into my ear: "Remember, for most of the people you will meet throughout your life, self-interest is their only interest."

As members luxuriated in their posh surroundings, I never heard them speak of the needs of ordinary people. Nor did I listen to discourses on loyalty to country or religion that went beyond platitudes.

They spoke endlessly and with boundless energy of oil, deals, money, and power. Anyone, anything, and any country deemed to stand in the way of achieving these goals automatically became their enemy. In their view that adversary took the form of Israel and, by extrapolation, the United States.

Without support from Washington, they declared again and again, the Jewish state could not have survived. Without American assistance, they exclaimed in heated phrases, the Palestinians could never have been dispersed to other Arab states to become a festering problem and a threat to stability in the Middle East and, consequently, a threat to the self-interest of the VIPs of the Equestrian Club.

Night after night I sipped sweet tea while seated on one of the innumerable comfortable couches while highly educated, enormously wealthy, and extremely ambitious men plotted a future which they would control. The dream envisioned a world in which the traditional and historical delineations such as states, nations, and peoples would be supplanted by multinational corporations for which the greatest good would be higher profits.

At no time during my frequent visits to the club did I find an individual who embraced the idea that what the Arabs needed to contain Israel was the Islamic fundamentalism being advanced by the Ayatollah and his followers. Rather, I found outspoken enthusiasm for the war with Iran that Iraq launched in 1980.

Saddam Hussein had used as an excuse to start the war a long-standing dispute over the sharing of the Shatt-al-Arab waterway bordering the two countries. After denouncing the 1975 pact he sent his army across the border into Iran. The Iraqi troops advanced to the important Iranian port of Khorramshahr and surrounded a vital oil complex at Abadan. But what Saddam had hoped would become a quick and decisive victory turned into a protracted struggle with terrible loss of lives on both sides and, finally, a stalemate.

The war bitterly split the Arab world, dividing those who backed the Khomeini revolution, mostly the ordinary Arab, and the Arab "establishment," which wished to blunt it, including the members of the Equestrian Club.

Although I did not consider myself an expert on the politics of the Middle East, I understood that the immediate interests of Israel and, therefore, my own, must lie in a continuation of the schism. Because Israeli leaders saw an advantage in favoring the Iranians, I reasoned that whatever I might pick up regarding the members' support for Iraq might be deemed worthy for Israel to pass on to Iran. This put me in the uncomfortable position of indirectly spying for Iran, for whose leaders and ideology I held no affection.

Only years later did I find out through the revelations of what came to be known as the "arms for hostages deal" that the Reagan administration had also helped Iran. While the knowledge that my own government and Israel had also trucked with the Iranians soothed my conscience somewhat, I could only shake my head in puzzlement over the intricacies of the politics of the Middle East.

"My guiding principle is quite simple," I said to my handler at another meeting in Rome. "I go by the old adage, 'The enemy of my enemy is my friend.' "

"Don't let our present policy toward Iran trouble you," he replied with a pat of my hand. "Once Saddam Hussein is finished with his adventure in Iran we shall find a way to put him back in his place. You just keep singing along with the anti-Khomeini, pro-Iraq crowd at that ritzy club of theirs and passing it all to us. We'll sort it out. And when the day comes that Saddam gets what's coming to him you will be able to say 'I had a part in socking it to the bad boy of Baghdad.' Meanwhile, if you have the chance to cozy up to the Iraqis and their Western friends at the Equestrian Club, by all means do so."

Such an opportunity occurred several weeks later. I had again returned to the Middle East, to the consternation of Ruth and my sons, who again complained of my frequent trips to such a danger- ous region. In Riyadh I telephoned my affable friend the colonel, counting on his suggesting that we dine at the club. I was confident that he would do so because I had nurtured our relationship, as was the custom of doing business in the Middle East, by plying him with gifts, favors, and flattery.

"You must be my guest tonight," he said. "There is to be a reception given by Sheik Yamani. It is in honor of Subhi Yassin, Iraq's minister of industry and minerals."

Struggling to control my excitement over this amazing bit of luck, I thought of the words of Rocky Graziano, "Somebody up there likes me."

"If my being there won't get you in trouble protocol-wise," I answered Colonel Halilli, "I'd be delighted to come."

"There is a bedouin saying," he said. " 'No matter the size of your tent you must always make room for a friend.' "

In accordance with his status the Iraqi minister brought an entourage that tested the confines of the club even with awnings unfurled. Among these lesser lights of Iraq I met an army general who had been seconded from battlefield command to take charge of the construction of a woefully behind-schedule power plant on the Euphrates River southwest of Baghdad at Al Musaiyib.

A major problem in delaying the work, he explained, had been the withdrawal of two European subcontractors whose business with Iran dwarfed their dealings with Iraq, proving once again that my father was right. Self-interest is the only interest.

Sensing a golden opportunity to promote my interest in helping Israel, I asked, "What's the nature of the work? If those firms have not yet been replaced, my company would like to have a crack at taking over some of the subcontracts. There are men at this dinner who can vouch for me. Colonel Halilli, for instance. Or ask Sheik Yamani about me."

"This is not necessary," he said, shaking a hand. "If you were not reliable and trustworthy, you would not be here. The companies have not been replaced. By all means, come to Baghdad and we will talk. Afterward, if we are both satisfied, you can go to the site and see for yourself if it is a project that you wish to undertake."

We agreed to meet two days later in his office in the Iraqi capital. Almost immediately I learned that financing for the $732-million project had been arranged by Great Britain's Export Credit, C. Itoh and Company of Japan, and the Korea Export and Import Bank.

Visiting the site in the historic valley of the Euphrates River, where civilized mankind first flourished thousands of years before the ascent of Saddam Hussein, I found the beginnings of a project that would be capable of generating 1.2 million kilowatts. A thermal plant, it would require three 300-ton-per-hour water treatment facilities, six 15,300-ton fuel oil tanks, four 300-megawatt turbine generators, and four 950-ton-per-hour boilers.

I reported these facts in yet another of my handlers' carefully selected and colorful meeting places.

"You are certain this plant is strictly thermal," he said, skimming my report, "not nuclear?"

I shook my head emphatically. "I know nuclear when I see it, believe me," I said. "When it looks like a duck, walks like a duck, and quacks like a duck, it is probably a duck. Take my word for it, this duck is not radioactive."

"Yes, of course,"he said apologetically. "But if you do ever pick up the slightest hint that Saddam is going nuclear, you will let us know?"

"I'll drop the Institute a postcard," I said.

"You've never been there, have you? To the Institute?"

"I've not had that privilege."

"Would you like to visit?"

"Would I like to win the New York lottery? Of course."

Pocketing my report, he winked. "Let me see what I can do about it. Hell, it's about time! Meanwhile, what are the chances that you could put together a list of outfits outside the Muslim world that are doing business with the Arabs, especially those that might be in a position to provide nuclear technology?"

"It will take a while, but it can be done. Do you want the names of their top people, too?"

Now he laughed.

Through painstaking culling of articles in construction industry journals and by looking up contracts filed with various agencies of the United Nations and the U.S. government, I put together over the next few months a list of firms doing business in the Arab world. Totaling hundreds, the firms engaged in providing Western expertise and hands-on assistance ranged around the globe, including some of the biggest and best companies in the United States.

From these same sources I compiled an inventory of Arab investments in America. They ranged from outright ownership of real estate to shares in a panoply of corporations from the Oklahoma Gas and Electric Company to JCPenney. Additionally, I gave my home base in Montreal a list of firms in Japan, Great Britain, Italy, France, Germany, and Canada whose names were a matter of public record in various international agencies, such as the World Bank.

I found most disconcerting that Germany was prominent among the countries. Several of its firms apparently saw nothing wrong in supplying enemies of the state of Israel the wherewithal to produce chemical weapons, as if there had never been a Dachau and Auschwitz.

In this roll call I had accounted for 170 German suppliers of chemical and other military technology to Arab governments, including Chemi GmbH, building a poison gas plant in Libya, and Karl Kolb GmbH, assisting with building pesticide and chemical weapons factories for Saddam Hussein, despite ample proof that Saddam had no qualms about using poison gas against dissident populations in his own country.

But as I considered these horrifying facts I thought back to the many evenings that I had whiled away at the Equestrian Club among men driven by money and power, not morality.

In soaking up conversations of the guests I also came to see the deep apprehension that gripped them concerning the Iranians which drove them to embrace Iraq. Despite public assertions of neutrality, Arab Gulf states provided Saddam Hussein with some $30 billion in aid. Openly supporting Iraq, Jordan permitted Iraq free use of the vital Red Sea port of Aqaba. Doing so allowed Iraq to resume the flow of oil that had been interrupted by the fighting around the Persian Gulf. Egypt sent enormous quantities of arms.

After skimming page after page of my written report on Western aid to Iraq, my debriefer sighed and muttered, "How different the world might be if God in His wisdom had given the oil fields to the children of Jacob instead of to the children of Ishmael. We, too, would have such generous friends and you and I would not have to conduct these clandestine meetings."

For this conference he had picked Café Alemagna, a monumental restaurant on Rome's Via del Corso bustling with shoppers taking a break for hurried lunches. As David had promised during our first meeting in Washington Square Park in 1974, I had dealt with several handlers. In most cases their job was to receive an oral as well as a written report. They did their work well, but from time to time I wondered if Langatazky and David assigned the men to me in the hope that they might learn techniques from me.

I understood that key intelligence officers such as Langatzky and David could not always meet with me. But as I met with their deputies I could almost feel the presence of Langatzky observing us, a conservatively dressed gentleman with a penchant for peering over half-moon reading glasses. By contrast, David presented a scholarly image, all tweeds and flannels.

Those whom Langatzky and David sent to debrief me seemed attuned not only to what one might expect, military tactics and weaponry and Middle East politics, but also to matters much more mundane, such as the status of the international stock markets, movies, television, celebrities, and trends in food and fashion. They also smoked an enormous number of cigarettes.

A handler called Ira preferred Camels. "I'm sure you recall my asking if you would be interested in paying a visit to the Institute," he said, puffing hard as he set aside my report on companies doing business in the Arab world. "It has been cleared at the very top. So when can you arrange to come to Israel?"

"There is no way that I can go traipsing off to Israel without bringing along my wife and a few close friends."

"Naturally. This will present no problem. The Ministry of Tourism will be delighted to accept their dollars. When you have worked out a date with your loved ones, our travel agency in New York will arrange everything, as usual."

By no means, however, could our arrival at Ben-Gurion Airport in Tel Aviv have been considered usual. We were greeted on board by a young man from the Institute who identified himself as Mr. Cohen. He said he was a representative of a firm with which my firm did business in Tel Aviv. We were then whisked off the plane ahead of all passengers, even those in first class. Moments later he escorted us past immigration without our passports being examined and, of course, a stamping signifying our presence in Israel. Leading us to a waiting station wagon with driver, he assured us that our luggage would follow directly, though he did not point out to Ruth and my friends that the baggage also would pass through customs without inspection.

Because I had told Ruth that the purpose of my trip to Israel was company business, my leaving her with our friends to fend for themselves the next day presented no difficulty. While they went sightseeing and shopping, Mr. Cohen picked me up at our hotel to escort me to the Institute.

Originally located within a large army compound in the heart of Tel Aviv, the burgeoning headquarters had been shifted to a building of its own across the road. Naturally, I did not expect to find a sign in front announcing that I was entering Mossad headquarters, but I did anticipate something more intriguing than the pedestrian office block one finds in countless corporate centers all over the United States. Nor did I find the corridors crowded with individuals whose bearing suggested that they spent their working hours carrying out skulduggeries.

If the Equestrian Club could be seen as a boys' club, one might describe agencies of the worldwide intelligence company in similar terms, including Israel's Mossad. Writers on the subject of the world's intelligence agencies noted that staffs consisted almost entirely of men. They attributed this to the fact that intelligence operations had been organized as part of nations' military organizations, traditionally male bastions. Israel was no exception. But compared to the number of employees in intelligence agencies in the United States, the Soviet Union, and Great Britain, the Institute's "boys' club" was small. I was told that its officers numbered about five hundred, supported by an office staff of about fifteen hundred. And Nigel West pointed out in *Games of Intelligence*, quoting a CIA report, that the Institute augmented its professional staff through a unique appeal to civilians to assist in intelligence work. It chose those who seemed motivated by what West called "Jewish racial or religious proclivities, pro-Zionism, dislike of anti-Semitism, anti-Soviet feelings, and humanitarian instincts."

In my readings on the world's intelligence services I noted that another aspect of Mossad's history that made it different from other secret services was the fact that many of Israel's politicians had served in the Institute or one of its predecessor services. Two of Israel's prime ministers had ties to Israel's intelligence apparatus: Menachem Begin (Irgun) and Yitzhak Shamir (ten years in Mossad). In contrast, Yuri Andropov had been the only boss of the KGB to move into the top job in the Kremlin and George Bush the only American president to serve in the CIA. As director of Central Intelligence for one year (1976–77), Bush had been the tenth man to head the CIA since it was founded in 1948. Since the reorganization of Israel's various secret services into Mossad in 1951, the Institute had had four directors: Isser Harel (1951–63), Meir Amit (1963–68), Zvi Zamir (1968–74), and Yitzhak Hofi, who took command in the same year that Colonel Langatzky suggested that I might play a role in the work of the Institute.

As a security officer cleared Mr. Cohen and me for entry into the headquarters building Cohen said, "Before I take you on the fifty-cent guided tour, there's another visitor from the United States who wants to say hello to you."

To my great surprise and delight, as I stepped into a windowless second-floor office Langatzky bounded across the room, his arms flung wide and a grin from ear to ear.

"Hershel, my friend," he exclaimed, bear-hugging me. "Long

time no see. But I get copies of your reports. Fan . . . tastic. I was most interested in the information you provided on the extent of the involvement of European firms with the government of Iraq, especially the French. As I recall, you have close connections to a Paris-based company."

"They've been very helpful in opening doors for me, yes."

"As for me, I have never felt much of a rapport with the French," he said, crinkling his nose as if he smelled a bad odor. "This is a terrible thing for me to say, being a Jew, but it's a prejudice. I am repelled by the willingness—the *eagerness*—that the French have shown in cozying up to Saddam Hussein. Perhaps this springs from what I know of the sorry history of some of the French in collaborating with the Nazis. Maybe my feelings go all the way back to the Dreyfus Affair of the last century. But in the back of my mind lurks the notion that France rests on a bed-rock of anti-Semitism. This is especially worrisome in view of the fact that France is a nuclear power. Frankly, I shudder at the thought that some Frenchie might see nothing wrong in sharing nuclear technology with Saddam Hussein."

Recalling that Ira had brought up the subject of an Iraqi nuclear capability, I began to wonder as I listened to Langatzky's tirade against the French if our meeting were coincidental after all. I asked, "Are you saying that the Institute wants me to find out if the French are helping Iraq go nuclear?"

"One of your many charms, Herschel, is your knack for cutting through bullshit. Of course that is what we desire. But I must never allow myself to forget that you are a volunteer. The rules have not changed. I cannot order you to do something."

"Can you tell me what information you may have on this subject?"

"We have nothing direct," he said with a shrug, adding, in a tone of utter exasperation, "All we have is *inklings*."

In those few, impatient words I suddenly realized that the legendary Mossad indeed had limitations.

In an instant of frustration, one of the great intelligence officers of the world demonstrated the truth of an observation regarding the Mossad that had been written by a veteran of America's intelligence services, Archie Roosevelt.

"One of the myths widely current in the United States is that of the efficacy of Israeli intelligence," he said in his memoirs, *For

Lust of Knowing. "It is simply not very reliable in its coverage of its primary target, the Arab world surrounding Israel's narrow boundaries. The Jewish communities that used to inhabit the Arab countries today are gathered in Israel, viewed by most Arabs with abhorrence. Thus Israeli intelligence can rarely count on ideological volunteers inside the Arab target. So they must try to find recruits without a local base, from afar."

People like me. Individuals who could use the cover of their everyday lives to winnow from unsuspecting and trusting sources information as to whether the French were assisting Iraq in obtaining nuclear technology.

Although no one had ever been able to prove it, Israel had won the race to introduce nuclear weapons to the Middle East long before Langatzky spoke to me of his concerns that Saddam Hussein might be getting nuclear technology through France. In achieving that success Mossad had pulled a spectacular disappearing act involving enough enriched uranium to build at least ten atomic bombs. Nearly one hundred kilos vanished from a nuclear plant in Apollo, Pennsylvania, in 1965 and wound up at Israel's Dimona research center in the Negev desert.

Through a combination of bits and pieces of conversation with Langatzky and various other handlers, reading books on the general subject of intelligence operations, and a little Sherlock Holmes deductive reasoning, I had some idea of Langatzky's past. I suspected that he had played a significant role in a 1969 enterprise to obtain uranium from another source. The purpose was to stymie Arab efforts to develop a nuclear capacity while Israel created a nuclear arsenal of its own. By asking me to tap my French connections he confirmed my feeling that this man who had inducted me into the Institute was of far higher rank in Mossad than I first believed.

In a moment that would never be repeated, Langatzky let slip the mask of the inscrutable, tight-lipped veteran of battles in no-telling-how-many intelligence wars. "I used to be an admirer of the French," he said. "Once upon a time I looked to them as true friends of Israel. No more."

For the first time I glimpsed the human being inside the lean, hard body. "What changed your mind?"

"Not what," he said. "Who."

"Okay. Who?"

He almost spat the answer. "Charles de Gaulle, that's who."

"What did he do? Or is it none of my business?"

"It's history," he said. "You could look it up."

Emboldened by his sudden openness, I answered, "I'd rather hear it from you."

"The year was 1967. A most auspicious date, no?"

I nodded.

"At that time we had to deal with France for a number of missile boats. They were being built in Cherbourg by Israeli workers, all with the cooperation of the French government. A handful had already been delivered, though not in time to be of any use in the war. Suddenly, de Gaulle became pro-Arab. I guess he was concerned about petrol for French motorists. Like the rest of the world he panicked over the oil embargo. So he pulled the plug on aid to Israel. He denounced what he called 'arrogance on the part of Jerusalem.' He ordered a cessation of sales of what he termed 'offensive weapons' to us. Just like that, he reneged on all our agreements. He imposed a total embargo. Well, in Israel, as with all honorable people, a deal is a deal. To make this long story short, we helped ourselves to the boats."

As he spoke I recalled reading newspaper stories describing how the Israelis in Cherbourg on January 4, 1969, simply sailed out of the port in the missile boats and took them to Israel.

"We called the operation Noah's Ark," Langatzky said with a tone that suggested to me that he had played a significant role in masterminding the plot.

As I said good-bye to him in the windowless room at Mossad headquarters, I felt flattered that he continued to take a personal interest in my activities, arranging to receive my reports even though I had been entrusted to other handlers. But as I thought more about it, I ought not to have been surprised that he was intimately apprised of my work and my progress as a volunteer agent. Whatever I did, if I succeeded or failed, inevitably had to reflect upon the person who brought me into an organization that was every bit as selective in its membership as the Equestrian Club of Riyadh.

12

Is This a Honeytrap?

 Shortly after my return home from Israel and the illuminating meeting with Langatzky, I got a surprise phone call from Riyadh.

"I need a big favor," Colonel Halilli said urgently. "You are the only one I can turn to. Please don't disappoint me!"

Immediately, I envisioned the high-ranking officer telling me that he had decided to defect.

"What can I do for you?" I asked eagerly.

"My boss, General Amir, has gotten it into his head to visit the United States next week," he said. "He has ordered me to make arrangements. Frankly, I haven't a clue as to where to begin on such short notice."

"Don't worry," I said. "I'll handle everything."

"It's not as easy as it sounds." He groaned. "The general will not be alone."

"Just give me the details."

For the next half hour he outlined a daunting challenge. The general intended to bring along an enormous entourage, including three "sisters" who were actually wives, his fifteen-year-old son, and a half-dozen assistants and servants. They were to accompany him on a three-week, coast-to-coast sightseeing tour starting at the Statue of Liberty and ending at the Golden Gate Bridge. Knowing General Amir, I realized that all of this meant first class, from stretch limos to private jets.

He also specified the St. Moritz Hotel, one of the poshest hotels overlooking Central Park. Booking the deluxe hotel was never an easy task. That the general's trip coincided with July Fourth, a peak time for tourism in New York City, compounded the problem.

Only after a full day of personal telephone calls to top executives in Manhattan real estate and a reshuffling of reservations by the hotel staff could I wangle the Presidential Suite for the general, his "sisters," and the son, with lesser rooms for all the others.

Satisfied with the arrangements, I joined the drivers of a small fleet of limousines at Kennedy Airport to greet the general and his band of followers and escort them in high style into the city. Unfortunately, this did not go according to my plan. First, the Saudia Air flight arrived several hours late. Second, the general was on crutches. He had broken a leg shortly before leaving and had not bothered to inform me. Finally, the group's luggage amounted to more than the trunks of three limos could hold. Handling such a mountain of luggage required the rental of a van at two o'clock in the morning, a chore requiring an hour.

While I handled the task, the general's party proceeded to the hotel and another fiasco that prompted me to wonder if I had stumbled into a poorly produced Arabian version of *The Man Who Came to Dinner.* Upon my arrival at the hotel I discovered to my horror that something had gone amiss regarding the arrangements that I had made for the rooms.

"I am so sorry, sir," the night manager said as he looked up the general's name in a computer, "but we have no record of any reservations."

Had this happened in the general's country I would have simply shrugged in the face of an *Enshallah* situation. But much more was at stake than the prospect of General Amir laying his head on the pillow of an inferior hotel. Blame for the foul-up might fall upon Colonel Halilli, upon whom I was relying for further successes as an intelligence agent.

Furthermore, I nurtured a hope that my efforts on behalf of General Amir might result in my cultivating *him* as a source both for business for my construction company and opportunities for gathering information to relay to the Institute.

Indeed, before I began making arrangements for the general I had notified the Institute of the situation, sending a written report on my unexpected involvement with Amir's travels to the Montreal office and requesting guidance.

The reply had come in a telegram:

Interested in visitor. A postcard will do.

"Postcard" signified a desire for a written report to be handled in a routine fashion unless I judged the information to be of an urgent nature.

At the moment, however, my urgency was directed at getting the general a place to stay. As he grew more impatient with each passing moment, I demanded that the night manager telephone his boss at home.

"If you do not and if this unfortunate situation is not cleared up right now to my satisfaction," I said, "I'm afraid that this may turn into an international incident. Not only that, this sorry mess will certainly be reported in the newspapers."

Bluffing, however, could not alter reality. There were no rooms available in the general's hotel of choice and there was nothing I could do to alter that fact. My only recourse was to find a suitable alternative hotel.

Awakened in his suburban home, the manager offered profuse apologies. "I'll make some calls to other hotels," he said. "If there is *anything* available in town I will find it."

To my relief he succeeded. To my dismay the only hotel he could find with ample space was considerably downscale.

Like a caravan of baggage-laden camels we moved crosstown. A very disgruntled general went to bed, and I drove back to my home to consider the ruination of my plans for cultivating the general as an intelligence source. I was still awake at the break of dawn when my bedside phone rang.

"Everything's been straightened out," exclaimed the manager of the hotel that had turned the general away. "It was a mixup in communications. The rooms you reserved were ready all the time. In entering the reservations in the computer the general's name got filed under his first name instead of the last."

I found the situation ironic. Never in all my travels in the Middle East had such a thing happened, even in the lowest-class hotels in which the staff spoke no English.

Returning to the city, I led a fuming General Amir back to the hotel, then went home again in hopes of spending a festive Fourth of July with my own family.

To my chagrin the general's aide-de-camp telephoned me late in the afternoon. "The general's son is ill."

"What's wrong with him?" I asked.

"The bellyache."

"I'm sure the hotel has medicine. Ask for some Alka-Seltzer. Or Pepto-Bismol."

"The general demands that you recommend a reliable doctor."

"This is a national holiday," I said. "I doubt that there is a private physician anywhere who is likely to be available. May I suggest that you take the boy to a hospital emergency room?"

"Impossible," said the aide. "This would be a *humiliation*. A man of the general's stature does not go to the emergency room. It comes to *him*."

The aide's tone had traversed from urgency to panic, impelled, no doubt, by visions of finding himself in a Saudi dungeon as soon as he returned to his country.

"You must have a personal physician on call," he asserted, as if I were an Arab potentate.

"I do know a doctor in Manhattan," I said. "But there is one thing you ought to know about him."

"Never mind that," the aide snapped. "Send him at once."

He hung up before I could tell him that the one thing he ought to know was that the physician whom I had in mind was a Jew, a steady contributor to Israeli fund-raisers and a lifelong Zionist. Because the doctor was an old friend of my own doctor in Rockland County, I felt certain that he could be persuaded to do me the favor of examining the boy. I was right.

"Don't worry," he said with a chuckle. "I'll rush right over to the hotel and burp the brat."

That night the general phoned me at my home in a state of agitation. "Did you know," he shouted, "that the doctor you sent to see my son was Jewish?"

I felt an impulse to yell, "So am I, you pampered, ungrateful son of a bitch."

Instead, I concentrated on the general's potential value to me as an intelligence source, recalling David quoting Winston Churchill on the justification of lying on behalf of a noble cause.

The next time I saw the doctor he took great pleasure in showing me the personal check that the general had given him in payment for an enormously inflated fee for treating his son's mildly upset stomach. Rather than cash the check, the doctor had it framed to hang like a trophy above his desk.

"The next time my old friend Golda Meir comes for a visit I'm going to show it to her," he said, laughing in anticipation.

A few days after the doctor's house call, I looked forward to bidding the general farewell as he departed for the next leg of his trip. Expecting to find him in a happy state of mind, I discovered when I arrived at the hotel that he was involved in an imbroglio over his bill. To settle a sum fit for a prince the general had handed the cashier a personal check. Informed that the hotel would accept payment only by credit card or travelers' checks, he thundered, "This is outrageous. I *own* this bank. *And* its eighty-six branches."

I resolved this problem by providing my American Express card as a guarantee for the bill should the general's check bounce, as unlikely an event as the oil fields of his country drying up that afternoon.

This was not the last bump in the course of Amir's American travels, however. Months after his return to Saudi Arabia I heard from Colonel Halilli that when the general reached Los Angeles he went to a hospital to have the cast removed from his leg.

"Now get this," Halilli said, laughing on the phone. "While he was waiting to see a doctor, a young man in a white coat told the general to take off his clothing and put on one of those backless hospital gowns. As the general did so, this Dr. Smith took the clothes, telling Amir that he would place them in a locker for safekeeping. But after Amir's cast was removed and he went to put on his clothes he found that his pants containing his wallet were gone."

Halilli's laughter was uproarious by now, as was mine.

"He got away with at least ten thousand dollars," he went on, gasping for breath. "But that loss was nothing compared to Amir's embarrassment at having to report to his boss, the minister of defense, that the crook also got Amir's identity papers and army credentials that were in the wallet."

Relishing the picture of a savvy swindler talking Amir out of his trousers, I wondered if the perpetrator had been an agent of some intelligence agency. Had someone in Tel Aviv or elsewhere had a change of mind concerning the general's importance? Could the Institute have assigned an agent of a special group known as the AL unit to accost him? Or had it really been a thief?

But in musing upon the fate of General Amir's wallet and personal documents and papers, I could not ignore a discomforting possibility. In the special relationship between the Institute and the CIA which began in 1951, my own activities on behalf of the Institute might have wound up in a file at Langley. Certainly, I could not dismiss the likelihood that if the man who robbed General Amir were carrying out a CIA surveillance operation the CIA might know about me.

When I next saw General Amir more than a year later he mentioned neither the incident at the Los Angeles hospital nor the hotel crisis in New York. Rather, he offered glowing praise for my efforts in his behalf. More important, regarding my dual purpose in wanting to get to know him, he vowed that in him I had found a friend who would do everything within his power to help me succeed as a businessman.

"And not only in Saudi Arabia," he bragged. "I am a man of great influence everywhere."

As if to validate this boast he introduced me to K. V. Rao, the chief engineer for Oman Shapoorji Construction Company, an Indian firm with a contract for building a dozen structures for a Jordanian army tank corps based near Amman. At General Amir's request, Rao invited me to tour the site immediately.

Visiting the project would have been an intelligence coup in itself. But within hours of my arrival I found myself reaping a windfall of information. It began when Rao thrust into my hands a set of plans for the expanded armor installation that were so detailed that the bundle of blueprints and a bulging project book even contained the specifications for the toilets. I received this data so that I might work up prices in order to submit a bid for supplying materials.

Rao then enhanced my treasure by giving permission for me to photograph the whole site. In doing so I discovered that the tank mobilization site stood adjacent to an airport that was in the process of being expanded.

Dating to the 1930s, the facility had been updated in the 1960s but had not kept up with the demands of the bigger and bigger aircraft of the 1970s, becoming virtually obsolete. To overcome this problem the Jordanian government had decreed a vast new passenger and cargo terminal. Capable of accommodating the largest aircraft the world had to offer, it included acres of parking aprons and three new runways, the longest being twelve thousand feet.

I reported to the Institute that besides being able to handle commercial 747s and L-1011s, the runways were perfectly suited for use by the Jordanian air force, other Arab air forces, and any of the aircraft currently flown by the Soviet Union.

Based on a subsequent conversation with General Amir, I was also able to report that the financing of the project had been underwritten by Saudi Arabia but that the motivation of the Saudis was rooted less in their concern about another war with Israel than in King Fahd's apprehensions regarding the intentions of Khomeini in Iran and Saddam Hussein in Iraq. Either might decide to make a grab for the Saudi oil fields.

Amir confided to me that if such a threat materialized, Saudi Arabia would be more likely to turn for assistance to the United States than to the Soviet Union, in which case the airport in Jordan would have to be able to accommodate the gigantic airlift capabilities of the U.S. Air Force.

"Wouldn't it be simpler," I asked, "to build another special airfield in Saudi Arabia?"

"That can never happen," Amir said emphatically. "This is the land of the holy city of Mecca. It would be unacceptable, an affront to all that is holy, to allow what the people would see as an infidel force to operate here."

A decade later I recalled Amir's impassioned words and wondered if he also remembered them as hundreds of thousands of infidel American, British, and French forces rushed to defend Saudi Arabia, the holy places, and the rest of the Arab world against another Muslim, Saddam Hussein.

As General Amir and I built our personal and professional relationship, I came to like him. Suddenly he revealed a side of his personality that erased my late-blooming sympathy for his tribulations during his luckless trip to the United States.

The occasion was a visit to a military prison where Amir's nephew, Tariq, had been interned. "He is an obstinate thorn in my side," Amir said with a look of disgust. "He has shamed me and his entire family. Rather than accept his military obligation, he has rebelled. He disregarded basic rules. Smoking. Talking back to his superiors. He needed to be taught a lesson."

Escorted by an armed guard to the young man's cell, we found him in a squalid cubicle, knee-deep in filthy water afloat with his own excrement. He peered vacant-eyed and grime-faced through a grid of steel slats that formed a window in a thick wooden door. When I looked at him I saw ugly facial bruises and clotted streaks of blood caking his black mustache.

Standing aside, I waited, expecting Amir to order the guard to open the door and release the youth. He stood still for a moment, then turned sharply and strode away without a word to his nephew.

As I caught up to him Amir said, "Did you see him? Did his eyes reveal even a trace of repentance? No. I saw only pride. But we shall see what a few more days will bring."

He stopped short. "You are shocked," he said.

"Well, the punishment does seem extreme," I said. "And he is a young man. Didn't you make mistakes when you were young?"

"I never disgraced my family's honor," he exclaimed, walking toward an exit at the end of a long, narrow corridor lined with reeking cells crowded with silent men. "As to punishment, he is lucky. He might have gotten much worse. That he had not been given even harsher treatment is due entirely to the fact that he is my nephew."

"How long must he stay here?"

"Until he understands," Amir said as a guard opened the door for us. "Until he accepts that he must be obedient. *Enshallah.*"

In my years of observing the Arab way of life, no incident demonstrated so forcefully that the family was the bedrock of Arab society and that the family required the support and loyalty of its members. General Amir's displeasure with his nephew lay not so much in Tariq's rebellion against being pressed into his country's military service as in the embarrassment he had caused his family.

Although the young man's imprisonment troubled me a great deal, I did not bring up the subject with General Amir until the evening of my departure two weeks later. The occasion was dinner at a Riyadh hotel for the top people of companies that had built a new air base.

"Excuse me for bringing up the subject," I said to Amir as I rode with him in his car en route to the dinner, "but I have been concerned about your nephew. I cannot leave the country without knowing what has happpened to him."

"There is no need to be concerned," he said. "The foolish boy came to his senses. He is now serving faithfully at a post at Abu'Arish near the North Yemen border."

Although Amir served as the official host of the dinner, Colonel Halilli had made the arrangements for a sumptuous meal and then performed the role of master of ceremonies. In that capacity he rose at the end of the long dinner, lit a Havana cigar, and with a twinkle in his eyes announced, "Gentlemen, it is time for the evening's entertainment."

Expecting after-dinner music and perhaps a performance of folk dancing or a belly dancer, I followed the others into the next room where we were greeted by six women. Introduced to us as British nurses, they were dressed for a party.

A thirtyish, statuesque redhead in a scarlet gown sidled up to me. "My name is Violet," she said.

Along the way to vanquishing sinister enemies, James Bond, the debonair bachelor with a license to kill, always encountered beautiful and accommodating women. Indeed, some of the most effective spies have been women. Of course, everyone has heard about the infamous Mata Hari in World War I. Fewer know about Ella Bartschatis, private secretary to the East German political boss but also working for West German intelligence. Then there was Ethel Gee, who provided shopping baskets full of files purloined from Britain's admiralty to the Russian spy Gordon Lonsdale until she was arrested at the Old Vic theater in London in 1962. And finally there was Sylvia Rafael, a beauty in ski pants and sweater and one of the best women agents in the service of Israel.

Noting that more than a few good agents had been compromised by women, my trainer had warned me that despite Islamic precepts about the purity and sanctity of women, Arab counterintelligence agencies exhibited no qualms concerning the use of women as honeytraps. "So if you can't be virtuous," he said with a wink, "be careful."

As the women paired off with the other guests, Violet and I retired arm-in-arm to a small sitting room. But the moment we found ourselves alone, she blurted, "Please, there has been a terrible mistake. I have been misled in being brought here by my friends. I'm not a party girl. I am not a whore."

If this had been meant to be a honeytrap, I thought, it was a mighty unusual one.

"I'm pretty embarrassed myself," I said. "I happen to be a very happily married man. All I want right now is to go back to my hotel and crawl into bed . . . alone."

"Thank you for understanding," she said. Then she laughed. "So now what?"

"Why don't we sit down," I said, "and have ourselves a civilized talk?"

The conversation lasted for well over an hour and when I did crawl into my bed at last—by myself—I considered the time I had spent with Violet one of the more pleasant experiences of my years as a secret agent.

The next morning, a taxi driver adjusted his flowing white headdress, swerved the Mercedes into oncoming traffic, answered the outraged curses of other drivers by screaming back in kind, performed a tire-squealing, heart-stopping U-turn, and headed for my next destination, another Saudi air base, and another meeting.

Madmen drivers were not the only danger facing me that morning of suffocating heat. Ahead of us the highway would be peppered with security roadblocks where I would be required to show my papers. Although they had been examined many times during this trip, I could not be sure that they would not be challenged. But just as important as having authentic-looking documents was how one acted during these inspections. The slightest hint of nervousness might trigger alarm.

I had long since developed a trick that involved looking busy and blasé, even bored. Sometimes I buried my face in the newspaper. Usually I kept my briefcase open on my lap as I leafed through official-looking papers, preferably bearing impressive-looking headings, seals, stamps, and stickers. The more official they seemed, the better.

In navigating roadblocks on this day I had the luxury of the genuine articles, passes issued by General Amir that cleared me to enter one of the country's most closely guarded installations. To my great relief, they were documents that the lowly, bored-looking guard stationed at a dusty roadblock was not about to challenge.

Arriving at the base, I was escorted into a meeting at which the first subject up for discussion was the recent signing of a multi-million-dollar deal. In the arrangement Britain had authorized delivery of Tornado fighter planes, which were being produced under license by West Germany. Because the subject was not my area of expertise and beyond the reason for my attending the meeting, I busied myself with the papers in my briefcase. Acting distracted, I did my best to look as though I were paying no attention to the animated talk going on around the large table. Of course, my ears were soaking up every word.

The talk then moved to a matter that I did know something about. As presented by Friedhelm Ost, a representative of the West German government, the project involved building within Saudi Arabia a plant that would produce artillery and tank ordnance. The work was to be undertaken by two German firms, Rheinmetall GmbH, and a unit of Thyssen AG.

I sat impassively for hours listening to the planning of a munitions works being designed and built by German firms for a government whose vowed international policy was to destroy the Jewish state. I could hardly wait to file a report on what I heard concerning architectural specifications, the layout of the airstrip, materials to be used, the number of aircraft that would operate out of the airstrip, and the number of personnel that would be required.

A few days later in Athens I presented the notes to my handler. I also gave him a message for Colonel Langatzky. "When you transmit this material to the Institute," I said, "inform him that I will be in Paris for the next several days to work on that special French assignment he gave me. Tell him that I plan to report my findings by way of Montreal as usual, but if I come up with gold he should expect to hear from me on an urgent basis through the Paris office."

With a professional's appreciation of compartmentation, the handler understood that I could tell him nothing more. "Consider the message delivered," he said.

Like many Americans, I held ambiguous feelings toward the French. The history books of my schooldays had imbued me with the stories of Lafayette in the American Revolution, the dashing, heroic American volunteers of the First World War declaring as they arrived in France, "Lafayette, we are here," and, of course, the Statue of Liberty, a gift of the French people to America. I also recalled that many of the French collaborated with the Nazis in the Second World War. I had also read of the Dreyfus Affair of the previous century. And in my travels to France I often sensed that the anti-Semitism that had been evident in the Dreyfus case remained deeply ingrained in the French character.

Therefore, these sentiments and the incident of the missile boats of Cherbourg as related to me by Colonel Langatzky erased any feelings of guilt or betrayal of my French business associates. I felt no qualms about trying to discover if there were any truth behind Colonel Langatzky's "inklings" about French assistance to Iraqis in obtaining nuclear technology.

As a further balm to my conscience, I reminded myself that France apparently had not exhibited any reluctance toward using its spies to ferret out nuclear secrets from the United States. To facilitate France's membership in the family of world nuclear powers, the Direction Générale de Sécurité Extérieur (DGSE) had set up a supersecret unit whose existence and purpose became known only after the defection to the CIA in 1961 of a Soviet double agent, Anatoli Golytsin.

Although I had taken advantage of my business relationships in France to facilitate my activities in the Middle East, I had always had good business reasons of my own in seeking assistance from my associates. They helped me to forward the legitimate interests of my construction business. Consequently, I did not feel that I had in any way done anything to harm them or their country in my pursuit of information that I deemed vital to the survival of Israel.

But going to them in the hope of obtaining information on French nuclear assistance to Iraq could not be defined except for what it was: straight-out, unadorned spying. By no means could I justify my purpose by claiming that whatever I did and whatever I learned was in the interests of my own firm.

There had been occasions in which my company had become involved in supplying building materials for projects that were partly or wholly nuclear in nature. As a result, I brought with me to Paris a respectable knowledge of the special requirements of building nuclear plants. I could spot the difference between a conventional power plant and a nuclear one in an instant.

Therefore, I arrived in Paris confident that if I brought up the subject of nuclear development in the Third World in general and the Middle East in particular I would not trigger suspicions in the minds of my associates.

I also appreciated, based on the experience of years in the

international marketplace, that I would have an easier time in playing the role of secret agent than I had had in the Middle East. Here I would have recourse to a spy's most useful device—the small talk of the cocktail party. The West's "happy hour" did not exist in Muslim countries. Acutely aware of the effect of alcohol in loosening lips, I drank only ginger ale or soda water. Fortunately, other guests proved less cautious.

Remaining in Paris for a week, I attended several functions either by invitation or by crashing affairs that seemed to have a potential for being informative. If I had picked up any skills as an intelligence agent, eavesdropping had to rank high among them. I had also developed a talent for eliciting information in the "hale fellow, well met" atmosphere of a social setting.

Two of these relaxed Parisian gatherings proved especially tempting because the invited guests included several highly placed officials of agencies of the French government related to France's nuclear program. Although I did not know French fluently, I was able to understand the gist of conversations and to attune my ears for words or phrases suggesting that the subject being discussed related to nuclear matters.

The second of these convivial, Scotch-, gin-, and vodka-fueled chats provided a chance for me to overhear a Frenchman and a German associate discuss a contract for the manufacture of a special lid for a container for the disposal of nuclear waste. As they conversed, I also heard the Frenchman say "Iraq," "nuclear," "core," and "La Seyne-sur-Mer."

Perusing a travel guide the following day, I learned that La Seyne-sur-Mer was a seaport on the Mediterranean coast about four miles from Toulon. The town of about 27,000 residents had been known primarily for sawmills and shipbuilding until the French government chose it as a site for manufacturing nuclear reactors and allied equipment.

Unfortunately, the guide did not provide a map of the town, so I postponed my planned departure from France in order to have a look at the place. I hoped to locate the factory and draw a map of my own. I would enclose it with a written report on what I overheard at the cocktail party and the name of the Frenchman who had uttered those intriguing words. I figured that if the information proved as fascinating to Colonel Langatzky and his associates as it had been to me, Institute resident agents in France could follow up.

Expecting that I might have to spend a few days exploring the seaside community, I was surprised and pleased to discover that the first person I encountered was quite willing to give me directions. The factory apparently represented a source of local pride. Emboldened by my success, I drove past the site as slowly as prudence permitted, snapping a dozen photos with my special camera of the exterior of the well-constructed building.

Returning to Paris that evening, I mailed the roll of film, a detailed sketch of the layout of the town, and my report at a mailbox in the Gare de l'Est. I found a room in a small hotel close to the Eiffel Tower, booked a next-day Air France flight to New York, enjoyed a late supper in a nearby café, and went to bed with a feeling that I had done a good day's work.

But as several weeks passed in which I heard nothing from the Institute regarding the report, my confidence that I had struck a blow at Saddam Hussein's dreams of possessing a nuclear arsenal dimmed.

Concluding that my report had proved worthless, I let Iraq, the factory at La Seyne-sur-Mer, and matters nuclear slip to the back of my mind, only to see the specter of a nuclear disaster suddenly cast its shadow across the world in the waning days of March 1979. It took the form of an accident in a reactor in an electric generating plant at Three Mile Island, near Harrisburg, Pennsylvania.

Like everyone I nervously followed the disaster day by day as efforts to contain it and prevent a meltdown of the reactor dominated news headlines. Then on April 6 a brief news item on the radio riveted my attention and catapulted my thoughts back to France. Early that morning at La Seyne-sur-Mer, a previously unknown group calling itself the French Ecological Group had blown up a warehouse containing parts for a nuclear reactor only hours before they were to be loaded aboard a freighter bound for Iraq.

The broadcaster continued, "In a telephone call to the Paris newspaper *Le Monde* an anonymous man claimed responsibility for the destruction, declaring that the action had been taken to draw attention to the dangers of nuclear power."

The destruction of the nuclear equipment destined for Iraq by ecological fanatics stretched the bounds of coincidence. Certain that the attack had been ordered by the Mossad, I broke into a satisfied smile.

Ruth gazed at me across the breakfast table. "What are you grinning about?" she asked.

"I'm happy," I said. "Can't a guy be happy?"

Because the radio account of the action had been brief, I searched the next day's *New York Times* for a fuller story. On an inside page, it too was scant on details. The account by the Associated Press, datelined April 6 at La Seyne-sur-Mer, said that saboteurs slipped into the plant and "neutralized machines dangerous to human life." Their intent, the item said, was to protect all humanity from future "Harrisburg catastrophes."

Only in later reports did French officials speculate that the attack might have been the work of Israeli agents. They cited evidence that the saboteurs had used "sophisticated explosives," which appeared beyond the abilities of ecological protesters.

I did not doubt that in doing the deed the Institute took advantage of the Three Mile Island disaster. It appeared to me that it had invented the mysterious ecology group and staged the claim of responsibility.

Although no one would ever provide it and the Institute could never confirm my assumption (compartmentation!), I drew deep satisfaction in holding in my hands the proof, albeit in the form of newspaper reports on the bombing of the reactor, that my eavesdropping in Paris salons and my picture-taking excursion to a seaside town had paid off handsomely.

That evening I went to sleep confident that my efforts on behalf of the Institute did not simply wind up in a file or become a footnote in a report seen by a handful of secrecy-bound Mossad officers. Only years later did I confirm that the information I had accumulated had been pieced together with other data to eliminate any possibility of doubt concerning the contents of the building at La Seyne-sur-Mer.

That was not the end of the affair. The following June brought news that the head of Iraq's atomic program had been shot in a Paris hotel. Reading the item in a newspaper, I tried to recall if I might have met the man at one of the parties in Paris. The name rang no bells of recognition. But that did not mean that I had not met him. Through years of experience as an intelligence agent I had come to expect that a name by which someone was introduced was not necessarily his true one.

Had I passed his name to a handler? I had provided so many that I occasionally felt as if I were a reporter for a newspaper society page. Had a particular name that meant nothing to me been spotted by an intelligence analyst at the Institute? Had information that I provided resulted in an order to a wet squad?

Only God and the Institute know.

13

Footloose in Canaan

 Long before I set out on my adventures as a spy for Israel in the Arab world, a well-meaning friend of mine had said, "If the mess in the Middle East is ever going to be settled, both sides are going to have to sit down and talk to one another like good Christians."

Despite its ludicrous simplicity, the remark had come back to me on an evening in Riyadh in 1977. The eyes of two boiled lambs' heads stared at me from atop a mountain of steaming rice in the center of a banquet table as my business associate Ahmad said, "I have nothing against the Jews whose ancestors lived in Palestine since the days of Abraham. But I shall always resist Zionism for as many years as I am allotted on this earth."

"It is historical fact," interjected Colonel Halilli, "that Arabs and Jews got along together until the Zionist conspiracy of European Jews interfered and brought war where there had been peace."

"With the help of countries who wished to take control of the oil," chimed in another of the guests.

This comment provoked a murmur of assent around the table and the vigorous bobbing of a dozen heads adorned by a flowing ghutra, the traditional headdress that designated social status in the kingdom of Saudi Arabia.

"We will not rest," Ahmad continued. "We will resist with all our hearts and with the blood of our men until the Zionists are destroyed and the people of Palestine are allowed to return to their rightful land."

Again the ghutras nodded.

"As the poet Mahmoud Darwish wrote," said a young man seated next to me,

" 'They conquered nothing.
Nothing.
They only kindled earthquakes.' "

As I listened to him I thought of the years that I had spent crisscrossing the Middle East. I had met no one on either side of the debate who seemed willing to concede the grievances of the other. I had been witness to a dialogue of the deaf. In listening to the Arab viewpoint as expressed at Ahmad's table and to the views on Arabs expressed by men of the Institute, I recalled that two thousand years before I became an agent for Israel the Roman author Plutarch wrote of a man taken to task by friends who could not understand why he had divorced.

"Was your wife not chaste?" they demanded. "Was she not fair? Was she not fruitful?"

The man held out a shoe and asked them whether it was not new and well made. "Yet," he added, "none of you can tell me where it pinches."

Although I never heard of my father having read Plutarch's *Lives*, he had made the same point to me when I was growing up. Wagging a finger under my nose, he said, "Don't judge any man until you have walked in that man's shoes."

I did my best to follow his advice throughout my life. However, I had never been called upon to test the precept in terms of an entire people whose sole purpose in life seemed to be the destruction of Israel. My previous relations with Arabs had developed out of business purposes. I had put politics aside when meeting them in offices and on construction sites and social situations related to business.

Now my undertakings on behalf of the Institute required me to seek a deeper understanding of the people who set themselves against Israel. If victory depended on knowing one's enemy, I had reasoned, I would have to put on the sandals of the Arab.

I had begun that venture by buying the book on Arabs at Grand Central Terminal on my way to Montreal to begin my training. But in the course of those few days in the house on rue Sanguinet, I received a more practical introduction to the subject of Arabs and the bedrock of their existence, the religion of Islam. My instructor called himself Caleb, after one of the twelve spies whom Moses sent into Canaan.

The biblical Caleb was the only one to come back and assure Moses that the Jews would do well to occupy the land. As it happened, Caleb had found himself outvoted. The Jews chose not to enter Canaan. They remained in the wilderness for another generation. But Caleb's reward came when God decreed that only Caleb and Joshua would eventually enter the Promised Land. Joshua then granted to Caleb the region of the country known as Hebron. History later named the region the West Bank, or, as my Arab associates called it, "the *occupied* West Bank."

At least twice the age of those in the safe house in Montreal who inducted me into the world of spycraft, the Institute's Caleb had been a member of Haganah, running the British blockade aboard a former U.S. Coast Guard cutter, USS Paducah, the ship spirited displaced Jews from postwar Europe to Israel, often running afoul of the Royal Navy. The British would arrest the crew members only to encounter them again and again as the Zionist masterminds of Haganah found ways to free the ship and its crew for another try. Regarded as a national hero in Israel and ostensibly enjoying well-deserved retirement, he found himself summoned back to duty to meet with me to draw aside the veil of the world of Arabs and Islam.

Handing me a Muslim calendar, he stressed the importance of the month of Ramadan, when no work was to be done after noon. He continued, "The work week runs from Saturday to Thursday, the holy day being from noon Friday to noon on Saturday. Try to stay out of sight during this time. And also make every effort to make yourself scarce during the five times a day devoted to prayers."

Undraping a blackboard, he revealed a list of words and phrases. "These are no-no's," he said with a frown. "Do not refer to the *Persian* Gulf, for example." He drew a chalk line through the phrase. "To a Muslim it is the *Arabian* Gulf. And by no means call a Muslim a Mohammedan. It's a racist term that harks back to the old days when the West dominated the region. Muslims resent it the way a Catholic feels about being called a papist."

As I came to my second meeting with Caleb he grabbed me by the shoulders and planted a kiss on each of my cheeks. "Get used to this," he said as I jerked away. "And don't be surprised if one of your Arab acquaintances takes your hand and holds it. This is a sign of friendship. It doesn't mean he's in love with you."

Yet as lighthearted and amusing as Caleb could be, his lectures turned dark and bitter when he explained why adherents of Islam turned to terrorism as a means of obtaining their goals. He expressed a belief that the willingness to dare all and die found its basis in the Muslim's conviction that a martyr's death assured immediate admittance to Paradise.

During my independent search for an understanding of the Arab people, I had devoured several books on the subject. As a businessman pursuing my own interests or as a spy on a specific mission, I carried with me in all my travels an intellectual appreciation of the plight in which the Arabs found themselves.

Through the long course of mankind's history, like people everywhere, they had played the cards that birth, geography, circumstance, events, religion, and politics had dealt them. Day by day, they did the best they could and hoped and prayed for something better. As I became known to many of them, they introduced me to their personal histories and those of their families dating back to a period when Arab states were regarded by outsiders as no more than tribes with flags.

As a result, I came to know men whose predecessors had dwelt in nomadic tents and lived to see their sons take a hand in the fates of international corporations, petrochemical firms, banks, and real estate holdings all over the world. Sons of Arabs who had counted their wealth in camels or goats, the men whom I met measured theirs in sums that surpassed the greatest fortunes of Judeo-Christian Europe and America. They invited me to share meals in resplendent houses in modern cities that surpassed the Gardens of Babylon and other citadels of the Bible.

In Jidda I met Abdullah, a dealer in petroleum. A descendant of pearl traders, he told me family yarns about ancestors trading with Indian and Chinese mariners. They navigated through monsoons in order to trade their treasures at Jidda, Mecca, and Medina. He spoke with pride and amusement of another ancestor, a jewelry dealer who smuggled gems and gold out of India. Abdullah's father had earned a living reaping oysters from the Red Sea and had sent his son to a university to learn engineering.

Abdullah said proudly, "Now my father lives in a big house that I bought him and sits overlooking the same water as other men do the work of his past."

Not to be outdone, another guest of Abdullah's regaled us with an epic that began with his father fishing for the family's next meal from a creaking dowh plying the waters of the Gulfs of Arabia and Suez. He concluded with the story of how the fisherman's son owned a chain of supermarkets.

On another occasion a friend of Colonel Halilli regaled me with stories of his grandfather, a bedouin. "At that time there were no paved roads and the ones we had were often obliterated by sandstorms," he said as proudly as an American father telling his son of having to walk miles through snow to get to school. "When we traveled it was either on foot or on a camel with only the stars to guide us. We slept on a blanket on the ground. Ah, believe me, there is nothing to compare to the bedouin life."

Another prosperous businessman, Ahmad, one of several Ahmads of my acquaintance, insisted that I listen to how he had risen from the life of a camel driver to become the owner of the largest automobile dealership in Saudi Arabia. "My house was a tent," he said. "Now I have not only this fine house here in Riyadh but a fine villa on the French Riviera and a condominium apartment on Park Avenue in New York City."

Fetched from my hotel to Ahmad's home in one of his seven Mercedes sedans, I entered the house through a foyer of polished travertine walls. They were adorned by exquisite Persian rugs and museum-quality paintings of scenes of an Arabia before the age of oil and a multiplication of men such as Ahmad. If the enemy of Israel were to be depicted with one face, it would not have been that of Arab leaders like Assad of Syria, Hussein of Iraq, or Arafat of the PLO. It would be Ahmad's, for it was he who had direct access to the corporate boardrooms and private offices of powerful men who in turn exerted great influence in the capitals of the non-Arab world.

Rising from leather chairs or from plush cushions placed upon the room's enormous carpet, four men like him greeted me in the main room of the house. Speaking English out of deference to my painfully forced and limited Arabic, they wasted little time on amenities. They immediately launched into a spirited discussion of the difficulties inherent in employing foreigners in their various businesses. By "foreigners" they meant the Pakistanis, Egyptians, Chinese, North Koreans, and, especially, Palestinians.

An immediate business conversation was unusual. The custom, as I had come to understand it, was to delay such discussions until after coffee had been served. Like many Arab customs, the ritual of imbibing the strong brew took getting used to. It began with the guest politely declining to accept the initial cup and insisting that the host drink the first. The host in turn urged the guest to drink up. At that point the guest could do so without fear of offending the host's sensibilities. Propriety dictated that three cups be consumed.

During this traditional charade the conversation was relaxed and the coffee drinkers off guard, providing an opportunity for an alert listener with an ulterior motive, such as I, to garner bits and pieces of valuable information.

In this manner I accumulated personal data on numerous important persons whose hands rested upon the helm of a worldwide network of corporations.

From an officer of the Saudi army I learned that a general in the army of Kuwait maintained at least four personal accounts in Swiss banks as insurance that he and his family would live in the manner to which they had become accustomed. He had taken out the "insurance" against Saddam Hussein taking it into his head to exercise an old Iraqi claim on the northern part of Kuwait and then proceed to take over the entire kingdom.

A similarly incautious Saudi banking official boasted over his third cup of coffee that he kept a treasure in jewelry, a cache of currency, and all of his personal and important business and government papers in an unlocked cabinet in his unguarded home. When I suggested the inherent risk he replied with confidence that the harsh penalties for burglary under Islamic law assured the safety of the cabinet's contents.

When I passed on this tidbit to my handler a few weeks later, the handler winked and said, "If everyone would be as cooperative as this guy, the break-in boys of the Nevlot section would have a hell of a lot easier job."

On my next visit to Ahmad's opulent house I learned that a burglary had occurred at the boastful banker's home and that the thief or thieves had taken not only the jewels and cash but every piece of paper in the cabinet.

"Unfortunately, the criminals have not been apprehended," Ahmad said, sipping his coffee.

I said nothing, assuming that the burglary had been done on orders from the Institute.

While it was impossible to carry out business of any kind in the Arab world without the accompanying coffee or sweet tea, I found that the Islamic taboo regarding the drinking of alcoholic beverages often was likely to be honored more in the breach than in practice. Time and again I found myself nursing a glass of the best bourbon, Scotch, gin, vodka, or wines. While this blatant disobedience to the tenets of their laws surprised and shocked me at first, it also provided me with valuable intelligence information.

In taking advantage of the opportunities which these social gatherings afforded, I reminded myself of an Arab saying: "It is written and so it must be."

I reasoned that if Arabs chose to reveal their secrets to an American businessman who concealed his identity as a Jew and an intelligence agent for Israel, it must have been so written and, having been written, so it had to be.

I could only hope and pray that it had *not* been written that I would run afoul of any Islamic tradition and start a chain of events that might lead to my being unmasked.

Just how easily I might stumble into the potential pitfalls that abounded in every country had been driven home to me during my first foray into espionage. The incident involved a young American whose job was supervising Palestinian laborers engaged in building storage facilities for a British petroleum consortium based in Riyadh.

Uncomplicated and thoroughly competent, Timothy Johnson went about his challenging work and the difficult business of living in Saudi Arabia with an unrestrained zest for the pure adventure of it. He also brought to the experience a determination to immerse himself in what he saw as a colorful and interesting society. He filled his mobile home with Arab art and artifacts, from the rugs on his floor to the pillows on his bed. The only thing about life in Saudi Arabia that irritated him was the ever-present desert sand.

Weary of the constant need to sweep and determined to check its inroads into his house, he installed tape around windows and doors and even plugged keyholes. But none of this prevented him from tracking sand into his home. To deal with the vexsome problem he decided to put down tiles outside the front door. In keeping with his compulsion to outfit his domicile with things Arabic he bought ceramic tiles of vivid colors in a local bazaar.

They were decorated with the graceful lettering of the Arabic alphabet.

Pleased and proud, he invited an Arab coworker to dinner with the idea of showing off the patio. The Arab refused to enter the home. Puzzled and hurt, Tim dined alone and went to bed, only to be awakened early the next morning by a pounding on his door.

Opening it, he found four dour-looking policemen and an even more severe-looking mutaw. A local guardian of the faith of Islam and one of the fundamentalist sect, Wahhabism, he had the duty to educate, encourage prayer, and to punish the crimes of smoking in public, looking lustfully at a woman, adultery, and a long list of other infractions. In effect, a mutaw was a religious policeman. Tim found himself arrested for disrespecting Islam.

He learned in court the Arabic writing on the tiles was of a religious nature. Treading on them was more than a serious crime. It amounted to blasphemy. The law required a sentence of two years in jail. Tim served one and then was expelled from the country. The embassy had been unable to help him, except to get the sentence reduced.

Shortly after learning of Tim's troubles, I witnessed the fate that befell another well-meaning American who had heard the siren song of Arabia. Dan Smith had gone to Saudi Arabia when the first Aramco oil wells started producing in the late 1940s. Because of the extremely hard conditions he had left his wife and children at home, promising to return a wealthy man.

He soon discovered that he liked his new surroundings. He became one of the permanent expatriates I had found scattered across the Arab world who had become more Arab than American. When I met him he held the title of manager for New Business Ventures in a firm owned by a Saudi sheik and lived in a palatial guest "cottage" on the sheik's estate near Dhahran.

In the thirty years prior to my meeting Dan Smith, his personal and business relationships had permitted him to accumulate a considerable fortune of his own. During a magnificent dinner at his house he reviewed with me the blueprints for a proposed expansion of supertanker facilities at Dhahran. He then said, "I love this place. I thought I would stay long enough to make a killing in oil and then go home. But this is my home now."

Because I had no reason to doubt him, I was stunned a few weeks later when he telephoned my office from his home in Saudi

Arabia. In tears, he told me that the sheik had accused him of embezzlement. "It's a lie," he said, his voice choking with sobs. "I felt sorry for him. We were friends. I would never do anything to hurt him. But it seems our friendship was one-sided. The whole damned thing is a setup. The sheik is covering his own miserable ass."

According to Dan's account, the sheik had made some rather poor investments. The loss of millions of dollars threatened the very survivial of his financial empire.

"He had to save face in his family," Dan continued, "so he put the blame on me. The son of a bitch actually stood before a court and turned his pockets inside out to show how he had been 'cleaned out,' as he put it, by an *infidel's* mismanagement."

I had come to know Dan as a scrupulous person. "Surely you can prove otherwise," I said.

He laughed bitterly. "What chance does an American have in a Muslim court?"

"Then my advice is to get the hell out of there," I said.

"It's impossible. The authorities confiscated my passport."

"Have you informed the American consulate?"

"Yes, and all I got was a shrug and 'Sorry, but as this is a private matter, we cannot interfere.' The consul told me that they would monitor the case. In short, they said, 'Here's your head' and 'Go check into a hotel.' I was actually told to leave the embassy with my bag or I would be put out on the street. I'm at a loss to know what to do. I was hoping you might have some ideas. Is there anything you can do to help me?"

Knowing that Dan came from the state of Washington, I contacted the offices of both of Washington's U.S. senators. I explained what happened and vouched for Dan's integrity. I then implored a Saudi attorney who had represented me and my firm on a few occasions to take Dan's case.

Eventually, the senators and the Saudi lawyer informed me that the matter could be settled by the posting of a $75,000 cash bond. This would permit Dan to leave the country and to return to the United States pending a trial.

"Naturally, no one expects that Mr. Smith will ever go back to Saudi," the lawyer said. "He will be tried in absentia and found guilty, with the proceeds of the bond paid to the sheik."

Dan accepted the deal reluctantly. His family posted the bond, wiping out their bank account. Returning to Washington for the first time in decades at the age of sixty, he became a morose and bitter man and died heartbroken the next year.

"Of course Smith was innocent," my friend Abdullah said during my next trip to Dan's adopted country. "What could one do?"

"You could have been a witness for him," I retorted.

"No, no, no," Abdullah said, shaking his head. "An Arab testifying against another Arab, taking sides with an outsider?"

"Outsider? Dan lived here for thirty years. He practically became an Arab."

Abdullah smiled. "We are a *people*," he said as he offered me coffee. "We are one and indivisible. Our unity lies in the faith of Islam, built on the pillars of purification, pilgrimage, fasting, prayer, and jihad, which means striving or exerting oneself in the way of God. One does not *become* an Arab."

On the way back to my hotel from Abdullah's mansionlike dwelling I came upon a scene that would become familiar to me in every Arab land. It raised for me questions and doubts about Arab unity as expressed by Abdullah and others who had become rich almost beyond the point of comprehension. My path took me to a village of ramshackle structures that looked as old as the land.

Before them, standing or hunkered down upon the hard and dusty ground, men stared at me as I passed by in a Mercedes. The women drew up their veils and turned away.

"What do they think of me?" I wondered as the car sped by. "Do they have any idea of the vast, modern world beyond their village and their country? Do they ever question? Might they, one day, rise up and demand of men such as Abdullah why, with all the riches that come out of their land, they remained so poor?"

Or would it forever be their lot to shrug their shoulders and resignedly mutter that it was God's will?

This question also concerned many of the Arabs whom I met in my travels. But the best answer came from Colonel Halilli. "We know that the West looks upon us as backward. We are not. We have a long and illustrious civilization. We reject the racist idea in the West that it is the West that will lift us up. We are not going to allow ourselves to be dictated to by great nations or small nations or dispersed nations."

All the thoughtful men with whom I conducted business or

simply encountered in my traveling insisted that nothing would change—nothing *could* change—until the issue of the Palestinians had been resolved.

"They are the symbol of our struggle," Halilli explained to me one evening at the Equestrian Club. "In the eyes of all Arabs the seizure of Palestine was a crime that was committed against all Arabs. It will not be forgiven nor forgotten. Until the Palestinians return to their homes, we are all Palestinians."

Although he spoke fervently, I knew from my own experience that his words and those of other champions of the Palestinian cause in Saudi Arabia were unmitigated hypocrisy. Despite the fact that their country ranked at the top of a list of oil-rich Arab nations, the Saudis had done almost nothing to alleviate the difficulties experienced by Palestinians, the majority of whom were to be found in the poorest countries of Egypt, Lebanon, Syria, and Jordan. The Saudis and the equally rich Kuwaitis had welcomed few Palestinians, and then only as laborers in the oil fields and construction sites, along with Yemenis, Indonesians, Koreans, and Filipinos.

Furthermore, since the advent of Islamic nationalism in Iran, the Saudis believed the presence of rootless Palestinians threatened the huge family enterprise that constituted the Saudi Arabian government. Increasingly nervous over the developments in Iran, the Saudi royal family had taken extraordinary steps to guard against uprisings that might produce a revolution and install in Saudi Arabia a dictator like Libya's Qadaffi.

No more convincing proof of the vulnerability of the Saudi government could be found than in an uprising by young fanatics in the holy city of Mecca in 1979. They stormed the Great Mosque and took it over, sending shock waves through the Saudi government, which detected on the incident the fingerprints of the Ayatollah Khomeini.

The next year saw a demonstration by Shiite Muslims during the Holy Feast of Sacrifice. In keeping with tradition but in open violation of Saudi law, the marchers flailed themselves with chains in a public procession. Police broke up the march, but when the news reached the Shiites in Qatif they broke loose in a rampage, attacking a police station and ransacking an armory. The national guard had to be sent to restore order.

Religion did not provide the only impetus behind concerns for the stability of the Saudi government. Sudden wealth and the headlong rush toward modern development also contributed to a general unease. The explosion of wealth made multimillionaires of about eight hundred Saudi princes but left out the general population. The boom in oil also spawned widespread ostentation as some of the senior princes built opulent palaces for themselves and splendid, exclusive spas such as the Equestrian Club.

Among the corrupt practices that I noted and reported to the Institute was a scheme in which the royal family granted huge parcels of desert land to princes who then sold the land back to the government at enormously inflated prices for development of projects like the Equestrian Club and modern superhighways. Those projects had nothing to do with the improvement of the lot of the ordinary Saudi.

In reporting these facts to my handlers I found that their interest extended beyond the pure intelligence value in my assessment of the political situation in the country. They seemed to be fascinated by gossip. They doted on stories about extravagant dinners at the Equestrian Club. They could not hear enough about personal rivalries and jealousies. Of course, knowledge of the personal peccadilloes of one's enemy, real or potential, carried with it a measure of relevance in terms of intelligence. Gossip might open the possibility of blackmail, always a useful tool in the world of intelligence. Nonetheless, I found it fascinating and amusing that my handlers encouraged me to dig it out with all the fervor of a snoop for a supermarket tabloid.

Of all the dominant circles in the Arab countries in which I gathered gossip, none offered such a rich harvest as the royal family of Saudi Arabia. They gave new meaning to the word "nepotism." The employment of members of the Saud family dwarfed the practice of the British royal family in providing jobs to relatives. What was known inside Buckingham Palace as "the Firm" paled in comparison to the Saud dynasty. Members of the family were sprinkled through governmental posts reaching down to the middle ranks of the bureaucracy and the military that a British royal might decline as being below his station.

I found relatives of King Fahd at nearly every turn. They presided everywhere, from grandiose office suites in ministries in Riyadh to spartan headquarters at army bases at Khamis Mushait, Al Khari, and King Khālid Military City.

I discovered, as Peter Mansfield noted in his book *The Arabs*, that the Saudi monarchy did not amount to an autocracy. The king operated through a consensus of family members. As a result, I reported to the Institute that the House of Saud appeared to me to be capable for the moment of withstanding internal threats that might arise, either from their own disgruntled population or from Khomeini-inspired Iranian fundamentalist zealots.

I also reported, based on my assessment of the Saudis with whom I dealt, that the country seemed considerably more vulnerable to threats beyond its borders than to an internal uprising.

"This may be an unfair question," a handler said as we sipped glasses of wine in a café near the Spanish Steps, "but what do you think the United States would do if Saudi Arabia were attacked by another Arab country? For example, Iraq?"

"The United States will do what they feel is politically right and necessary at the time," I said confidently. "The real question is, What would Israel do?"

14

A Day at the Races, Camel, That Is

  In September 1979 an Alitalia jetliner brought me across the Mediterranean and descended above the sparkling blue waters of the gulf of Sidra toward the capital city of Libya. The passport and other documents in my luggage had been crafted by counterfeiting wizards of the Institute. They identified me as a subcontractor from Canada who represented a West German company with interests in obtaining contracts in Libya.

"This guy Qaddafi is nobody to mess around with," my handler had said at a meeting in Rome at which he provided me the bogus passport and supporting papers. "While we at the Institute appreciate your volunteering to go to Libya, we feel obliged to warn you that you will be entering the most dangerous spot in the world. Libya is ruled by perhaps the most frightening fanatic on earth. Before I hand over the material that you requested, I must insist that you study a briefing paper on Libya and Qaddafi drawn up by our Libya desk just for you."

He handed me four typewritten pages. "Read it now, please," he said, lighting a cigarette. "Take your time."

The document began with a one-page summation of the recent history of Qaddafi's international record of support for terrorism that included his support of the bloodthirsty Idi Amin of Uganda; providing heroes' burials for four Palestinian terrorists who were shot during the massacre of Israeli athletes at the 1972 Munich Olympics; and his military adventures in neighboring Chad.

The brief summary was followed by a one-page biography of Qaddafi and two pages offering a psychological profile of the man. Among the observations: knowing that an Arab assassin would have trouble shooting a woman, he surrounded himself with female bodyguards; because of a paranoid belief that many "infidels" were out to kill him, he never slept in the same bed two nights in a row. He showed signs of a middle-age crisis. His behavior was rooted in bedouin religious fanaticism, austerity, intense personal pride, and xenophobia.

As I returned the document to my handler he said, "What this means is that if you are caught spying, Qaddafi won't slap you on the wrist and kick you out. You'll disappear without a trace."

"I appreciate the concern and the warning. I assure you I will be as careful as I can. An invitation to this country may not be available again, so I don't think I can refuse to go."

Of all the countries I had visited in my dual capacity as a legitimate seeker of building contracts and a collector of intelligence information, none had seemed as daunting. Except for the Ayatollah Khomeini, no leader so thoroughly embraced the puritan Islamic revolution that threatened overthrow of the established order of Islam while expunging the vestiges of Western dominance.

In pursuit of these goals Qaddafi had expounded a "Third Way" ideology, contained in three volumes of what was known as the Green Book. Published between 1975 and 1979, it rested on the idea that "whoever possesses your needs controls or exploits you." Simply defined, the Third Way was a blueprint for turning Libya into an Arab-style socialist state that rejected the capitalism of the West and the communism of the Soviet Union. Under Qaddafi's plan he would become the arbiter of all facets of Libyan life.

His decrees included an order requiring that the passports of all visitors to Libya be written in Arabic as well as French and English. After examining mine, a stern-looking young man of the "popular committee" that ran the customs and immigration station at Tripoli airport stamped his approval, admitting me to the country. In doing so, he unknowingly handed the forgers of the Institute a compliment on the quality of their work. He then presented me with a booklet, also written in Arabic, English, and French, containing a code of behavior for visitors to the Socialist People's Libyan Arab Jamahiriya.

Sharing a taxi with four citizens of Qaddafi's "mass state," I was conveyed into Tripoli by a driver who appeared to share the suicidal penchant for speed of his Arab cousins in the Mideast. I decided that whoever coined the phrases "Getting there is half the fun" and "Having a great time, wish you were here" had never set foot in the capital of Libya. No major Arabian city that I had visited had appeared as bleak and the people on the streets as cheerless. In his zeal to establish Islamic revolution Qaddafi had erased all forms of popular diversions that could be found in Egypt, such as bars, nightclubs, and movie theaters. I had seen television antennas poking up from rooftops of countless homes in other Arab cities. In contrast, in Libya's capital I found few, and those households received only those programs authorized by the government to promulgate the Third Way.

My hotel proved to be no less diligent in adhering to the Qaddafi line. His portraits alternated on walls with posters proclaiming the revolution, not only in the lobby and corridors but in the rooms. Although my third-floor room offered a spectacular view of the famed shores of Tripoli, I first looked for spying devices and for places that might be converted into slicks. I also searched for places to hide myself. This practice had by now become a compulsion. Unfortunately, the room provided no place where I could conceal myself or anything else.

I kept what I had first organized as a traveler's survival kit in a canvas backpack next to my bed. It was packed with items that I might not find in the Middle East, such as my preferred brand of toothpaste, a small first-aid kit, and a few cans of food. To these I had added a compass, a Swiss army knife, extra sunglasses, a map, a spare hat, two large plastic bottles of water, and a small leather coin purse containing four South African gold coins, in case I needed to bribe someone.

My only recourse should I feel a need to flee was a narrow coping four feet beneath the window, followed by a leap to a steeply slanting roof one floor lower. One story below I saw a narrow walled garden whose only exit led through an adjoining house. I had no ready answer as to how I might get out of the garden and, after that, out of the country.

Morning arrived to the blaring loudspeakers of at least half a dozen mosques awakening the faithful and infidel alike to their responsibilities to God and mammon. The day began at ten o'clock in a meeting with the official in charge of all construction in the immediate vicinity of Tripoli. Because the conference had been planned as an introduction, I did not expect to leave Tripoli carrying nuggets of intelligence gold. Indeed, while that turned out to be the case, I learned about a pair of Pakistani brothers who held contracts for a power plant in Libya.

In following up on this information I learned that Ikram Khan and his brother Haseeb operated out of a small office in a village overlooking the Rhine south of the West German capital. They had been doing so for years, conducting business in all the Arab countries.

Having introduced myself in Libya and having promised that I would submit bids on two small storage buildings planned for the airport, I returned to Rome to inform the Institute about the Khans. My handler told me that the Khans had long been suspected of illicit dealings in nuclear technologies.

"We have not been able to prove anything concerning the Khans," he said, "but we believe the two of them are like spiders spinning a web. Its strands reach into all the Muslim countries showing an interesting in getting into the nuclear game. Pakistan, Iraq, and Libya."

"Would it be useful if I got to know these guys?" I asked.

"Of course it would," he said. "But I can't issue you an order. This must be strictly voluntary, as always."

Presently, through my contacts in West Germany, I arranged to meet the Khans on the pretext of having been referred to them by officials in Tripoli. We met at their office. Although Ikram presented himself as aloof and cautious, I found Haseeb to be vain and boastful. These were two of the most dangerous traits for someone engaged in keeping secrets, but they were most welcome characteristics to someone seeking them out. Over several months of contacts in person or by telephone, I forwarded to the Institute morsels of information directly connecting the Khans to the Pakistan Institute of Science and Technology (Pinstech). A heavily fortified compound north of the capital, Islamabad, it contained a uranium enrichment plant.

Equipment for this and other Pakistani nuclear projects had been acquired on the open market by the Khans, with the financing provided by Saudi Arabia. Technical assistance had been supplied by experts in France through the Khan front. Thousands of components for the nuclear facilities flowed to Pakistan from dozens of small companies in Europe via Switzerland in a transshipment route charted by the Khans.

Then Haseeb let slip something that proved more alarming to me as an American than all of this intricate wheeling and dealing between nuclear-hungry Muslim dictatorships and greedy Europeans. In another remarkable demonstration of loose lips, he bragged in detail about his "important connections" in the United States. The names read like a report on the *Fortune 500*. He peppered his boasts with specifics concerning the methods employed by him, his brother, and their American allies to circumvent U.S. trading laws. That night I spent hours drawing a chart showing that the Khans were indeed at the center of an international spiderweb of nuclear merchandising.

I found it alarming that the dealing in instruments of mass death that could be aimed at Israel was carried out in Germany. The chart connected the Khans to scores of German firms engaged in activities that had been made illegal under the West German constitution. They included the large Taii Project Consortium, which made artillery and other armaments and sold them throughout the Mideast; the chemical companies Chemie GmbH and Karl Kolb GmbH, providing technologies for pesticide manufacturing in Libya that could be easily converted to making poison gases; and H & H Metalform GmbH, shipping components to Iraq for gas centrifuges that could be employed in nuclear weapons development.

Therefore, it was with profound relief that a few months after I forwarded my chart on the Khan business network to the Institute, I read newspaper accounts of investigations by the FBI and other federal agencies that led to the expulsion of the Khan brothers' enterprises in the United States. Again I believed this had to be more than a coincidence. I knew that my mentor, Langatzky, was still on duty at the Israeli embassy in Washington. Certainly, I reasoned, he would have been aware of the Khan data that I provided and recognized the advantages in passing the information to the CIA and other agencies of the American intelligence community.

Soon after the downfall of the Pakistanis I returned to the land of my first venture into espionage in 1974, Saudi Arabia. Since then, I had witnessed great advances in terms of the Saudi Arabian infrastructure, not the least of which was the King Abdul Aziz International Airport at Jidda, now ranked among the largest in the world.

Yet after a speedy delivery by taxi to the Red Sea Palace Hotel, I had only to walk a block off King Aziz Street to the city's old bazaar to plunge back to an ancient epoch that existed long before the discovery of oil beneath the desert. I had wandered through souks in most of the great cities and many of the smallest towns of Arabia, from Morocco to the Persian Gulf, but none as extensive as Jidda's.

A maze of alleyways and narrow passages, it was lined with shops offering goods made on the spot or imported thousands of miles from Bangladesh in the Far East, But unlike those of the bazaars of Cairo and Riyadh, the Jidda merchants rarely had had to deal with foreign tourists. In my Western clothing I stood out among those visitors who looked for bargains while wearing the traditional garb of the Middle East, whether they came to the souk from Basra in Iraq or merely a street away.

I had to fend off scores of eager sellers and persistent hawkers before reaching my destination, a restaurant at the far side of the souk. There I was to meet General Ahmad Al-Ayun. A Saudi air force officer overseeing several projects, he had been brought to my attention by my old friend Colonel Halilli.

The projects ranged from a mess hall and kitchen with a capacity for feeding three thousand airmen at Al-Khurj to a nationwide microwave communications system linking Riyadh to Hail in the north and Najran on the border with Yemen. Ayun also had charge of planning a new military school at Kassin and facilities at an air academy and technical studies institute at Dhahran that had to be upgraded to handle instruction in F-15 fighters being supplied by the United States in its latest effort to court the Saudis.

Ushered through an ornate doorway and up narrow stairs to the second-floor restaurant, I found General Ayun accompanied by four junior officers. They wore crisp khaki uniforms and the distinctive flowing red-and-white headdresses of the Saudis. As they rose to greet me I saw in Ayun's lean young aides the cold, calculating eyes that would not blink at carrying out the orders of the Four Horsemen of the Apocalypse.

In Ayun I found the middle-aged bulk and bearing of Gilbert and Sullivan's "very model of the modern major general." More interested in the food than business, he put off any talk of work until hours later, when we went to his office. There he pointed to a stack of blueprints, bid documents, and books of specifications for his projects. "Here is all you need to know to submit bids," he said. "I am informed by friends that you know what you are doing. So pick those plans you need to quote our requirements."

As I tried to conceal a triumphant smile, my heart raced with excitement. "If I may, I'd like to have time to properly review everything."

"Whatever you require. I shall have one of these young men bring the entire pile to your hotel. Take them back home. Study them to your heart's content. Then let me know which projects interest you the most. I can arrange for you to obtain the necessary copies."

Astonished by my luck, I muttered, *"Enshallah."*

"I know from Colonel Halilli that you come to Saudi Arabia often," he said. "He thinks you are at heart an Arab. Have you ever been to a camel race?"

"Not that I recall," I said. "I'm sure I would remember."

"In America they race horses. The best of these horses are bred from Arabian stock, no?"

"So I've been told."

"I, too, like horse racing. But believe me, there is nothing like a good camel race. Did you know that a Sudanese camel can reach speeds of up to twenty kilometers an hour?"

"Very impressive."

"You do not believe me." He bellowed a laugh. "You will see, my friend. You will come to a race. My guest. Sunday. I will pick you up."

On the way, he regaled me with the history of the sport. "It all started in the marketplaces, of course. Everything begins in the marketplace, eh? The bedouin came in from their desert tents with their best camels. Naturally, each man bragged that his camel was the best. But they can't all be the best, right? So they raced. Not for money, of course. They raced for the pride that comes with winning."

The race was to be held at Janadriyah. "It is the longest camel-racing track in the world," Ayun boasted.

By the time we arrived I had heard more than I cared to know about camel racing. But with the crack of the starting gun for the first race of the morning, I was caught up by the colorfully dressed crowd's excitement as ugly and ungainly animals lurched forward. Within seconds they attained a brisk trot, their long necks stretched, the humps quivering, flanks stinging from the whips of jockeys with faces shrouded against the sandstorm kicked up by their mounts. How the riders stayed on the beasts, even with the saddles used in modern times in the interests of safety, amazed me.

By the end of the fifth and final race I cheered the winner with as much enthusiasm as Ayun. Scenes that had unfolded around me and in the end embraced me had been going on for centuries. Then I heard a familiar drone as the young winner of the last race proudly received his prize, a traditional wooden mallet that signified his triumph and bestowed upon him the bragging rights of his bedouin village.

Looking up and squinting against the glaring sun, I watched a formation of four American-made F-15 fighters breaking the sound barrier above us. Nothing before that moment or since drove home to me as forcefully the enduring reality of the Middle East. Past and future clashing in the present. The camel represented nostalgia for the past. The F-15 was a commitment to an uncertain future.

I made a quick study of the plans Ayun had given me. I had decided to press my luck by asking the general to see the various methods of construction the Koreans were using at the communications facility that was being built at Hail. Again, he seemed to be an intelligence agent's godsend.

"I've been meaning to inspect the work," he exclaimed. "We will go up together."

Measured by a straight line on a map of Saudi Arabia, Hail, the principal city of Saudi Arabia's central plateau, stood about five hundred miles northwest of Riyadh. But getting to the remote spot on the southern edge of the Great Nafud Desert by car involved a trip over twisting roads cut through three imposing mountain ranges, the Jabal Shammar, Jabal Aja, and Jabal Selma. The area had been described in a guidebook as a place "for die-hard Arab buffs." The region had been populated for thousands of years by ancestors of colorful nomads who gazed back at me from the backs of loping camels while I studied them from the air-conditioned comfort of the rear seat of General Ayun's Mercedes.

"That is Hail just ahead," Ayun said as the car came down from a craggy foothill onto a stretch of flatland. "You see? The water tower?"

A few miles distant, its top looked like a giant mushroom cap against a deep blue sky crisscrossed by long strings of puffy white contrails left by jets of the Royal Saudi Air Force.

"Training maneuvers," Ayun said, peering up. "The pilots fly toward the Iraqi border then turn back." He laughed. "It makes the Iraqis scramble. Then we listen to their radio chatter. When our planes fly toward the border with Jordan, they provoke the same response from the Israelis, who are not that far away."

I pictured my map of Saudi Arabia. If I were to continue the straight line on the map of Saudi Arabia drawn between Riyadh and Hail by another five hundred miles, the line would cross the Hashemite kingdom of Jordan and proceed directly over Jerusalem to Tel Aviv. In an air force jet of either country such a flight would be measured in minutes.

We entered Hail at dusk and proceeded north on the city's main thoroughfare, flanked by trees and neat white, single-story buildings. Passing through Commercial District Square, we came to our hotel.

"Ah, you are in luck," General Ayun exclaimed. He gestured toward a sprawl of bedouin tents adjacent to the modern hotel. "Have you ever been to a bedouin wedding?"

I shook my head.

"You are in for something special."

Like a narrator in travelogues that played in movie theaters when I was growing up in Spring Valley, New York, he described the traditions, which I found fascinating. The affair had begun a few days before, he explained, with the bridegroom arriving on a white horse. He was accompanied by family, friends, and servants on camels, horses, and donkeys and a rat-a-tat-tat of vintage rifles and modern firearms being shot into the air.

"This is where the food is made ready," he said, pointing to a huge tent in which veiled women toiled among billows of steam and smoke and the scents of garlic, cinnamon, and saffron. He added, "This is for women only, of course."

A second large tent accommodated several men who reclined on cushions and camel saddles or sat on rugs that had been laid upon the ground. Resplendent in tribal garb and flowing headdresses, they sucked on stems of bubbling water pipes, which they passed among themselves. They looked like figures in the etchings found in old books about Arabia.

While I looked into the tent, one of the men rose from an ornate pillow and beckoned Ayun inside. After they spoke for a moment, the general returned to my side.

"He is the father of the groom," he explained, nodding at the grinning figure returning to his pillow. "He has done you the great honor of inviting you to partake of the wedding meal."

I had never been a fan of Middle East cooking that always seemed to come from a restaurant where the bugs had to be picked out before the food was served. However, I could not refuse his generous offer. To do so would have insulted not just the man who had invited me but General Ayun as well. I smiled and nodded my acceptance at the beaming father of the groom.

I stepped into a main tent that was crowded with family and friends. I soon discovered that when it came to celebrations the Arabs could put on a display as ostentatious as any given for Jewish weddings and bar mitzvahs.

Before eating came a ritual washing of hands, a custom that I welcomed. I knew from experience that the food being carried into the tent by the women would be eaten with fingers directly from the bowls and trays. I saw enormous heaps of food: tahini, hummus, deep-fried balls of crushed wheat and chick peas, stuffed grape leaves, peppers, eggplant, rice, olives, beans, almonds, and the main course of lamb, served on gigantic trays and garnished by lambs' eyes and testicles. Dessert consisted of peaches, grapes, bananas, melons, pastries crammed with nuts and honey, and a huge variety of sweet, sticky cakes.

Because of the general's status we were invited to partake of the festivities that followed the meal. Lasting well past midnight, these included dancing by the men that was punctuated every few minutes by bursts of gunfire. The women could be heard making clucking noises and shrill shrieks, using their tongues to trill the notes. I looked for the bride and groom but could not find them in the throng of attendants. These festivities did not stop until the call to prayer floated across the city at dawn.

"I trust you had a good time and slept well," said General Ayun as we met in the lobby of the hotel at mid-morning. "The guns did not keep you awake, I hope?"

"I slept like a baby," I said, which was a lie.

"Good. Because we have a busy day ahead," he said, gesturing toward his waiting Mercedes. "I intend to take advantage of your presence by picking your brains about all that you see. Frankly, we are running slightly behind schedule on the project. I hope that you will have some helpful suggestions."

As we drove out to the construction site I mused upon the irony of the situation. Here I was, an agent of Israel being taken on a guided tour of a supersecret Arab communications system that might be used against Israel and being solicited for advice in getting the project back on its timetable by the general in charge.

If I offered advice that I knew would serve to put the work even further behind schedule, I might jeopardize my reputation and ruin my chances for future opportunities to collect intelligence. But if I helped General Ayun with his problem, would I eventually damage Israel? As the general's car proceeded out of Hail into rugged countryside, I suddenly felt a keen appreciation for those in the world of intelligence who operated as double agents, though why anyone would do so escaped my understanding.

Arriving at the site, I saw that Ayun's project reeked of incompetence. It flowed from the top in the form of the project's civilian supervisors. Because Saudis do not do physical labor, the work was being carried out by an assortment of Pakistanis, Indonesians, and Koreans.

"You've got a morale problem," I said to Ayun as we took a break for lunch. "Your labor force obviously resents bosses who are getting paid a lot of money to stand around shouting orders. Frankly, what the hell do these imported men care about this project? What's in it for them, except money? They have no feelings of pride. Without pride you get shoddy work."

As I spoke, I felt the stirrings of a devilish idea that I felt would permit me to appear to be helpful to Ayun and at the same time throw a monkey wrench into his project, at least temporarily. "You would do better with a Taiwanese work force," I said. "My advice is to get rid of the outside labor, replace the civilian bosses, and put military officers in charge."

"If I were to do that," he said, "it would mean bringing the entire project to a halt until I could bring in the new people."

"It would. But it's your only recourse, as I see it."

"I'm sure it's good advice," he said, shaking his head. "But it cannot be done. My superiors wouldn't understand. And who can tell what the Palestinians might do?"

Apparently, no problem in the Middle East could be resolved without considering the Palestinians.

I had also witnessed, not for the first time, another problem affecting the progress of a job. That everybody involved in Ayun's enterprise stopped working several times a day for the devotions required by the Muslim religion did not contribute to high productivity. Of course, there was nothing that anyone could do about that.

Later in the evening Ayun got down to business. "If you wish to become involved in any of my projects, I would be honored to have such a distinguished and valued person as an associate. It could be a superb and very profitable partnership for both sides."

I had listened to similar flatteries often, but invariably followed by an unabashed solicitation of a bribe. Because I knew the claiming of baksheesh had been the way of doing business for centuries in the Middle East, I never felt shocked or scandalized. My objections to bribery as a way of doing business rested on a more practical foundation. Quite simply, I had never found a situation in which a payoff might advance my objectives. In the first instance, I saw it as risky. The slightest slip might lead to unpleasant legal entanglements, including expulsion from the country in question, thus nullifying my chances of acting as an intelligence gatherer. Second, the haggling required served to delay things. Bribery of one official inevitably led to bribes for others. The word traveled fast.

Finally, engaging in an under-the-table deal opened the possibility that someone who was left out would hold a grudge and seek revenge.

After weighing these negatives, I always rejected the baksheesh game. In the case of General Ayun my only interest in his projects extended to gathering information. I had no desire to go into business with him. Therefore, I decided to short-circuit what I interpreted to be his opening gambit in a bid for a bribe.

"Before I can enter into any agreement with you," I said, "I'll have to discuss the details with officials of my firm. If I'm not able to work with you, I'll recommend someone capable."

Ayun reared back. "But I thought you were the boss."

"I am, but I have partners. They call themselves bankers! Before I enter into any arrangement as extensive as ours would be, the money men have to get in their two cents worth."

"This is a great pity. What do bankers know about building? They know the cost of everything and the value of nothing. But if you must confer with them, so be it. If there is anything I can do to assist you in persuading them, you need only ask."

In making this offer he had no idea that he was letting a fox into his chicken coop. Over the next several days I took him at his word. After my first meeting with him at the restaurant at the souk in Jidda, I had been allowed to borrow the plans for his projects, including the supersecret communications system. I thus had the opportunity to photograph the most important ones in the security of my motel room.

I requested complete copies of Ayun's plans, along with books of detailed specifications that I had not been able to photograph. He gladly handed them over.

Two days later I presented them to a debriefer who called himself Seth. "It's a privilege to meet you," he said. "You are such a legend at the Institute that there is a waiting list of agents who wish to work with you. We all feel that we can learn from you. Everyone is astonished by your ability to get people to just hand over their secrets. You ought to be teaching a training course at the Institute!"

Feeling embarrassed, I looked at my watch. I was booked on a four o'clock flight to New York. "Look at the time! I've got a plane to catch."

I scanned the café for a waiter. I wanted the check. I saw many. But none seemed to notice me.

"I believe I see how you manage to be so good at your work," Seth said with a laugh. "You have a way of coming across as just an ordinary man. You are exactly what William Colby of the CIA described as the perfect agent."

"That's very interesting," I said, waving at two waiters without effect. "And what is the perfect spy?"

"Colby said that the best spy is a gray-haired man who has a hard time catching the eye of a waiter in a restaurant."

15

A Very Nice Concert

 To borrow a phrase from Charles Dickens, being a spy in the Middle East from the mid-1970s to the late 1980s was the best of times and the worst of times.

On the bright side, the region witnessed a petroleum-fueled explosion in development projects, both civilian and military, that presented rich pickings for a spy in the guise of a middle-aged businessman who had to struggle to get the attention of a waiter.

Regarding the darker side, no period in the history of the Middle East had been fraught with more peril for the nations of the region and individuals residing or traveling here. This was especially true for visitors from the West.

Terrorism had become a new battlefield of the East-West contest known as the Cold War in which the Middle East became a key arena. Gun-toting, bomb-planting killers spread out from the Middle East to stalk the entire world. Hardly a day passed without a new atrocity to read of or hear about. The wanton murders of innocent people had become, in the words of Claire Sterling in her book *The Terror Network*, "a continuation of war by other means: cheaper, safer, and no less portentous. Its uses were nowhere plainer than in Iran."

Since I had offered my services to Israel in 1973, terror groups, frequently bankrolled by the Soviet Union, fanned out to perpetrate their outrages anywhere a target of opportunity arose. In my years working for the Institute I did not have one meeting with a handler that did not include an update on the activities of Arab terrorists. The purpose was to keep me apprised of the assassins who specialized in attacks upon traveling civilians, grabbing Westerners off the streets of Middle East cities and holding them hostage. Those were situations in which I felt most vulnerable.

202

Despite this threatening atmosphere, I felt compelled to resist the pleas of my family for me to stay at home. I returned again and again to the Middle East, like a moth to a bright light, even if it turned out to be a flame.

Nonetheless, between my excursions I did have a family to support and a business to run. I also found myself called upon to consult with counterparts in large international corporations who respected my reputation, personal and professional.

One such person contacted me late in 1979.

Except for his exquisitely tailored pin-striped suit, Mr. Oh bore a striking resemblance to the hard-headed and stiffly proud Japanese colonel in the movie *The Bridge on the River Kwai* whose favorite saying was "Be happy in your work." As Oh rose to greet me in the Rockefeller Center offices of his construction firm, he certainly seemed content in his labors.

"So happy to welcome you," he said, speaking slowly, as if painfully translating each word before uttering it. "I have heard only praise concerning you and your company." he said. "I hope we can do business together."

As I drew up a chair, I said, "As President Calvin Coolidge observed, the business of America is business."

"The same is true for Japan," he replied. His smile revealed a gold front tooth. "It is the single most valuable lesson we in Japan have learned from America since the war."

Almost forty years had passed since the Japanese sneak attack on Pearl Harbor. However, like most Americans who were alive at the time, I had never been able to encounter a Japanese of Mr. Oh's age without wondering what role he played in the war.

Oh and I had been introduced by a mutual business associate at the Equestrian Club in Saudi Arabia. We had encountered one another in Iraq at various work sites. These projects included a Sheraton Hotel near Baghdad and a smaller development at Basra for which his company had supplied hundreds of Japanese workers.

"Your letter concerning your company's new project was a little vague," I said, "but I gather that you feel that my firm might be of assistance and that time is of the essence."

"Exactly so. The project involves a large building. For many reasons you would appreciate, we are far behind schedule. It is very embarrassing. No one likes to lose face."

"Where is the project"

"Outside Baghdad. A place called Tuwaitha-Osirak."

I had been to the capital of Iraq, but not there. "Your letter said it is to be some kind of manufacturing building," I said.

"Correct."

"What kind of products?" I said.

Oh paused a moment before answering what I considered to be a straightforward question.

"It is very technical," he said at last. "The entire thing is very advanced. Much of the work falls in areas that are not within the expertise of my company. That is why I am interested in bringing your expertise to bear. We are well aware of your reputation for getting things done. So if you feel this is a project worthy of your valuable time, we are ready to negotiate the necessary contracts that will bring you in as a consultant. Once that is accomplished, you and I will be free to get down to, uh, what is the term? Nitty-gritty?"

"That's it," I said.

Proud of himself, he grinned broadly.

After several days of paperwork to formalize our business relationship, in which I would advise as needed, he showed me plans for what appeared to be run-of-the-mill buildings. But on the third day as we turned to details of the main structure he pointed to a large space on a blueprint on which the data had been inscribed in Japanese.

Tapping a stubby finger on the oddly shaped space, he said, "Here is the reactor room."

While he casually spoke the words, what I saw before me in the plans required no translation. Anyone with even a beginner's knowledge of how to read the blueprints would have recognized the purpose of the facility.

The plans specified doors capable of withstanding an atomic blast. They showed extensive built-in security measures and an intricate complex of external guard towers, concrete barriers, and electrified fences that were clearly superfluous to a civilian power plant. The water system far exceeded ordinary needs. These took into consideration the special requirements for cooling a nuclear reactor.

The project that lay before me was a nuclear plant for a country that luxuriated in conventional power!

From all that I knew of Iraq and its ruthless leader, the purpose of a nuclear reactor was not to provide Iraqis with abundant, cheap electric power. With two great rivers running through the country, the Tigris and Euphrates, they had plenty of power. The only purpose I could see for this reactor was to make nuclear weapons. I could think of nothing more potentially disastrous for Israel.

Suddenly I grasped the reason for all the urgency. Oh feared that his company's work on the building would not be ready in time for the delivery of the core of the reactor. Manufactured in France, the core was ahead of schedule while Oh's part of the job had fallen woefully behind. Saddam had never been a man to accept disappointment gracefully.

Here was information that I had to provide to the Institute as quickly as possible. But I needed as many specifics as I could obtain.

"I wish you had told me sooner that this was to be a nuclear plant," I said to Mr. Oh as forcefully but as calmly as possible. "It puts a whole new slant on things."

"How so?" he asked.

"Isn't it obvious?" I replied. "This means nuclear-proof doors, walls. Special materials. Different procedures than I had expected. This is going to require a complete review. I must see *all* of the architectural blueprints. I must have access to *all* the specifications."

"I will have to consult about this with my superiors in Tokyo," Oh said hesitantly.

"Consult with anyone you care to," I responded politely. "But every minute that passes is going to put you that much further behind schedule."

He paused to think over what I had said. "I understand that you believe you must confer with your superiors," I went on soothingly. "All I need is a couple of hours alone and a desk to work at uninterrupted. Give me all the blueprints and I'll be done before you know it."

After a few moments of rumination he reached deep into a briefcase, handed me its contents, and spoke the most satisfying words imaginable. "You may use the room next door."

Unfortunately, I did not have a camera. But when I entered the room I nearly let out a whoop of joy. In the corner of the unoccupied room filled with drafting tables stood a photocopying machine. Nearly two hours later I had produced duplicates of the important pages. After concealing the copies among other papers in my briefcase, I returned to Oh's office and put the originals on his desk.

"I believe I can help you overcome your problem." I said. "I will call you in a few days."

After I hand these plans over to Israel, I thought.

Evidently relieved, Oh smiled and bowed, then escorted me to the door, unaware that the slender briefcase which I had brought to his office now exhibited a considerable bulge. Returning to my office, I phoned Ruth to inform her that I would not be home for dinner because of pressing work, an excuse she had often accepted. Then, spreading out the photocopied plans on the floor, I pored over them again and again, as if to convince myself that they were real.

As I did so I found that the drawings were so detailed that they even included the specifications for the work camp to be occupied by Oh's Japanese labor force. But most important by far were drawings of the infrastructure suitable only for housing a nuclear reactor that Iraq did not require. A considerable part of the plant, I noted, had been designed to be hidden in underground structures. Surely, I concluded, no such specifications would be required in a design for a simple power plant.

With mounting excitement I realized that in all my rummaging through architectural materials, I had never until now found material worthy of forwarding to the Institute with the highest classification code. Now, with Iraq's plan to build a nuclear plant, I had information that required instant transmittal to Tel Aviv: "top priority, confirmed hard copy." Because I did not dare entrust the material to the mail, I decided to deliver it in person to the house on rue Sanguinet in Montreal.

Arriving the next afternoon, unannounced, I created quite a stir within. Standard operating procedure required advance notice of a visit or accompaniment by my handler. "I don't have authority to admit you," growled a middle-aged man whom I had met once and knew as Moshe, a low-echelon security officer. "I must follow protocol. I can't let people walk in like this."

"I certainly have a good reason for doing so," I said, clutching the brown paper shopping bag that contained the plans. "But I will explain why only to whoever happens to be the chief of station. What I've got is for his eyes only. It's top priority, confirmed hard copy."

Rising abruptly, he grumbled, "Wait here."

After five minutes of eerie silence as I was watched by a second security man, I heard the door open and then the familiar voice of my first handler, the man who had trained me in this very house.

"Hershel," David said, enveloping me in a bear hug. "Where's the fire? It's not like you to raise such a fuss. It certainly isn't your style to show up unannounced. What's got your wind up all of a sudden? Tell me all about it. Come in and sit down."

"You're the one who'd better have a seat," I said, reaching into the shopping bag. "I think you'll find this interesting."

He went through the material quickly, stuffed it back into the bag, stood, and shook my hand. "To call this *interesting*," he said with a smile, "has to be the understatement of the year. Please wait here."

Without a further word he left the room with the weighty shopping bag hugged to his chest.

A moment later the security officer returned. "You will be contacted," he said, politely but firmly convincing me to let him escort me out of the room and the building.

I had learned that it is the lot of a spy to never know directly whether his work paid off. But surely, I told myself as I flew back to New York, that could not happen with the information I had handed over to David. I was certain that my report would be on its way to Israel right away. I also understood that I could not expect direct acknowledgment of its receipt. That Israel would do something, I had no doubt.

Nearly a year passed between my giving David the shopping bag and a newspaper headline of June 8, 1981:

ISRAELI PLANES ATTACK
IRAQI NUCLEAR REACTOR

According to the paper, the raid had been carried by fourteen American-built planes. Six F-15 fighters acted as escorts for eight F-16s carrying two 2,000-pound bombs. Each returned safely.

The Israeli government revealed that the attack had been carried out on a Sunday "on the assumption that the 100 to 150 foreign experts who were active on the reactor would not be there on the Christian day of rest." Only one person was killed during the attack, a watchman.

Reading the news account, I thought of Mr. Oh. All of his work and worry had gone for naught. Of course, I could not call him up on the phone and tell him the role he had inadvertently played in bringing about the attack on the reactor. When I did speak to him a few days later he exploded in anger, denouncing Israel as an outlaw country populated by trigger-happy paranoiacs.

"This was a peaceful project," he exclaimed. "It is a terrible outrage. What treachery."

As I listened to him I needed all the restraint that I could muster to keep from reminding him of December 7, 1941.

He joined a worldwide chorus of denunciations of Israel's action. Libya's Qaddafi called for an Arab raid on Israel's own nuclear facilities. The Kuwait government demanded "collective Arab action." Saudi Arabia cited the raid as "the peak of international terrorism." Egypt called the attack "irresponsible and unjustified."

The Soviet Union saw "ruling circles of the United States of America" as "direct accomplices." France's President François Mitterrand, whose government had sold the reactor to Iraq, stated, "Even though there is a latent state of war between Iraq and Israel, it is not acceptable for a country, however just its cause, to settle its dispute by military intervention."

A U.S. State Department official condemned the air strike, stating that its unprecedented character added "to the already tense situation in the area." This comment was followed by Secretary of State Alexander Haig suspending delivery of four F-16 fighters that had been ordered by Israel.

Prime Minister Begin answered, "Israel acted in self-defense against threats to its existence by Iraq, which declares itself to be in a state of war with Israel since 1948. Iraqi leaders have voiced time and again their enmity and aggressive intentions towards Israel. They neither restricted nor disguised their plans to use any weapons, be they conventional or nonconventional, against Israel."

Begin justified the attack as a way of preventing devastation of the Jewish people surpassing that of the Nazi Holocaust. He pointed out that with three atomic bombs of twenty kilotons each, the Iraqis could have destroyed Israel's industrial, commercial, agricultural, and cultural life.

"Six hundred thousand casualties we would suffer," Begin went on, "which would mean, in terms of the United States, forty-four million casualties, in terms of Egypt, over eight million casualties. Where is the country which would tolerate such a danger knocking at its door?"

While these events unfolded I could not tell Ruth or my sons of the part I had played in the Israeli victory. Certainly I knew that there could never be a public recognition by Israel of my role in the affair.

Accordingly, I did not expect to be greeted by anyone from the Institute when Ruth and I arrived in Israel several months later for a strictly personal visit with relatives. But when I was met at Ben-Gurion Airport by a young man who claimed to be a representative of the travel agency that had arranged our trip, I knew he had to have been sent by the Institute. Although we had never met, he had no trouble picking me out of the throng of passengers.

The manner in which he greeted me also signalled connection with the Institute. "Welcome to Israel, Hershel," he said. He then whisked us past the usual customs and immigrations posts to a car that he had arranged to take us to Jerusalem, another clue that he represented the home office.

As modern as any highway in the United States or Europe, the road from Tel Aviv to Jerusalem at first rolled eastward through green flatlands. Soon it began a steady climb into the spine of mountains that runs the length of Israel. At turnoffs, road signs announced the names of places as ancient as the Old Testament: Lod, Rehovot, Ramala, Ashkelon, Ashdod, Beersheba. All around, steep hillsides were scattered with stones as white as the bones of prophets.

But as the highway twisted and turned, always climbing toward the city, we saw artifacts of later history in the form of the burnt and rusting relics of the 1948 War of Independence. Israel had won the city only to have to fight for it again, for the last time, in 1967.

Shortly after arriving at our hotel I got a phone call. "I hope you are available tomorrow for a meeting," said the male voice. "We'll send a car."

Suddenly I saw that my having been met at the airport had to have been more than a courtesy. I felt that such a summons without prior warning had been prompted by something unusual.

"Please set aside the whole day," the caller said.

What should I say to Ruth? I made up a story about an unexpected business meeting.

"It will be only the one day," I said. "I'll catch up with you the day after tomorrow."

As always, Ruth accepted the disruption in our plans without complaint. When the car came to pick me up she was well on her way to what I hoped would be a festive occasion that would not be spoiled by her husband's absence. I could only wonder what Ruth and our relatives would say if they knew the real reason for my not accompanying her.

Meanwhile, I arrived at the unobtrusive building on King Saul Street that served as Institute headquarters and proceeded directly to an office on the second floor. As my escort opened the door I saw Colonel Langatzky standing in the middle of the room, obviously expecting me.

"Sorry for all the cloak-and-dagger theatrics," he said, extending a hand, "but since we had a rather short notice that you were coming to Israel for a personal visit, we did not have time to go through channels to arrange a meeting. But when your visit to the Institute is over I'm sure you will forgive this infringement on your time with your family."

Though his words puzzled me, he offered no explanation as he conducted me on a tour of the headquarters, taking a great deal of time in showing me a computer center that had been added since my last visit. While I found it interesting, I had a feeling that Langatzky's guided tour had been intended to pass the time and that something else lay in store for me.

Presently, a young man approached us, saluted, and said, "The car is here, Colonel."

"It was great to see you again, Hershel," Langatzky said, shaking my hand. "Now please accompany this officer."

Within a few minutes I found myself being driven back along the Tel Aviv–Jerusalem highway. But the driver turned off the highway and proceeded to Kfar-Sirkin, a large air base east of Tel Aviv.

As I stepped from the car, an officer saluted. "Follow me, please, sir," he said, gesturing toward a helicopter.

Shortly after we took off, I found myself looking down at the kibbutz where Ruth was visiting our relatives, and expecting the pilot to deposit me there. But the chopper flew on, dipping low over a paratroopers' training school, the naval commando unit at Ahlit, and a portion of southern Lebanon occupied by Israeli defense forces. Finally, he set us down at Hatsim Air Base near Beersheba, from which the raid upon Iraq's nuclear facility had originated.

I thought as I waited to be escorted into the office of the base commander, "If I'm lucky I'll get a chance to meet some of the pilots."

As General Moshe Dorot rose from behind his desk to greet me, he caught me off guard by snapping a salute.

I simply smiled.

"Come with me, Hershel," he said, opening a door. "I want to introduce you to some people."

Stepping into the next room, I found a crowd of air force officers standing at attention. In a row of civilians I spotted members of the Institute, including several of my handlers.

An aide to General Dorot handed him a small black box. "In appreciation of your recent services," said the general, flipping it open, "the Joint Military and the Institute wish to present you with a memento."

He drew a small bronze disk from the box.

"This is the medal that was struck to honor the squadron that carried out the recent mission to destroy Iraq's nuclear plant," he said, handing it to me. "By accepting this, you have become an honorary member of the squadron that knocked out what the Iraqis called Complex 17."

From somewhere in the room a voice barked, "Attention!"

As if one man, the assembled officers saluted. I returned their gesture as best I could.

At that point a lanky officer with brown hair and eyes and wearing the rank of colonel come forward to shake my hand. The general introduced him as Aviem Sella. One of the stars of the Israeli Air Force, he was born in Haifa in 1946. Entering the service in 1964, he had flown Mystere jets during the Six-Day War of 1967. As first deputy to a Phantom squadron, he engaged in numerous combat missions during the Yom Kippur War, going on to command the 201st Fighter-Bomber Squadron between 1976 and 1979. From 1980 to 1983 he was chief of air force operations.

"Colonel Sella," the general said, "was in charge of the raid on Osirak."

As several other officers stepped forward, Sella introduced them as the pilots who had carried out the mission.

"You fellows do good work," I said with a grin.

"We try," Sella said with a laugh. "Of course, we could not have done it without the information that you provided. It was right on target, so to speak."

"It must have been quite a show," I said. "I would have loved to have seen it."

"We've got the next best thing," Sella said. His brown eyes sparkled like those of a boy who had just hit a winning home run. "If you'll come with us into the next room, you'll find it well worth your while."

Immediately upon entering a room that appeared half office and half theater, I found myself looking at a scale model of the Iraqi nuclear plant.

"This was built from the blueprints you provided," General Dorot said while Colonel Sella drew aside a blue curtain to reveal a motion picture screen.

"If you'll take a seat, Hershel," Dorot said, "we've got some home movies to show you. It's a silent film, of course, but all of us will take turns narrating."

Sella began. "The time is four-oh-one in the afternoon of seven June," he said as the black-and-white film showed a pilot's view of the runway while his plane sped toward takeoff. "It takes almost a mile to get up to speed." he continued. "The payload is much heavier than was designed for these aircraft."

From behind me someone interjected, "Plus the weight of the extra fuel tanks that we needed." The speaker was Squadron Leader Zev Raz, who admitted to me later that he was "excited" to have taken part in the attack. "The F-16 was not designed to fly more that 580 miles. Our mission was 600," he explained as the film continued. "So we had to add extra wing tanks. It was a big risk to take. We did not know if the undercarriages of the plane would bear that weight. But we had to try."

"Nobody slept very well the night before," said another pilot from the back of the room.

"The mission is now a 'go,' " said colonel Sella while the screen showed images filmed by a camera in the nose of an F-16 as it rose from the ground. "We flew at maximum speed, about 150 feet above the ground, crossing Jordan and the northwestern part of Saudi Arabia. To conceal our presence from ground radars we flew beneath a refueling tanker that had been disguised to look like a Boeing 707."

Next came a time in the mission second in danger only to the bombing run itself. Over the Saudi desert, pilots had to jettison the expended extra fuel tanks.

"We did not know if they would break loose and hit the bombs," someone said from behind me. "Happily for us, they didn't."

"We were so low to the ground," Zev Raz continued, "that we could see the people on the ground. I saw some bedouins with their camels. We were going too fast to see faces. We were all smoking along the ground. The 707, which was painted for the mission like an AerLingus airliner, flew cover for us so that we would seem like one aircraft. We refueled once on the way to ensure enough fuel for the return flight."

Entering Iraqi air space and bearing down on the target, the raiders encountered antiaircraft fire as their planes zoomed upward to attain attack altitude. Looking ahead, they found the reactor surrounded by huge earthworks out of which spewed what Raz called "triple-A," for antiaircraft artillery. Also nearby stood surface-to-air missile batteries and three Iraqi air force bases. "I saw the triple-A," said Raz, "and I saw the target. There was no problem identifying it. In that moment you see nothing but your gunsight and your target. Gunsight and target. Gunsight and target. When they meet, you release your bombs. A computer shows its fall. A device that we call the 'pickle jar' lights up. It is the moment of truth."

From behind me in the darkened room as the screen showed the target being hit by the bombs, the calm, steady voice of one of the pilots said, "I looked back to see what I had done. Who could go there and not want to see the result? I felt as if I were at a very nice concert with a very good orchestra with a very good conductor. I felt like singing."

In completing their round-trip to Baghdad the men around me had traversed more than a thousand miles of Arab air space.

Despite protestations from Saddam Hussein and others that the plant had been designed for peaceful purposes, I had no doubt that had it become operational the material it produced would have been turned to military use, and that the target would be Israel.

I had seen the dreadful possibility from the start.

That such a disaster had been averted as the result of an action on my part meant infinitely more to me than any medal, though I was, of course, proud to have received it.

"I hope you can find the time to polish this once in a while," the general said, pointing to the medal in its box.

"Don't worry," I said with a hearty laugh. "I shall do it myself."

The honor could not be made known outside the Institute. Were anyone but those immediately around me to know, my work for Israel would be finished. Like everything I had done over the past several years, the medal had to remain a secret.

16

Endgame

 Although the United States government joined the rest of the world in lodging protests against the Israeli raid on the Iraqi nuclear plant, I suspected that there must have been a collective sigh of relief at the White House.

Certainly the brash Israeli initiative was in line with the spirit of an assertive foreign policy that Ronald Reagan had brought to Washington. Before he took office on January 20, 1981, Americans had been held hostage in Iran for 444 days while the Carter administration appeared to be weak and indecisive. Moreover, the Soviet Union seemed to have gotten away with an invasion of Afghanistan, to which the Carter administration responded with a grain embargo that hurt American farmers. The military capability of the United States had deteriorated so badly that an attempt to free the hostages in Tehran had to be aborted because there had not been enough backup military hardware to replace an incapacitated helicopter.

In the Middle East the reaction to the signing of the Camp David Accords by President Sadat and Prime Minister Begin under the auspices of President Carter had been greeted with an ugly upsurge in terrorism. It would attain new heights of daring with a murderous attack on a U.S. Marine barracks in Beirut, Lebanon, in 1983 that killed 260 GIs and severely embarrassed Reagan. By the start of his fourth year in office, Iranian-backed terror groups acted with such impunity that they kidnapped the CIA station chief in Beirut, William Buckley, and then killed him. That March they also grabbed correspondent Jeremy Levin. In May they seized the Reverend Benjamin Weir. December brought the taking of American University librarian Peter Kilburn. A month later it was the Reverend Lawrence Jenco.

215

These acts of terror were followed by a lonely bright spot, the escape on February 15, 1985, by Jeremy Levin. But a month later he was replaced on the hostage list by Associated Press correspondent Terry Anderson. And on May 28, hospital official David Jacobsen was captured.

Although I had long since struck Lebanon from my list of countries to be visited in the Middle East, I did not know whether a terrorist would not look at me and see a prize worth grabbing. Therefore, when I set out at the end of May 1985, four years after the raid on Iraq's nuclear plant, on another journey to check out the Arab world, I did so with a deeper sense of apprehension than at any time in my eleven years of working with the Institute.

I had two destinations. The first was Germany. The other was Iraq. Four years had passed since the raid on Osirak had dealt a blow to Saddam Hussein's dreams of building a nuclear weapon, yet reports persisted in the press and in international construction circles that he had not given up. Moreover, rather than being shunned as an international outlaw, he had found himself courted by a world that was considerably more worried about Iran than Iraq. In the war between the neighboring countries the nations of the West had been providing Saddam with all sorts of assistance, including armaments and advice in expanding his military.

One of the projects undertaken by my French contacts was an expansion of an air base at Al-Falluja and modernizing radar systems at Basra. I had been asked to make a preliminary survey of blueprints for both sites, concentrating on plans to obtain exact coordinates of the military barracks.

I felt misgivings about going to the country that had been bombed by Israel, in part because of information provided by me. I had no idea whether the Iraqis knew of my role. Was my name on a list for retaliation? Might I be arrested the second I stepped from an airplane? In weighing my decision, these questions tipped the balance against going. But on the other side, Al-Falluja was a major base a few miles west of Baghdad. Basra lay several hundred miles to the south, close to the borders of Iran and Kuwait, and was also a significant military site. To explore both areas was a golden opportunity that I could not miss. I made up my mind that if I got out in one piece, I would never go back.

A trip to Libya had been canceled by David. The Institute had wanted me to check on a report that Libya had worked out a deal with the Hyundai company in which the South Korean firm had agreed to provide a large-scale technical training program for workers involved in power and desalinization plants. David also hoped to find out more about Qaddafi's support for terrorist groups. But David decided the risk in going had become too great.

What I learned from a German businessman immediately before the cancellation was that Qaddafi had become even more paranoid, going to extraordinary lengths to assure his personal security. He now lived in tents in the most remote areas of the desert and made last-minute changes in his quarters to thwart what Qaddafi believed to be a top priority of the Mossad, namely, his assassination—a possibility he also feared from Arab governments.

In just a few days of conversations with the Germans and other businessmen who had been to Libya recently, I felt confident in reporting that the rumor concerning Hyundai had been true. I also was told that terrorist groups had established training bases deep in the desert south of Tripoli and that Qaddafi often visited the camps because he felt safe from assassination attempts there.

During a brief stopover in Athens on my way to Baghdad, I was met at the airport by a handler who caught my attention in a crowd of taxi and limousine drivers soliciting business. I had been instructed by the Rome office to look for a man holding a sign bearing the name Joseph. We had arranged a bit of identifying dialogue.

He said, "I am the best guide in all of Athens."

I said, "Are you expensive?"

To which he replied, "Yes, but I'm worth it."

He debriefed me on my Libyan information in his car as he drove me into the city.

"When Qaddafi picks the place where he's going to spend the night," I said, "he makes sure that the tent where he sleeps is in the center of a group of tents used by his children and wife."

"That's typical of him," Joseph replied with a tight smile. "He hides behind skirts."

I had arranged to meet with Joseph in Athens rather than Rome for both business and personal reasons. One of my French associates had offices in the Greek capital. He planned to brief me on the Al-Falluja and Basra projects. My plan was to have a quick debriefing session with Joseph and conclude my conference with the French associate in one day. I would then spend a few more days getting over the arduousness of acquiring the Libyan information by relaxing in and around Athens, always one of my favorite cities. I made my base at the Hotel Grande Bretagne in the heart of the city and within easy walking distance of markets and the main tourist sites, the Plaka and the Acropolis. I also intended to take an excursion to Pireaus, famed for its seafood and as the locale for the movie *Never on Sunday*.

Because the song of the same title had become known around the world, it was impossible to enjoy a meal at any of the many colorful harborside restaurants without being serenaded by a strolling singer accompanying himself on the Greek version of a mandolin. Nor could I finish the savory seafood without fending off women and old men hawking lacework tablecloths and other local handicrafts, making their way from table to table while the serenaders took intermissions.

Ordinarily I would have accepted these intrusions good-naturedly as indispensable atmosphere, but as I ate I noticed that a young man seemed to be watching me from the sidewalk. At first glance he appeared to be a Greek. But as I snatched glimpses of him he looked more like an Arab.

"This is ridiculous," I thought. "You're becoming even more paranoid than Qaddafi!"

Leaving the open-air restaurant, I strolled beneath shady trees, breathing the fresh sea air, and proceeded to the end of the curving sidewalk to an abandoned amusement park.

I paused to snap pictures of a small rusting locomotive that once had pulled tiny wagons for the delight of children touring with their parents. I noted that the young man had followed me, but at a distance. Seeing me looking at him while he lit a cigarette, he jerked as if he were a puppet.

At such a moment an ordinary tourist might have wondered if the young man were a thief waiting for the most auspicious moment to pull a stickup. But years of espionage invoked a far different scenario in my imagination. I pictured him either as an assassin or one of a group plotting my kidnapping.

As I moved deeper into the eerie emptiness of the park, I sensed he was behind me. I looked for ways to escape. But I felt outrage rising within me. I thought, "I am not going to run from this guy."

But what should I do? I had not brought my gun. But I did have a Swiss army knife. Ducking behind a dilapidated shed, I yanked the knife from a pocket and held it out as it were the barrel of a gun. A moment later the young man turned the corner of the shed.

Grabbing his right arm, I pulled him toward me. With my right hand I held the metal against his Adam's apple.

"Take it easy," he blurted. "I have a message from Joseph."

I poked his neck.

"Is that so? If you know Joseph, you know my name. What is it, please?"

"Hershel," he gasped.

Still unsure of him, I tightened my hold on his arm.

"Give me another proof," I demanded, twisting his arm. He gurgled. "What proof do you want?"

"Anything that will keep me from killing you."

He blurted, "I am the best guide in all of Athens."

I relaxed the pressure. "Are you expensive?"

"Yes," he grunted, "but I'm worth it."

I let him go. "What's the message from Joseph?"

"It's a warning, actually," he said, rubbing his arm. "The home office has sent an alert to all its agents in the eastern Mediterranean sector. We are advised to expect an action by the Abu Nidal group. We are to be ready for a possible attack at an airport, possibly a hostage-taking. It may involve Athens."

"Thank you," I said. "I hope I didn't hurt you."

"I deserved it," he said, smiling sheepishly. "I asked for it. You are one tough cookie."

The following day I stepped onto the soil of a country whose leader had used terrorism to subdue its own people and dreamed of annihilating Israel with nuclear weapons, Saddam Hussein's Iraq. Despite apprehensions concerning being arrested, I passed customs and immigration with only customary delays. Half an hour later I was in a hotel room checking for hidden microphones and cameras.

In the morning I presented myself to an official of the Iraqi air force and found that I was expected. My associates in Paris and Athens had done their jobs well. "All is arranged," he said. "There is a car waiting to drive you to Al-Falluja. A visit to Basra has been scheduled for the day after tomorrow. Please feel free to call on me anytime if you need assistance."

"As you know, I'm here to conduct a site survey. It would be very helpful if I could take photographs. Is it permitted?"

"There are, of course, some restrictions. We are at war, as you know." He smiled. "When in doubt, ask your guide."

Of all the Arab countries that I had toured over the previous decade none had bristled with as much military preparedness as the Baghdad I observed the next morning when an air force car made its way out of the city. It seemed that every rooftop held an antiaircraft gun. Sandbags flanked doorways. Gun-toting soldiers manned every intersection. Tanks stood at each end of the bridges spanning the Euphrates River and beside the main road out of the city. From time to time we had to stop at military checkpoints.

The entrance to the air base at Al-Falluja was also heavily guarded. But this vigilance relaxed once we were admitted. And when the driver stopped at the site of the proposed expansion of the facility, the few guards on hand busied themselves welcoming him. A few minutes later a call to prayer blared out of a loud-speaker and they all turned away from me and toward Mecca.

Slipping my hand into my carryall bag, I took out my camera. As they prayed, I quickly shot half a roll of film, shooting aircraft parked nearby, a control tower, and hangars that I assumed I would not have been allowed to photograph if I had asked permission. In snapping shots of the proposed construction site I had no problem in getting the driver's okay. But he watched me closely, making certain that I concentrated on an expanse of empty desert and nothing beyond.

Expecting this scrupulous officer to accompany me to Basra, I did not anticipate productive photography. But to my surprise and delight, the driver who picked me up at the hotel for the trip south turned out to be concerned only with getting me to our destination. He was oblivious to what I did after we arrived. As a result, I reaped a rich harvest of pictures for the processing labs of the Institute.

As I handed the rolls of film to Joseph in Athens, he said, "The first driver was undoubtedly one of Saddam's Republican Guard. The second was probably a regular. Maybe even a draftee. Or perhaps he never got the word about photography. Iraq's army is like all the others. There's always some jerk who doesn't get the word. Thank God."

"What about that advisory from the home office?" I asked. "Are we still on alert?"

"Nothing has changed," Joseph said. "So be careful."

Two weeks later, June 14, 1985, TWA flight 847 was hijacked after leaving Athens airport. In the course of the seventeen-day crisis a young American sailor, Robert Stethem, was murdered and his body tossed onto the tarmac like so much garbage.

That evening as Ruth and I watched the horrible tragedy unfold on television, she turned to me with an expression of concern that I had never witnessed.

"This is the last straw," she said sternly. "You must not go over there again. I don't care how good these trips are for the business, the situation is getting too dangerous. Think of your children. Think of me. We need you."

Of course, she was right to be worried.

Yet even while I told her that I would take her concern to heart, I knew that if I believed that my going might be important to Israel, I would go. I would have no choice.

Indeed, only a few days later it appeared that such an occasion had presented itself. The phone rang while I was shaving.

Ruth answered it in the kitchen. "It's for you," she called to me. "It's the office."

Which office? I wondered.

The distraught voice on the line belonged to my secretary. "Mr. Schack, you'd better come in at once."

I had never known her to be so upset. "What's the problem?"

"We've had a burglary," she said tearfully. "I've already called the police."

When I arrived, three blue-and-white cruisers of the Spring Valley Police Department were parked in front of the office. A uniformed policeman stood beside the entrance. The scene struck me as being as unreal as a TV movie of the week. I half expected Peter Falk to introduce himself as Lieutenant Columbo.

A considerably better-dressed detective greeted me at the door to my office. "Whoever it was, he made quite a mess," he said. "We are hoping you'll be able to tell us what's missing, if anything."

I quickly surveyed the scene. Apparently the burglars wanted to know how an international corporation operated. A safe had been opened. Stock books had been removed from shelves and studied. A folder of letters of credit had been taken out of the safe and rifled. Routine correspondence had been gone through. As I examined these materials, I concluded the search through these pedestrian business documents had served as a disguise for the real intent of the intruders. This was not a burglary. This was espionage.

I informed the detective that nothing appeared to have been stolen. I could not tell him what I suspected. The burglars had not entered in the hope of finding money or equipment that could be sold. Nor had these men been looking for information on the business of my company. The hard-to-believe truth that cried out to me from the evidence was that my offices had been rifled by people who wanted to find out about *me*.

What people?

I noticed faint impressions in the blotter atop my desk and recognized them as having been left by a tripod camera used for document copying. The camera was similar to the one that had been provided to me by the photography instructor at the house on rue Sanguinet in Montreal. I assumed that blueprints and specification documents had been taken from storage bins and photographed.

I then noted with relief that the cabinets where I kept the records of my work for the Institute had not been opened. Keys to them were not kept in the office. I carried them with me at all times. Other keys that had been removed from a storage cabinet had been put back, but not until impressions had been made. As I studied them I found that traces of the wax employed for that purpose clung to the keys. The same type of wax that had been supplied to me.

If the break-in had been an Institute job, why had it been ordered? I saw two possibilities, neither very satisfying.

First, the raid might have been a Mossad training operation. Such things happened, but whoever arranged it had run a terrible risk in not alerting me first.

Second, I had heard of a special group known as the AL unit, which operated in the United States without any connection to Israel's embassy or consulates. I could not understand why an AL unit might have targeted me. The only explanation I could think of was that there must have been a breakdown in internal communications at the Institute. Had someone not gotten the word? Or believe I did not realize the potential value of the documents in my possession?

Then a third explanation occurred to me. The break-in could have been carried out by someone who knew Institute methods and used them to make it *seem* as if this were a Mossad operation, that is, our enemies. The break-in could have been carried out by any of a number of Arab intelligence services.

All of these possibilities both enraged and sickened me. However, I dared not tell the police what I knew and what I suspected. I decided to dismiss the incident as an ordinary crime.

I said to the detective, "Whatever these people hoped for, they were disappointed. We don't keep money around. We run on paperwork. And as far as I can see no equipment was taken. I guess you should put this down as some drug addict looking for a way to pay for his next fix who went away disappointed."

"You may be right, Mr. Schack," the detective replied. "But since this is a firm involved in international business I thought it wise to call in the FBI."

This news hit me like a fist to the stomach. The last thing I wanted was federal agents poking around my office. But to try to persuade the police to call off the FBI might seem strange indeed. I had to agree to see the agents. They investigated in the manner I had expected, crisply, deliberately, and efficiently. To my relief they departed as had the police, attributing the burglary to "person or persons unknown."

Determined to get to the bottom of things myself, I shot off what some people in the intelligence community call "a distress rocket." In my case it was a call placed from a pay telephone several miles from my office.

While I spoke in code to the person who answered, I knew that standard operating procedures dictated that the message be entered into a computer, ciphered, and sent directly to home base.

My message was brief:

HERSHEL NEEDS IMMEDIATE INFORMATION FOR FURNITURE
SHIPMENT. REPEAT IMMEDIATE INFORMATION.

A few hours later, a familiar voice on my phone said, "In two. Hamburgers and fries."

His work name was Sidney. He meant for us to meet in two hours at McDonald's on East Twenty-third Street in Manhattan. It was one of several places previously agreed upon should I ever need a crash meeting. In my nearly dozen years as an agent this was the first.

I assumed that Sidney would not attend alone, that he would bring people to watch our backs. One occupied a nearby table and took his time devouring a Big Mac. The second pretended to be waiting for someone just outside the entrance.

"Well, fancy meeting you here," Sidney exclaimed as I pretended to pass his table. A half-eaten hamburger lay before him. He looked like a harried businessman suffering from a bad case of heartburn. "Long time no see."

I sat opposite him. "Hello, Sidney," I said grimly.

As I told him about the burglary and spelled out what I saw as the possible explanations, his expression turned grimmer than mine. He tapped the table, making the staccato sound of an old-fashioned Western Union telegraph key.

"If this was an Institute operation," I concluded, "I think I am entitled to an explanation. In fact, I *demand* one."

My anger was rising. As I struggled to keep my voice down, the watcher at an adjacent table showed signs of nervousness. I supposed he carried an Uzi machine gun under his long coat.

"Do you know how many jobs I have done?" I demanded. "In the hundreds. Just how many items do you suppose I've dug up? How many rolls of film have I shot? Hell, I'd bet that in his entire career Cecil B. DeMille didn't use as much, including *The Ten Commandments*. And the remake."

Sidney shifted nervously in his chair. "I'm glad to see that you haven't lost your sense of humor," he said. "Look, Hershel, it definitely was not us. And I just cannot believe that this unfortunate incident was an AL thing."

"You can't be sure, can you?"

"In all honesty, Hershel, no. Those guys are pretty much on their own. But I promise you I will look into it."

"It's tough enough having to peek over my shoulder all the time for people who'd just as soon slit my throat." I said. "I'd hate to think I now have to look out for friends who might stab me in the back."

"Hershel, please. That's rather harsh."

"If the people at home office don't trust me anymore, let them say so," I retorted. "I'll fold up my tent like a bedouin looking for better pastures. But if this was some crazy, stupid stunt by a rogue AL unit, somebody had better set them straight. I assure you that if the American people ever find out they were being spied on by Israel, there will be hell to pay."

Although I never found out who broke into my office nor what transpired after the meeting with Sidney, I was unable to shake off the appalling idea that I had been betrayed.

A month later I was still bothered about the event when I got a phone call from General Ayun. He invited me to go to Saudi Arabia so that he might introduce me to a high-ranking officer of the Iraqi air force. He was looking for an outside consultant on a procurement problem at the Al-Falluja military base.

Had I not acquired so much experience in the Middle East, I might have viewed the proposition as peculiar—an Iraqi officer turning to a Saudi general for help in finding a consultant. But having done business in the Middle East, I immediately understood that the arrangement between the men would certainly end in the enrichment of both men through the timeless institution of baksheesh. I had no intention of ultimately committing my company or myself to a consulting contract with the Iraqis. At the same time, I could not brush aside an opportunity to go to the country whose hopes for joining the world's nuclear club I had helped dash.

I had only one reservation, that the Iraqi government had discovered my connection to the raid on the Osirak reactor and that I was being set up. The burglary might have been the first stage in a plan to somehow discredit me and make it look like a commonplace crime. But as I weighed that likelihood I became convinced that I was imagining a danger that did not exist. If Saddam Hussein's secret service knew about me and wished to settle a score, they had had their chance while I was in Baghdad. Furthermore, Iraq had the service of a worldwide network of terrorists at its command.

Just how daring and vicious the terrorists could be became evident during three days in October. On the seventh, the Abu Nidal group took over the cruise ship *Achille Lauro* and proceeded to murder Leon Klinghoffer, an elderly American Jew who was confined to a wheelchair. He was brutally killed and tossed into the sea along with the chair as the terrorists sought haven in Egypt.

What happened next left Ruth, me, and the world breathless.

The crisis team at the White House discovered that the terrorists had arranged a deal with the Egyptians and planned to leave the country on a commercial 737 airliner. They ordered four U.S. F-14 navy Tomcats from the aircraft carrier *USS Saratoga* to intercept the jet. The navy planes forced the jetliner with the terrorists to land at a NATO base in Sicily. They were promptly arrested and turned over to Italian authorities. This astonishing capture brought the *New York Daily News* headline:

WE BAGGED THE BUMS

As I followed this amazing feat I knew in my heart that it could not have succeeded without the assistance of the Institute. As the *Achille Lauro* faded from the headlines in November 1985, I received an early-morning phone call from Sidney. I had not seen him since the crash meeting at McDonald's after the break-in at my office. Calling me at home on an unsafe phone was not an ordinary event. It broke all the rules.

"We need to talk," he said anxiously. "Right away, Hershel. Same place as before. Noon."

This time there was no pretending that we met by chance. The moment I walked into the crowded restaurant he stood to wave me to him. Even before we sat in a remote corner he was talking.

"To use an old American expression," he said, "the shit is about to hit the fan. I want you to hear about the trouble from me before it goes public."

He paused for a deep breath and a quick glance at the same watchers who had attended the previous meeting.

"The thing that you were so worried about last time has happened. Federal agents have picked up an American citizen on a charge of selling American secrets to Israel. It's going to be all over the news at any minute. You're a smart man, Hershel. I do not think I have to spell out the implications for the rest of us."

"Do I know this man they've arrested? What's his name?"

"Jonathan Pollard. You do not know him. Our people, that is, those you have worked with, were not involved. But there's no getting away from the fact that the heat is going to be on every aspect of the Institute's work. We are going to be under a microscope. I and everyone whom you've been dealing with are bound to be ordered back to home office. That means we will be suspending operations involving American citizens until further notice. Meanwhile, here is a phone number that you may use to contact Langatzky. But only if you feel you must."

The area code, I noted, was Washington, D.C.

As I drove back to Rockland County with my radio tuned to an all-news station, the story of Pollard's arrest came on. The item was brief, stating only that the thirty-one-year-old intelligence analyst for the Naval Investigative Service had been arrested and charged with theft of government property, illegal possession of classified documents, and selling code information to Israel.

The next day, his wife, Anne L. Henderson Pollard, was also arrested and charged with unauthorized possession of government secrets.

Over the next few days it became painfully apparent to me that Israel and the United States had become entangled in the greatest crisis of confidence between two governments since Israel had joined Britain and France in the surprise attack on Egypt in 1956. It seemed to me that each newscast and every edition of the *New York Times* brought a revelation that deepened the mystery.

State Department spokesman Charles Redman declared, "We are shocked and saddened at the notion that something like this might occur. We have been in touch with the Israelis to try and get to the bottom of this."

At first the Israeli government denied any knowledge of Pollard. Then it staged a clandestine recall of several diplomats from its embassy in Washington that angered officials in the State Department who had been promised access to the diplomats.

On November 12, 1985, Redman said, "We are dismayed that the government of Israel was not as forthcoming as we would have hoped and expected."

On hearing of the diplomats' withdrawal, I concluded that such extraordinary steps could only mean that Israel had lied. I assumed Pollard had been a spy and that the Israeli government had issued a denial to buy time until efforts could be made at damage control. It seemed clear to me that in pulling out the members of its Washington embassy staff the Israelis had hoped to throw up roadblocks in the unfolding investigation. They wanted to short-circuit additional probes that might lead to the discovery of Institute activities and Israeli intelligence agencies that might have engaged other American citizens.

I decided to seek advice because such a broadened inquiry might stumble upon my own connection with the Institute. Using a pay phone in another town in Rockland, I called the special number in Washington that Sidney had provided. I gave the switchboard operator the name "Mr. Hershel" and asked to speak to Colonel Langatzky, calling him "Mr. David."

"I'm sorry, sir," the operator replied coldly, "but there is no such person at this number, and never has been."

The only interpretation that I could give to this blatant lie was that Langatzky had been among those who had decamped for Israel. If my assumption were true, and given the fact that I knew Langatzky to be a high-ranking officer of the Institute, I could draw only one reasonable deduction. Langatzky had been involved with Pollard.

I read Pollard's confession as well as interviews conducted by Washington journalist Wolf Blitzer in his 1989 book *Territory of Lies*. I saw how Pollard and I might have had mutual acquaintances in the tightly enclosed universe of the Institute. To my astonishment, I found out that his first handler had been Colonel Sella, the Israeli air force officer whom I had met only once, when he showed me the films of the raid on the Iraqi nuclear plant.

According to Blitzer's account, Sella had been introduced to Pollard by a wealthy New York stockbroker, Steven E. Stern. Stern had attended a lecture by Sella in which Sella recounted the Osirak raid for a group of potential investors in Israeli bonds. This liaison prompted Pollard to approach the Israeli government about providing Israel with information. Rebuffed by the Institute, he contacted the Office of Scientific Liaison, Lishka le-Kishrei Mada (Lakam).

"Despite the Mossad's decision to stay away [from Pollard]," Wolf Blitzer wrote, "Rafael 'Rafi' Eitan, the politically well-connected and mysterious head of Lakam and a legendary spymaster in his own right, decided that it might still be worthwhile to see what Pollard had in mind."

Eitan advised Sella to contact Pollard. He did so, opening a relationship that lasted until Pollard's arrest on November 21, 1985. Although we both worked for Israel in that time, what we did and why we did it were worlds apart. We both volunteered. I did so because I was a Jew who had been outraged by the Arab attack on Israel on Yom Kippur in 1973. In contrast, Pollard, also a Jew, had become a "walk in" out of resentment at what he considered to be shabby treatment of him by the U.S. government regarding his security clearance. While I insisted on not being paid for my services, Pollard sought to line his pockets. I never engaged in activities that could be even remotely harmful to my country. Pollard offered to dispense, virtually wholesale, secrets allegedly damaging to the United States, not only to Israel but to other countries, including Pakistan.

As the details of the Pollard case became known to me in the press and on TV, I had to agree with David Durenberger, chairman of the Senate Select Committee on Intelligence. He said, "This treacherous and traitorous act by a trusted employee motivated simply by money is appalling."

I had never accepted money from the Institute, not even for expenses. In fact, if payment had been pressed upon me, or even suggested, I would have terminated my activities.

It may never be known whether Pollard's offer to provide the Institute with secrets had been declined by the Mossad or if the Institute had engaged in a case of plausible deniability. The Israeli government did offer a formal apology to the United States on December 1, 1985, although the statement by Prime Minister Shimon Peres contained the words "to the extent that it [Pollard's working for Israel] did take place." He then pledged that the Israelis would dismantle any government agency involved in the espionage "if the allegations are confirmed." He also pledged that Israel would disclose all the facts "no matter where the trail may lead."

According to American prosecutors, the trail led to Sella. They indicted him. But by the time the indictment was handed up, Sella was safely back in Israel, presently to be promoted to the rank of brigadier general and given command of Tel Nof air base. However, the higher rank was revoked in 1987, apparently after strenuous protests from the United States.

In his last appearance before his men Sella declared, "I'd like you to know that what occurred was in the national security of the state of Israel. What was at stake was the saving of many Jews' lives."

Sella went on to become head of the Israel Defense Forces staff college. Pollard received a sentence of life in prison. His wife got a term of five years. Langatzky's name never came up publicly in connection with the scandal.

"There have been some very real repercussions from the Pollard affair," Blitzer wrote in his book on the case. "In the relationship between Israel and the American Jewish community, it has been a truly watershed event. Together with other decisions and actions taken by Israel in recent years, the affair has ensured that American Jews are now far more ready to criticize Israel. They still overwhelmingly support that country, but not nearly as blindly as they once did."

While I found that the Pollard case had affected a previously unquestioning devotion of some Jews toward Israel, I also encountered scores of American Jews who believed that Pollard had been treated much too harshly. Committees formed to pressure the U.S. government to lighten his sentence or even to cancel it.

As the Pollard case unfolded, my thoughts returned to the break-in at my offices. Based on what I came to learn about the investigation and surveillance of Pollard by the American government, I also had to consider the possibility that my office might have been entered by federal agents who had learned about my activities while working on the Pollard case.

Whether the break-in had been carried out by Americans or by Israelis, rogues or agents, because of the Pollard affair ultimately made no difference to me. My work for the Institute came to an abrupt ending as a result of the crisis the Pollard case created between the U.S. and Israel. I became a sideline spectator to the astonishing events that unfolded over the next year.

They began on December 27, 1985. Abu Nidal gunmen at Rome and Vienna airports killed fourteen people with grenades and machine guns. Four months later Libyan terrorists exploded a bomb in the Belle Disco in Berlin, killing an American serviceman and wounding fifty civilians. The American response took the form of bombers from bases in England. They crossed Qaddafi's "line of Death" in the Gulf of Sidra to carry out an attack that narrowly missed killing Qaddafi as he bedded down in a tent surrounded by those of his family. Two days later Qaddafi retaliated in the only way he could. He ordered the murder of Peter Kilburn, an American hostage in Lebanon.

Despite my idleness as a spy for Israel, I maintained a keen interest in the events affecting the region. As I watched the American-led, worldwide showdown with Saddam Hussein on television during Operation Desert Storm, I felt confident that the information and the photographs that I had brought out of Iraq in 1985 had added to data gathered by U.S. spy satellites.

In Riyadh American and Saudi Arabian military briefers at their headquarters showed the world pictures and videotapes of the war in progress. As they did so, I took note that several of the Iraqi targets that had been hit had been included in my report, from strategically important bridges across the Euphrates River to militarily vital sites in and around Baghdad. I felt a surge of satisfaction when American planes and missiles targeted the air base at Al-Falluja and the installations at Basra, which I had described in reports to the Institute. But I could barely contain my outrage as I watched news reports carried by the Cable News Network (CNN) describing an alleged bombing of a building in the Iraqi capital, which Saddam Hussein's government persuaded some gullible members of the press was a bomb shelter for ordinary Iraqis. I knew the claim to be false.

I had also seen and forwarded to the Institute evidence that the subbasements of the Baghdad luxury hotel where Western correspondents stayed during the 1991 Gulf War housed a military command center. Yet Iraqis denied this claim on American television. As a result of meetings I had with Iraqis, I had no doubt that a portion of a chemical plant in Baghdad had been converted to production of chemical warfare agents. Nonetheless, Iraqis insisted to impressionable reporters that it was a factory for making baby formula.

Despite these facts, I felt that I could not come forward to assert this firsthand knowledge at the time. I had no desire to go public with the story of my work for the Mossad in the midst of such dramatic events, even though doing so might have blunted Iraq's public relations campaign aimed at making the Gulf War coalition into monsters intent on denying babies their milk.

Equally as important in my rationale was a realization that the Gulf War had placed Israel in a difficult position. The last thing anyone wanted at the height of the crisis was to see Israel drawn into the war directly. In a delicate moment when Israel had to restrain itself to keep from responding to Iraq's Scud rocket attacks, I had no wish to come forward with tales of my work as an intelligence agent on behalf of Israel against Saudi Arabia, the country from which a large portion of Operation Desert Storm was being waged. Finally, I realized that that part of my life was finished. I had done what I saw to be my duty. It was time to move on.

When the last shot was fired in the Gulf War of 1991 I was a lot younger in mind and body than the calendar on my desk indicated. In the nearly eighteen years since the events of the Yom Kippur War propelled me to volunteer my services to Israel I had gone from middle age to the threshold of senior citizenry. Such a cross-roads serves to divide one's attention between the years of youth that had seemed limitless and the reality that those of the future are numbered. It is a moment that requires decisions.

My first was to devote more time to a family who had seen less of me than they deserved. Accordingly, I relinquished direct control of my business and became an independent consultant to the many international firms with which I had been associated. In doing so I set up a nearby office. The result was to bring Ruth closer to my business activites than at any time. She became my informal partner. Independence also freed me from the tyranny of a calendar. I could now arrange all of my work to accommodate the needs of Ruth and my family, rather than the other way around. Because overseas trips no longer had a dual purpose, I could take Ruth along. Vacations were important to her and I did not have to cancel or delay them so I could dash to the Middle East on an intelligence mission. Ruth was delighted. So was I.

Like millions of other people who led active lives, I soon realized that my consulting business and my family would not fill up my calendar. I always knew that I could never retire. Suddenly I recognized that I was not even suited for *semi*retirement. But what might I do?

One project practically demanded my attention. In stepping aside from the daily demands of running my business, I had moved all of my files to my new office. Dozens of boxes, crates, and file cabinets cluttered the storage spaces. These included the locked cabinets containing the materials I had accumulated while working for the Institute. I decided to go through them with the intention of choosing what to dispose of and what for a variety of reasons ought to be kept.

In the wake of the Pollard affair, I thought a time could come when I might have to prove that I had done nothing to harm the interests of the United States. We live in an investigatory era. Other files might be required by the Institute. Some seemed worth saving as personal souvenirs. I would keep other papers as proof that I was not making up stories, should a day arrive when I felt comfortable in telling my grandchildren about my life as an intelligence agent for the legendary secret service of Israel.

Eventually I saw the notes, diaries, copies of my reports, and scores of photographs as more than personal mementos. The files in my hands were history in the raw. Did I have the right to dispose of them? Was I under an obligation to preserve them? And was it incumbent upon me to share them? In thinking about these questions I recalled the ethical will that I had written for my family in the hope that after my death they might find guidance for their lives in mine. Now I wondered if that document could have any real meaning if my descendants knew nothing about the years I had spent in the service of Israel.

I began writing. But as the work progressed I began to see that I was writing more than personal adventures. It was also a story of Israel during some of the most dangerous decades of its existence. More and more, I thought that in writing my story I could tell another chapter of Israel's history. What I had planned as purely a family document assumed wider dimensions. I found myself writing a book and hoping that it might be published someday. In pursuing this dream I found inspiration in the words of Ralph Waldo Emerson. "There is no proper history; only biography."

The writing became so involving that I took the thickening manuscript with me in the summer of 1991 when Ruth and I traveled to Cape May, New Jersey. Ruth had planned an extended vacation for us. While she enjoyed the sun and sea air, she could not fail to notice that I spent most of my time going through stacks of papers. On the third day she stood by the table where I was working and looked down at me quizzically. "This is supposed to be a vacation," she said. "What are you doing?"

Without looking up, I said, "I'm writing a book."

"A *book*? What kind of book."

I realized at that moment that my answer had to be more than, "Autobiographical." To Ruth I was a husband, father, grandfather, and businessman. She had always been an avid reader. To her my life could hardly be viewed as stuff for autobiography. Of course, she did not know the truth. I had kept it from her for more than twenty years.

"Sit down, please," I said, pulling up a chair. "I have something to tell you." She sat without a word. I took a deep breath and said, "Have you ever heard of the Mossad?"

"Of course I have," she said. "It's Israel's CIA."

With a little laugh, I said, "Actually, it's much better." I squeezed her hand and took another breath. "I know a lot about the Mossad. I collected intelligence for them."

She looked at me suspiciously. "Harvey," she said, using her pet name for me, "is this another one of your jokes?"

"I'm not kidding," I said, slowly shaking my head. "I have never been more serious in my life." I looked down at the manuscript lying between us on the table. "It's all here," I said, patting the papers. "I'm halfway through."

Her eyes went wide. In a rising voice, she said, "Are you telling me you were a spy like Pollard?"

"Shh," I said, looking around at people seated nearby. "I was not a Pollard. I did all my work in the Middle East and only against Arab countries. My business trips were perfect cover."

"You *aren't* kidding," she said. As her hand trembled slightly in mine, she asked, "When did all this go on?"

"I contacted Israel in 1973, during the Yom Kippur War."

Her eyes glinted. "That trip you took to Washington."

"Yes. My last mission was around the time that Pollard was caught. The Institute panicked."

"The Institute?"

"Mossad. We called it the Institute. Or the home office. I'll tell you everything. But not now. Not here. When we're alone. Read the book." I smiled. "You can be my editor."

"I have to ask you one thing right now," she said firmly. "It can't wait. Why didn't you tell me before this?"

"I think you already have the answer."

She thought for a moment, then nodded her head. "You didn't want me to worry."

Leaning toward her, I whispered, "Yes."

"One more question now," she said. "Is it finished?"

"The book?"

"The spying."

"Yes," I said, kissing her cheek. "It's over."

And so it was. The world had changed. The combination of the stunning defeat of Saddam Hussein and the spectacular and unexpected ending of the Cold War suddenly altered the dynamics of the Middle East. After more than four decades of war between Arabs and Israel, all sides seemed to be moving toward some version of peace, led by President George Bush and Secretary of State James Baker. I welcomed the peace talks.

In my years in the Middle East I had developed friendships in the ranks of those from whom I secretly secured information. At no time had I regarded them as personal enemies. They had been the enemies of a country in whose defense I had enlisted, but I never hated them as individuals nor as a people. If my intelligence work contributed a little to bringing about the peace talks that followed the Gulf War, then it must follow as day comes after night that I had contributed something that would benefit them as well as Israel. If the first real chance at peace in the Middle East forced me into early retirement, I told myself, "It is God's will." Or, as my Arab friends would say over a glass of sweet tea, "*Enshallah*."

Epilogue:
A Meeting in Helsinki

 With the demise of the Soviet Union and the Desert Storm victory, a lot of people who had made their living out of crises suddenly turned into potential business partners. Adversaries who had labored to keep or obtain one another's secrets now openly swapped information on how to make a killing off the bones of the late and unlamented Soviet empire. By the winter of 1991 birds of prey were flocking to pick the corpse clean. I saw them everywhere. They flocked to the banking offices of the Western world. I ran into them in Europe as they looked for ways to turn themselves and former Kremlin commissars into millionaires faster than if they had won the New York State lottery.

In the Arab world a long flirtation with the Soviets had come a cropper. For decades the Nassers, Assads, Qaddafis, Husseins, Arafats, and others had sought to exploit the Cold War. They had looked to the Kremlin to supply their arsenals and to bankroll their terrorists in a long twilight war against Israel. In those years their rallying cries had been "down with Zionists," "death to Israel," and "remember the Palestinians."

But in seeking advantage through alliances with the Soviets, they had wound up on the wrong side.

And what of the pawns in the Arab-Israeli conflict, the Palestinians? In the showdown with Saddam Hussein they had miscalculated, leaving them no choice but to bargain with Israel under the auspices of the world's only superpower, the United States.

While President Bush spoke of "a new world order," many ex-agents put away their cloaks and daggers in favor of pin-striped suits and briefcases stuffed with order books. In the jigsaw-puzzle map of the post–Cold War world, they laid out a smorgasbord of weaponry as good as new and ideal for settling ancient squabbles that the "old order" had stifled. For sale or barter they provided everything from rifles to surface-to-air missiles. They did not lack takers. Contentious factions in what used to be Yugoslavia and scores of other hot spots around the globe gobbled them up.

Meanwhile, other entrepreneurs plunged into the uncharted future with a vision of cashing in on a market for the plowshares that were required by the people of the new world, from super-computers to supermarkets. Smart guys in smart suits roamed a high-tech world like the traveling salesmen of past centuries.

On the other hand there were businessmen like myself, seeing in the ashes of world communism and its equally and justly repudi-ated half-brother, socialism, a need to construct brand-new infra-structures on the rubble of the old regimes. Acting as a consultant, I looked forward to helping to build this new world. If I could also make a few honest dollars, why not?

Pursuing my own plan for the future, I departed New York for Helsinki, Finland, to consult on matters related to various world-wide enterprises. In several ways the journey was bittersweet. It brought flashes of memory of travels on behalf of the Institute and the realization that I carried with me only one passport—mine, legitimately obtained.

Being so close to Russia, I was mindful that my ancestors had fled that country through Finland to escape the pogroms. They had found a better life in America, though it never equaled the good life that came to me as their heir. I felt that I had evened the score a bit for them. I had been able to help Israel, a country my ancestors could only dream about as they spoke the Passover vow, "Next year in Jerusalem."

My purpose in Helsinki was a conference with a Russian whom I knew had been a colonel in the KGB, although he insisted that he had not been in the directorate that ran agents in the Middle East. Now he headed a loose consortium of Russians who had been on the losing side in the coup against Mikhail Gorbachev. His name was Andropov, no relation to the man who had headed the KGB and then took the helm in the Kremlin, briefly. We were to meet in a café in my hotel.

As I entered I heard my name shouted. In the past I would have followed Institute training and not acknowledged that greeting. But all that was over. I turned around to find myself looking across the large and crowded room at the smiling face of the last of my handlers, who called himself Sidney. I had not seen him since our rushed and fateful meeting at the McDonald's on Twenty-third Street in 1985 as the Pollard case was exploding in everyone's face.

"It's like old times," he said, embracing me and slapping me on the back. "The good old days. All those secret meetings about how to put the screws to the Arabs."

"Maybe now that the Communists aren't around to back up the enemies of Israel and the Palestinians are talking we can have peace in the Middle East," I said.

"We'll see," Sidney replied with a shrug. "Sit with me. Let me treat you to a cup of coffee."

"So what brings you to Finland?" I asked as I sat down in the middle of the crowded café. I lowered my voice to a whisper, as in the old days. "Or shouldn't I ask? Should I assume you're here on Institute business?"

"Those days are gone forever for me. This is strictly personal, Hershel."

"Is that so?" I said dubiously, assuming that "personal" was cover and that he remained in harness.

"It's the truth. I've left the firm. I got out about a year ago." Now he sounded truthful. And more than a little wistful.

"Why was that?" I asked. "You were one of the best handlers I ever had."

"Halcyon days," he said, lighting a cigarette. Holding it out, he seemed to be studying it. "These days I'm making a fortune out of these."

"I thought cigarettes were on everyone's list of very bad habits."

"The Russkies are nuts about American cigarettes. It is amazing. They are so hard up that they sell all their clothing, except what's on their backs, yet they spend their rubles for cigarettes and vodka. Someday when we both have the time I'll educate you on all the ins and outs of the cigarette trade."

He dragged deeply on his. "The world is full of formers," he said, exhaling the words on a plume of smoke. "The *former* Cold War. The *former* Soviet Union. The *former* Mideast crisis." He cracked a smile. "So now I'm a *former*. A former spymaster. There are plenty of us around, by the way. Former KGB men. Former CIA men. Former this. Former that."

"It sounds as if you really are nostalgic for the way things used to be," I said, looking around the café as I had done so many times with Sidney and other handlers. "What are you fellows doing, meeting to plot how to change things back?"

For an instant Sidney's eyes twinkled. He smiled the way he had when giving me an assignment in the old days. I suspected that in my joke about going back to the old ways I somehow had struck close to the truth.

"We would welcome you into the club, Hershel," he said. "I can promise you that you'll meet a lot of old pals. The one who scouted you, Langatzky, is with us. He was your first handler, I believe. And the one whom you knew as David is also with us."

"They're no longer with the Institute?"

As he surveyed the room I detected the old wariness, the look that took in everyone and everything in a closed space or an open one, searching for a likely enemy.

"They've all retired," he said.

"Well at least *they* have pensions," I said jokingly.

"You could have walked away with plenty of money," he said. "The Institute would have paid you handsomely for the stuff you gave them for nothing. I never understood that about you."

"I didn't want money."

"You could make a bundle now, if you'd join us," he said as his eyes came back to mine. "We can use a man with your smarts. And that extra sense of yours about what was important and what wasn't that made you so famous around the home office. What do you say? Would you care to come on board?"

"No thanks, Sidney," I said. "I like the way things have changed. I don't want to go back. The world isn't perfect by any means, but I do think it's better off than it was in 1973 when I volunteered my services. I like to think I helped make it so."

"You did a great job for us. I hope somebody took the time along the way to tell you just how great."

"I did what I could," I said with a shrug.

He reached out to touch my sleeve. "Don't you *miss* it, Hershel? Not a teensy bit?"

"Not really," I said. "It's finished. All that is behind me. I'd never go back, Sidney."

"Too bad."

"I'm not a 'former' anything," I said. "I'm a 'future.' Now, if you'll excuse me, I have a meeting."

"Be careful, Hershel," he said as I stood to leave. "It's a dangerous place out there."

"Helsinki? Dangerous?"

"Not Helsinki," he said, laughing. "The future."

Index